Economics After Capitalism

Economics
After Capitalism

A Guide to the Ruins and
a Road to the Future

Derek Wall

Forewords by David Bollier and Nandor Tanczos

PlutoPress
www.plutobooks.com

First published as *Babylon and Beyond*, 2005
This revised expanded edition first published 2015 by Pluto Press
345 Archway Road, London N6 5AA

www.plutobooks.com

British Library Cataloguing in Publication Data
A catalogue record for this book is available from the British Library

ISBN   978 0 7453 3508 7   Hardback
ISBN   978 0 7453 3507 0   Paperback
ISBN   978 1 7837 1302 8   PDF eBook
ISBN   978 1 7837 1304 2   Kindle eBook
ISBN   978 1 7837 1303 5   EPUB eBook

This book is printed on paper suitable for recycling and made from
fully managed and sustained forest sources. Logging, pulping and
manufacturing processes are expected to conform to the environmental
standards of the country of origin.

10   9   8   7   6   5   4   3   2   1

Typeset by Stanford DTP Services, Northampton, England
Text design by Melanie Patrick
Simultaneously printed by CPI Antony Rowe, Chippenham, UK
and Edwards Bros in the United States of America

CONTENTS

Mr. Lebeziatnikov who keeps up with modern ideas explained the other day that compassion is forbidden nowadays by science itself, and that that's what is done now in England, where there is political economy.

Dostoevsky 1993: 14

FOREWORD TO
THE NEW EDITION

David Bollier

As a cascading series of crises converge – economic, ecological, social – what better time to review the long history of anti-capitalist thinking? The past is rich with important lessons, ones that can help orient us to grapple with present-day challenges, refine our strategic judgement and develop practical alternatives.

History can be instructive in a double sense: it can show us what worked and what didn't work, and so guide our own efforts, but it can also reveal that the past does not define the scope of realistic ambitions today. The future is not yet written. If *Economics After Capitalism* demonstrates anything, it is that we must step bravely into history with our own creative energies and seize the unique opportunities of our time. But because time is short and the challenges are great, we must do so with intelligence and resolve.

Although our mainstream institutions are loath to admit it, we are in the midst of a civilisational crisis. Existing structures and practices are crumbling. The moral and political legitimacy of the nation state and international governance bodies is waning. The relentless promises of economic growth, consumerism and 'progress' are being exposed as utopian fantasies. The neo-liberal vision can now be seen as not only grossly unfair and unattainable, but deeply destructive of our planet and human well-being.

But how to move forward?

It is helpful to revisit the many traditions of anti-capitalist critique, dissent and creative world-making, as outlined in the pages below. 'The past is never dead,' wrote William Faulkner. 'It's not even past.' From reformist finance to green economics, anarchism to ecofeminism, and Marxist economics to the commons, we actually have a rich palette of experiences, ideas and alternatives to draw upon. Some of these anti-capitalist traditions seem deeply rooted in their times and therefore feel remote, while others are perennial and timeless, ready to be thrust into action immediately. Some approaches feel highly prescriptive and run the risk of becoming totalising, rigid ideologies, while other challenges to capitalism function more as open-ended templates that invite creative improvisation.

I see great potential in the commons as an attractive framing paradigm and discourse because it is not just a critique of capitalism but a constellation of constructive, working alternatives. It consists of general design principles, ethical norms and a diverse array of actual projects that resemble fractal variations on a theme. The commons is less of an ideology or critique than a meta-framework of principles and values that describes a wide variety of collective action projects, each with their own situational politics, cultural and geographic circumstances, and intellectual character. Indeed, the commons is already serving as a staging area in which numerous movements of self-identified commoners are working out the details of what the commons means to them in their particular local, political, economic and ecological circumstances.

Despite a diverse range of on-the-ground realities for commoners, they adhere to a general principle of 'unity in diversity'. This is entirely appropriate not just in a time when globalised capitalist markets have penetrated most corners of the earth, but at a time when most of humanity is now interconnected through a single network of networks, the Internet, which for the first time brings us together (fitfully) as a single human species. The commons seizes this moment in global culture by offering us a vision of human society that is inclusivist, ecologically minded, and committed to social justice and basic human needs. It demonstrates that, *pace* the claims of economists that we are all *Homo economicus*, selfish, utility-maximising individuals, human beings can in fact self-organise themselves to create fair, sustainable systems of governance and management for their shared wealth. This has in fact been the primary mode of self-governance throughout human history. Unlike the nation state and capitalist market, which have trouble respecting ecological limits and minimising social conflict, the commons is predisposed to internalise negative economic externalities, welcome participation by ordinary people and cultivate an ethic of sufficiency. No wonder it is seen as an attractive alternative to bureaucratic systems and predatory markets.

Unfortunately, the commons has long been eclipsed by the destructive interventions of the market/state duopoly, otherwise known as 'enclosures'. It has also been crippled by the smear that it is an inherently impractical, failed model for managing resources – a brilliant cover story to justify the private appropriation of the common wealth. That tradition was given new life in 1968 when biologist Garrett Hardin published his famous essay, 'The Tragedy of the Commons'. Few people then or now have dared to consider that Hardin was not really describing a commons; he was describing an open-access regime – a free-for-all in which there is no community, no rules, no monitoring of the resource and no penalties for those who violate community rules. This, of course, is a scenario that more closely resembles the normal working of unfettered 'free markets' than the that of the commons – the tragedy of the market, one might say.

The 'tragedy of the commons' parable has nonetheless been embraced by conservative ideologues and property-rights advocates for nearly fifty years, as a useful way to discredit collective action to protect shared wealth. As a result, exiled from the circle of respectable policy making and politics, the commons has remained largely invisible, and the state and the market are routinely portrayed as the only two serious systems of governance and production.

Margaret Thatcher famously declared, 'There is no alternative' – a phrase memorialised in the acronym TINA. She was keen to forestall any challenges to her neo-liberal agenda and to bully dissenters into submission. In truth, the more accurate acronym for our time is TAPAS – 'There are plenty of alternatives.' In the years since the 2008 financial and economic crisis, there has been a stunning efflorescence of creative projects, intellectual critiques and political movements dedicated to forging a new path forward.

These can be seen in the many citizen movements in New York City (Occupy), Madrid (*Indignados*), Athens (anti-austerity protests), Istanbul (Taksim Square uprisings), Cairo (Arab Spring) and Rome (Teatro Valle occupation), all of which were and are less intent with negotiating with mainstream political institutions than with changing corrupt, rigged systems of governance. The *system* itself is the problem, in other words. With similar intent, political parties such as Syriza in Greece, Podemos in Spain and the international Pirate Party are trying to achieve fundamental change through elections. Efforts in Ecuador and Bolivia are promoting *Buen Vivir* – the ethic of 'good living' – as an alternative to neo-extractivist policies.

Beyond these groundswells of political action, there are many serious economic and social movements gaining strength and focus. Most of these challenge capitalist logic and culture in some fashion, but most are also careful not to be defined or limited by the narrow terms of capitalist discourse. These creative, boundary-stretching movements include the Social and Solidarity Economy, which is pioneering new models of social provisioning and mutualism, especially in Europe and Brazil. There is the Degrowth movement, which is developing a new vocabulary of simplicity, autonomy, conviviality and care as key elements of a new economy. There is the burgeoning Transition Towns movement, which is anticipating the impact of 'Peak Oil' and climate change by re-imagining and building more self-sufficient local economies. There is the Sharing Economy movement, which apart from its venture capital-driven sector, is dedicated to developing projects and policies that enable people, especially city-dwellers, to cooperate and share their personal lives, neighbourhood spaces, productive activities and offices.

While some elements in the cooperative movement have lost track of its original vision, there are heartening signs of public-spirited innovation in this world, too, especially with multi-stakeholder cooperatives and new vehicles for community development and finance. The world of Internet-based peer production is exploding, going well beyond familiar open source software and social networking models to include developing open design and manufacturing of cars, furniture and farm equipment; open data collectives; open source computer boards and electronic equipment, and wiki-style humanitarian relief services. The global sharing of knowledge and design is being joined to local, modular, customisable production, pointing to new, more convivial modes of non-capitalist production. In Barcelona alone, for example, there are now more than a dozen 'Fab Labs', with special fields of expertise – all linked to a global network of Fab Labs and the Maker movement.

One can also point to the many food-related movements that are challenging the global apparatus of capitalist agriculture and food distribution: the anti-GMO activists, the seed-sharing collectives, Community-Supported Agriculture, permaculture, agroecology and agroforestry, the Slow Food movement, La Via Campesina, relocalisation projects, among many others. One could name many other transformation-minded movements – the environmental justice movement, the many coalitions fighting for climate change policies, and opponents of rapacious, anti-democratic free trade and investment treaties.

The truly encouraging news is that these many movements are no longer content to work in isolation from each other; they are finding out that they have a great deal in common as victims of market enclosures and as co-creators of a new sort of economy and society. New federations of cooperation are arising, and new synergies are developing – between digital commoners and natural resource commoners, between commoners of the industrialised North and citizen movements of the global South, and between indigenous peoples and activists. The relentless urgency of climate change is acting as an accelerant for many such collaborations, spurring new political action and convergence among movements.

It is the burden of those who wish to displace capitalism to demonstrate that there are indeed humane, fair alternatives. It must be shown that a different logic and ethic will not only work, and work well, but that they can prevail in practical settings, in real-world politics and in formal law and policy making. This is precisely what it is happening now, but it is a ragged, provisional frontier – one that must be consolidated, defended and pushed forward.

Given the declining legitimacy and efficacy of the neo-liberal capitalist agenda – its myths and logic no longer make sense; its ecological and social devastation can no longer be sustained – it is impossible to ignore the fresh, practical, sophisticated visions of these various movements. No one can tell precisely *how* the structural disabilities of a troubled, recalcitrant capitalist system will be addressed and replaced. It is not self-evident how a more humane, eco-sensitive set of institutions, legal principles, social practices and cultural norms will take root, flourish and rebuff the logic of capitalism. Surely much will depend on how each of us engages personally with the epic transition ahead, hopefully with a deep understanding of the movements that have preceded us. For that, please read on ...

David Bollier
Commons Strategies Group
Amherst, Massachusetts

FOREWORD TO
THE FIRST EDITION

Nandor Tanczos

Human beings face the greatest challenge in the history of our species. We face the destruction of the life support systems on which our very existence depends, and we face it because of our own activity.

There are some who deny or diminish that threat. They mostly either retreat into fairy tale thinking – that technology, or the 'free' market, or UFOs will save us – or hope that by closing their eyes they can make it go away.

Yet the evidence is mounting almost daily that the threats are very real and are gathering momentum. A new report from the UK is saying that if we don't turn carbon emissions around in the next decade, we will not be able to stop runaway climate change whatever we do.

Authoritative voices are warning us that we are very close to the point where world demand for oil will outstrip the capacity of the oilfields to supply. Our total dependence on fossil fuels, the use of which has provided the energy for an enormous expansion of human activity and population, is like a chemical addiction. And as the US has recently confirmed in Iraq, strip a junkie of their supply and the temptation to turn to crime can be irresistible.

'The American way of life' said George Bush Sr, 'is not negotiable.'

A time of crisis, however, is also the time of greatest opportunity. More and more people are waking up to the need to change, to change at a fundamental level, and to change right now. People are waking up to the fact that the institutions of society that so many have put their trust in are failing us. Government won't do it. Big business can't do it.

Because the challenge we are facing is about more than changing a few policies or practices. It requires a fundamental rethink of what it means to be a human being. Government and business can become allies, but the power to make real change lies in the hearts and the lives of ordinary people.

It is already happening. The international people's movement against genetically engineered (GE) plants and animals has demonstrated how the reckless agenda of multinational corporations, aided and abetted by our own governments, can be stopped in its tracks and rolled back. One conglomerate has been outed bribing government regulatory officials in Indonesia, GE companies are pulling out of the EU and Australia, and GE agriculture firms are facing massive stock market losses. The promised gold rush is proving to be a fantasy, largely because of global consumer resistance.

While the campaign has significant support in the scientific community, for many ordinary people it began as a sense that something just didn't feel right. That feeling is often quickly backed up by investigation, but the sense of something being fundamentally arrogant and wrong about GE is the key – it is our humanness talking to us.

What is it to be human? Western society, at least, defines us as individuals whose value can be judged by what job we have, what colour credit card we have, what kind of car we drive and the label on our clothes.

Yet beneath these displays of status, real people are emotional, social and spiritual beings – intrinsic characteristics that cannot be considered in isolation from each other. We seem to have forgotten that our relationships – with one another and all the other beings with whom we share this beautiful planet – are fundamental to who we are.

There is a passage in the Bible that says 'where there is no vision, the people perish.' The inability to step back and clearly see and understand the 'big picture' is the central problem that we face in the world today. The main motivations for western industrial society for the past few hundred years – belief in unlimited growth and technology as the solution to all problems – are the very things that are killing us.

We cannot grow forever on a finite planet. If we continue to assume that endless growth and consumption is possible, and disregard the biosphere's capacity to meet our greed, and if we continue to neglect social justice and fair and sustainable wealth distribution, we will reap a bitter harvest.

Neither will technology on its own fix the problem. Yes, we need better technology, more efficient technology that uses non-polluting cyclical processes and that does not depend on fossil fuels. But just more technology will not do, because the problem is in us and the way we see ourselves in the world.

We humans think that we can own the planet, as if fleas could own a dog. Our concepts of property ownership are vastly different from traditional practices of recognising use rights over various resources. A right to grow or gather food or other resources in a particular place is about meeting needs. Property ownership is about the ability to live on one side of the world and speculate on resources on the other, possibly without ever seeing it, without regard to need or consequence.

The ability to 'own' property is fundamental to capitalism. Since the first limited liability companies – the Dutch and British East India Companies – were formed, we have seen the kidnapping and enslavement of 20–60 million African people and the rape, murder and exploitation of indigenous people around the world. Colonisation was primarily about mercantile empires, not political ones. It was all about forcing indigenous, communitarian people to accept private individual ownership of resources, which could then be alienated, either by being bought or stolen. The subsequent political colonisation was just about how to enforce that ownership.

Today property rights are being extended through the General Agreement on Tariffs and Trade (GATT) and trade-related aspects of intellectual prosperity rights agreements (TRIPS) and through institutions such as the World Trade Organization (WTO) and the World Bank. Private property rights are being imposed over public assets such as water, intellectual property and, through genetic engineering and biopiracy, on DNA sequences. Even traditional healing plants are under threat. In Aotearoa – New Zealand – we have had multinationals attempting to patent pikopiko and other native plants. This is all part of the 'free' trade corporate globalisation agenda – to create tradable rights over our common wealth, accumulate ownership and then sell back to us what is already ours.

This is only possible because we have lost our place in the scheme of things. We think of the environment as something 'over there', as something separate from human activity, something to either be exploited or protected. The reality is that we are as much part of the environment and the planet as the trees, insects and birds.

It is time to relearn what it means to be human.

Nandor Tanczos served as a Green Party MP in Aotearoa/New Zealand Green Party between 1999 and 2008, and wrote this foreword for the first edition of this book in 2005.

ACKNOWLEDGEMENTS

My wife Emily Blyth has read drafts of this book, and been immensely supportive, while Nandor Tanczos and David Bollier have been generous in providing introductory material. Romayne Phoenix, Freda Davis and Mária Dokupilová all provided useful suggestions for improving the text. And a shout out to Chris Kraft. And to Alex for the zazen.

1

WARM CONSPIRACIES
AND COLD CONCEPTS

The capitalist epoch will come to be seen as one in which we relied on incredibly crude economic mechanisms called 'markets'. Markets are like machines for coordinating and relaying information, but they are only effective in relaying limited kinds of information in very circuitous ways. Markets are often thought to be highly efficient, but in the future they will be seen as highly inefficient and costly. Markets not only fail to take account of social and environmental costs, but they also generate instability, insecurity, inequality, antisocial egotism, frenetic lifestyles, cultural impoverishment, beggar-thy-neighbour greed and oppression of difference. (Albritton 1999: 180)

Frank Knight is often described as the founder of the Chicago School. The economics department at the University of Chicago, famous for Milton Friedman and other neo-liberal economists, inspired Mrs Thatcher, Ronald Reagan and other right-wing politicians. It could be said that their neo-liberalism, which promotes capitalism above all else, has transformed the world and now dominates our planet. Democrats from Obama to Clinton, and Labour leaders from Bob Hawke to Tony Blair, accepted many of the Chicago School's key assumptions and the 'Washington consensus' of deregulation, privatisation, tax cuts (at least for corporations), slashed welfare, and reduced trade union rights, based on Chicago School economic sentiments, remain almost universal today.

However, in 1932, on the evening before the US presidential election of that year, Frank Knight did something very odd indeed. He gave a lecture entitled 'The Case for Communism: From the Standpoint of an Ex-liberal', and opened it by suggesting 'those who want a change and wish to vote intelligently should vote Communist' (Burgin 2009: 517). For most of his career, Knight was a committed free marketer, who was known for converting socialists like James Buchanan into fervent advocates of capitalism. Milton Friedman referred to him as 'our great and revered teacher' (Nelson 2001: 119). Knight was a richly paradoxical character; no simple free marketeer, he believed in capitalism but was aware of its innate contradictions. He argued that luck and inheritance, as well as hard work, determine how well we do. He saw capitalism as leading to increasing inequality and tending towards crisis, and was also sceptical of ideas of economic rationality (Burgin 2009). In the 1930s, capitalism was in crisis, a severe economic depression occurred and even the likes of Frank Knight, in his case both dramatically and briefly, were looking for alternatives.

In 2015, the world economy is growing but capitalism has been tarnished. In 2008, a financial crisis, caused by deregulation of banking in line with neo-liberal principles, led to a world recession. Neo-liberalism has led to increased inequality in the US and UK. To keep us spending, despite slower wage growth, there was a massive expansion of personal credit. Capitalism, after all, has many contradictions, but one of the most significant is the wage relationship. If wages rise, firms face greater costs and less profit, neo-liberalism has made it easier for companies to reduce wages by cutting trade union power and relocating to low wage economies. If wages fall, firms face more difficulty in finding consumers (who after all generally have to work to afford to buy products), and see profits decrease. There is, of course, no single unique contradiction; the geographer David Harvey (2014) has identified 17, and his list may not be exhaustive. The contradiction between wages, costs and consumption, means increased credit becomes vital as a way of allowing consumers to borrow to spend despite stagnant wages. Virtually fraudulent 'subprime' mortgages were sold to poor householders, most notoriously in Florida. Subprime is jargon, meaning mortgages for people who can't afford them. The mortgages started with ultra-low teaser interest rates which then rapidly increased. You don't have to be a genius to see that this would end in tears. Mortgage debt, as Michael Lewis in his beautifully written book, *The Big Short* (2010), was re-packaged and sold on, so that banks in Britain, such as Northern Rock, ended up with toxic debt from the US. Banks and other financial institutions descended into crisis, governments stepped in to bail them out, markets took fright, economic growth became negative and millions of us lost homes, jobs and incomes. The inequalities of capitalism contributed to the crisis, the mantra of deregulation meant that risks were allowed to build up and calls for an end to neo-liberalism grew loud. This book is about alternatives to neo-liberalism, and argues that capitalism is merely one way of running the economy, that capitalism doesn't work and that alternatives are possible.

In writing this book I am, in a sense, taking the Frank Knight wager. Knight argued that capitalism was flawed but ultimately, despite his socialist origins and his 1932 episode of communist advocacy, he felt that there was no alternative. I enjoy reading Knight immensely; along with the free market feminist economists Deirdre McCloskey, he is an example of an intelligent advocate of capitalism, aware of its problems and committed to a society that works not simply for the rich and powerful, but for all of us. How can we create practical alternatives to capitalism that work to put food on the table, providing long-term material well-being not only for a minority but a whole planet?

Commentators predicted a new economics, and in 2009 Elinor Ostrom, the first woman to win the Nobel Prize for economics, delivered a lecture boldly entitled 'Beyond Markets and States'; however, the orthodoxy retained its power (Wall 2014). The journalist Richard Seymour, in *Against Austerity* (2014), argued that the neo-liberals retained a virtual monopoly on economics, there were few clearly articulated alternatives and the rich and powerful worked to turn a crisis into an opportunity. He noted that the growth of government debt was used to justify more cuts in public spending, and in countries like Britain ever more deeply market-based policies are justified as a source of growth.

The future looks both clear and bleak. The economic system we have at present cannot cope with climate change, cannot reduce inequality, and it attempts to overcome its contradictions by insisting upon more of the same. The left, strong in Frank Knight's day, seems weaker than ever. Greater inequality and reduced standards of workers' protection, along with the sale of institutions and assets such as the British National Health Service and even Greek beaches, will lead to greater misery. Increasing police powers and surveillance will be used to stifle dissent. Discontent is, at least in Europe, leading to the growth of far right parties. It's easier to explain falling living standards as being a result of immigration than the workings of economic theories and bond markets, so politicians are prepared to use race, nationalism, or sectarian religious sentiments to gather votes. From India, where the right-wing People's Party, or BJP, won the 2014 general election in the world's biggest democracy, to the emergence of the Tea Party in the US, to the rise of Islamic fundamentalists such as ISIS in Syria, economic and ecological crisis is fuelling hate-filled, regressive movements rather than positive change.

In the wake of the 2008 crisis, there were calls for an inclusive, compassionate capitalism. Some of these calls seem genuine and progressive, others a little absurd. In July 2014, it was reported by the *Evening Standard* that

A London summit on 'caring capitalism' that attracted Prince Charles and Bill Clinton as speakers became embroiled in a bitter legal dispute.

Philanthropist Lady Lynn Forester de Rothschild, who says the one-day conference was her idea, has launched a £187,000 High Court claim against the think-tank that helped stage the event ...Lady de Rothschild claims HJS, a registered charity, and its executive director Alan Mendoza are holding £137,000 of 'surplus funds' from the conference that should be returned to the couple's investment company EL Rothschild ... It also says HJS must give her control of websites connected with the conference and other assets such as a contacts database which she says 'does not belong to' HJS.

(www.standard.co.uk/news/london/lady-de-rothschild-sues-thinktank-over-funds-from-caring-capitalism-summit-9625722.html)

Pleas for such inclusive capitalism have come from those who argue that rising inequality is impossible to sustain. US billionaire Nick Hanauer dramatically warned fellow 'plutocrats' in June 2014 that the pitchforks were coming:

> Some inequality is intrinsic to any high-functioning capitalist economy. The problem is that inequality is at historically high levels and getting worse every day. Our country is rapidly becoming less a capitalist society and more a feudal society. Unless our policies change dramatically, the middle class will disappear, and we will be back to late 18th-century France. Before the revolution.
>
> And so I have a message for my fellow filthy rich, for all of us who live in our gated bubble worlds: Wake up, people. It won't last.
>
> If we don't do something to fix the glaring inequities in this economy, the pitchforks are going to come for us. No society can sustain this kind of rising inequality. In fact, there is no example in human history where wealth accumulated like this and the pitchforks didn't eventually come out. You show me a highly unequal society, and I will show you a police state. Or an uprising. There are no counterexamples. None. It's not if, it's when.
>
> (www.politico.com/magazine/story/2014/06/the-pitchforks-are-coming-for-us-plutocrats-108014.html)

However, more intensive rather than more inclusive capitalism is apparently on its way. What seems now to be taking hold, at least on the part of right-wing governments, such as the Conservatives in Canada, UK and Australia, is a kind of 'catastrophe capitalism'. With these right-wing governments committed to capitalism, the crisis can only be solved by introducing more capitalism, which creates more chaos, leading to more capitalism! As I write, the UK government is busily privatising the state-owned National Health Service, an icon of socialism in Britain. Workers can no longer gain funds for unfair dismissal cases, so firms can, if they wish, increasingly bully employees with impunity if they so desire. A Deregulation Bill, passed with the support of the opposition Labour Party, allows public green space to be sold off to private companies. Increasingly, profit is the goal of life in Britain, a sacred principle for politicians of most parties. Fracking, which poisons water and accelerates climate change by releasing methane gas, is being heavily supported with tax cuts, subsidies and planning changes that allow fracking companies to operate below people's homes and land. In Australia, while forest fires have been linked to climate change, the carbon tax has been abolished by a prime minister in denial. In Canada, the highly polluting tar sands sites are being expanded. Workers' rights are being weakened all over the world. Meanwhile, bankers' bonuses are defended to the death in another element of this system which appears almost designed to fail.

The creation of crises, as various writers on the left have pointed out, leads to new opportunities for corporations. The future unfolding is likely to be characterised by more conflict, but also more contracts for capitalists. Providing an alternative based on the common good, rather than the needs of the 1 percent, is challenging. However, anti-capitalism has deep roots, has never been removed and has the potential to flower.

The Anti-capitalist Movement

Anti-capitalist sentiments pre-date capitalism as it is understood as an advanced industrial or post-industrial system based on profit and investment. Given that centuries before capitalism existed, Jesus threw the moneylenders out of the temple, one wonders how he would have reacted to contemporary church towers being used as mobile phone masts or the corporate enthusiasms of some American Protestants. Five centuries before Christ entered the temple, the Buddha, Gautama Siddhartha, set up a philosophical system in opposition to the notion of economic (wo)man and the desire for ever more consumer goods. The fact that the Buddha's holiness was indicated, amongst other signs, by his long ear lobes, a symbol of nobility enjoyed by the then Nepalese ruling class whose lavish jewellery distended their ears, suggests that Zen is only half of the process. Challenging organised religion, the philosopher Spinoza argued that, shorn of superstition, the true faith advocated obedience to the principle of mutual love or the common good. Rebellion against empire has a long history too. The Spartacus uprising, where the slaves attempted to overthrow Roman power, deserves a mention, immortalised as it was by Rosa Luxemburg's brave but failed Spartacist revolution of 1919 and put into celluloid by the Marxist scriptwriter Howard Fast (Bronner 1987; Fast 1990). From the peasant revolutionaries such as John Ball to the Anabaptists who took on and nearly defeated the Saxon Lutheran princes, there is a tradition of struggle against established economic and political power that stretches back centuries (Strayer 1991).

In Britain during the eighteenth century, small producers, farmers and workers who insisted instead on the maintenance of a moral economy that placed need before greed used direct action to oppose the power of the rich and powerful (Tilly 1978). Land enclosure was fought with a series of peasant revolts and oppressive landlords were shamed in the seventeenth century by ritual processions known as 'charivari or skimmingtons' (Wall 2004). In Ireland, oppressive landowners were humiliated by hunger strikers who starved themselves to death at their gates in the nineteenth century. The so-called 'utopian socialists' continued the habit of resistance to the market, particularly in Britain and France. It is worth mentioning Robert Owen, the factory-owning radical, who attempted to build a socialist commonwealth in the early nineteenth century (Taylor 1982). Karl Marx, who spent his entire adult life attempting to understand capitalism at the very time it was maturing, sought to create a system to help fight it (Harvey 1990; Wheen 2000). Marx's attitude to capitalism was complex; while he attacked it as exploitative, he also saw it as a progressive force, which by developing the means of production would pave the way to a new society. For good and sometimes for ill, the twentieth century saw Marxist-inspired revolutions over much of the globe. In turn, Marx's anarchist detractors created militant movements opposed to capitalism during the nineteenth and twentieth centuries (Woodcock 1963).

The Frankfurt School of western Marxists, based around figures such as Adorno, Horkheimer and Marcuse, saw capitalism as a totalitarian system that controlled the working class via parliamentary democracy and consumerism (Jay 1973). According to Marcuse, representative democracy seduces the public into thinking that they can participate politically, when in fact they are being manipulated by a capitalist elite who choose the real rulers of society. Marcuse partly helped inspire the student uprisings of the late 1960s and early 1970s, particularly in Paris in 1968 (Brown 1974).

Drawing upon both the Frankfurt School and feminism, green movements have crystallised during the last quarter of the twentieth century to argue that a society focused on market economics diminishes human beings and manipulates spiritual and social needs into forms of consumerism (Snyder 1974). Greens have attacked capitalism, above all, because of its emphasis on economic growth, which they have seen as ecologically unsustainable (Douthwaite 1993; Porritt 1984). Activists have increasingly targeted corporations as a source of ecological and human injustice. From the boycott of Nestlé over its high-pressure selling of powdered milk to mothers whose lack of access to clean water resulted in raised infant mortality, to animal rights campaigns against vivisecting companies, anti-corporate protest has grown more diverse.

The Zapatista uprising of January 1994 is pivotal to the revival of anti-cap-italism in recent decades. This previously obscure guerrilla army occupied five southern Mexican provinces to protest at the introduction of the North American Free Trade Agreement (NAFTA), which they believed would lead to the loss of their land to multinationals. Their spokesperson Marcos argued, 'NAFTA is a death sentence because it leads to competition based on your level of skill, and what skill level can illiterate people have? And look at this land. How can we compete with farms in California and Canada?' (Russell 1995: 6). The Zapatistas were reported as stating: 'There are those with white skins and a dark sorrow. Our struggle walks with these skins. There are those who have dark skins and a white arrogance; against them is our fire. Our armed path is not against skin colour but against the colour of money' (*Earth First! Update* 53, November 1994: 3).

The Zapatistas fought to prevent these '*ejidos*', or communal landholdings, from being sold to private landowners. The Zapatista Army of National Liberation began as a local militia to defend the poorest people of Mexico's poorest provinces, but mutated into a wider campaign against capitalism, motivated by fear that free trade would create even greater suffering in the Chiapas. The Zapatistas exploited the power of the Internet, a product of capitalism and driving force of globalisation, to help kickstart the anti-capitalist mobilisation during the 1990s and the early years of this century (Anon. 1998; Holloway and Pelaez 1998).

Following 9/11 and the second Iraq War, anti-capitalist protests waned; however, the emergence of left governments in Latin America, including Venezuela, Bolivia and Ecuador, has promoted an alternative to neo-liberal globalisation. The financial crisis of 2008–09 and the resulting recession had contradictory effects. The Occupy protests and new anti-capitalists political parties like Podemos in Spain and Syriza in Greece are products, at least in part, of this crisis. Yet while the intellectual arguments for unrestrained capitalism were undermined, at the same time, programmes of austerity were used to deregulate economies and promote neo-liberalism. There are a number of cogent arguments for a market economy and capitalism, to which we shall now turn.

Globalisation, Capitalism and the Arguments for Neo-liberalism

It is important to define the key terms and to explore, albeit briefly, the arguments used to defend economic orthodoxy. Globalisation is a much-debated term but can be defined straightforwardly as the decline in the power of nation states and the growing flow of resources on a planetary scale. While technology, culture and other factors come into play, globalisation is first and foremost an economic process driven by market forces. The market is a system in which we buy and sell items. In theory, the market is made up of thousands of competing firms, whose desire for profit means they provide goods and services. Even some supposed 'anti-capitalists' such as David Korten, author of *When Corporations Rule the World* (2001), view the market as a positive and practical way of organising economic activity. However, the market tends to evolve into capitalism. Capitalism is, essentially, a system where profits are made within a market-based context and reinvested in new capital equipment, that is, machines and information technology (IT) used to produce even more goods and services. Some theorists have suggested that forms of 'state capitalism' can also be identified, where the state, rather than private companies, exploits workers and the environment.

However, capitalism is based not on the intense competition between thousands of companies, but on the creation of markets dominated by a handful of enormous firms. Food retailing is a good example of this process. In Britain, thousands of bakeries, greengrocers and corner shops have disappeared since the 1950s, and four or five large supermarkets now control much of the market. To survive under capitalism, a firm must, generally, make profit. Profit is reinvested to expand the size of the firm; if profit were frittered away rather than reinvested, the firm would risk being put out of business by more efficient rivals. Investment allows a firm to expand its market share, and as it sells more items it can exploit economies of scale. This concept is based on the idea that as a firm grows larger, production costs fall per item produced. Such economies occur because larger firms can bulk-buy raw materials more cheaply than smaller firms; larger firms can make more efficient use of machinery, employ specialist staff and more easily gain funds for expansion in the form of bank loans. Smaller firms generally have higher costs and tend to be pushed out of business. There are numerous linked processes that help explain the evolution of markets into capitalist systems. The creation of public limited companies allows firms to borrow money in return for giving others a 'share'. Such share ownership allows swift expansion but aids the process of replacing small businesses owned by individual entrepreneurs with faceless corporations. Public companies gain an institutional existence, have the legal status of individuals and, like all good bureaucracies, tend to be self-perpetuating.

The capitalist system, as we shall see in subsequent chapters, is complex. Workers must be made to work and consumers must be persuaded to consume to sustain growth. Ever more complex financial instruments are used to allow capitalism to grow and change in order to survive. Banks, to cut a long story short, lend money from depositors to borrowers and create more money in the process. Banking has been one target of anti-capitalist concern because of the banks' ability to make money out of money and use this power to shape society. Share ownership and the basic banking functions are the first steps on a ladder of increasing financial abstraction, with ever more esoteric devices being used to make money out of money and, at the same time, to support capitalist growth. The drive for profit fuels globalisation as firms seek new markets to sell their products and new sources of cheap raw materials and labour. The creation of global markets is also strongly conditioned by the financial side of capitalist growth. 'Hot money', so-called because it moves from one country to another and is transformed from one currency to another and then back again, erodes the barrier between nations. If a country introduces policies hostile to capitalism, currency tends to flow out, creating an economic crisis. To maintain a strong exchange rate, pro-capitalist policies are often a necessity.

Hedge funds are an increasingly important financial institution. Hedging started by meeting a practical need but soon changed into something much more complex. Hedging is a way of providing security, as in the phrase 'hedging a bet'. For example, an investor concerned that the exchange rate for the pound sterling will fall, can buy the right to sell pounds in three months' time at the present value, so if the currency crashes, losses will be prevented. For a fee, risk is removed. Various forms of right-to-buy, such as a right to hedge are bought and sold, including varied financial 'options' and 'derivatives'. Essentially, mathematically complex forms of betting have become an increasingly important global economic activity.

Supporters of capitalist globalisation are often termed 'neo-liberals' supposedly because of their renewed faith in the 'liberal' unconstrained free market. Yet neo-liberalism is associated increasingly with the celebration of powerful corporations rather than competitive markets with many relatively small firms. Neo-liberals are confident that the pursuit of financial gain, the accumulation of private property and the race for personal wealth are to be welcomed (Bhagwati 2004; Wolf 2004). They believe that capitalism is the road to prosperity, pleasure, freedom, justice and all that is beneficial. Capitalism, because it is based on market forces, is both natural and good. For the advocates of unrestrained capitalism, the only alternative to market forces is government planning and control. They consider intervention inefficient because government planners cannot take into account all the thousands of pieces of information necessary for an economy to function well. In the Soviet Union, it is assumed, the state's planning did not meet the needs of consumers, and provided no incentive for workers to work hard so as to raise production.

In contrast to bureaucratic planning, the market regulates the economy via forces of demand and supply. Adam Smith, whose book *The Wealth of Nations* launched market-based economics in 1776, believed that these market forces manage wealth for the good of the community. If consumers demand goods and are prepared to back up their desire with hard cash, firms will supply their wants in order to make a profit. Competition between firms means that neither consumers nor workers will be exploited. If a firm cuts its wages, workers will sell their labour to a rival and maintain their standard of living. Wage rises can be used to encourage workers to retrain, to work harder and to raise production through greater participation. Likewise, market forces benefit shoppers: if a firm provides shoddy or expensive goods, consumers will go elsewhere. The market is freedom. It is a tool of liberation for workers, who can choose to work for the firm that pays the highest wage.

The market system leads to capitalism, because firms have an incentive to invest in new technology to produce cheaper goods to undercut rivals and maintain profits. The market system is based on greed, but greed fuels the common good and drives progress forward as industrialists strive to create new products and new production techniques. Capitalism is a source of new ideas and products. Such growth tends to spread prosperity to the entire community via a process labelled 'trickle down' economics. Even if a wealthy minority do exist, they must use their wealth to purchase goods and services from others, and in so doing, they create jobs and the basis for growing prosperity.

The market is seen as a force for democracy because it breaks up the power of the old feudal elements of society. Monarchs lose their power and companies must respect the rest of the community if they wish to gain customers and attract staff. Money is profoundly democratic because whatever the social rank, gender, or ethnicity of the person spending it, it still has the same value for firms seeking profit. The notion of private property, a precondition for and goal of the market, makes it difficult for the state to control private citizens.

The pro-capitalist messengers believe that the system brings ever greater benefits. The classic free market is decentralised, with economic decisions being taken at a grass-roots level. The market, according to advocates, also provides a cleaner environment because consumers can purchase greener goods, and, as levels of prosperity rise, societies generally become more environmentally aware. Bjørn Lomborg, the Danish statistician, has argued that resources such as oil and fish are increasing in quantity while pollution is being defeated by prosperity (Lomborg 2001).

Responding to critics of capitalism, Graeme Leech in *City A.M.* argues that capitalism rests on culture and institutions; blaming the economic system for problems is like blaming one's car for a crash. Drive it properly and it will speed you to your destination without danger:

> Capitalism is the greatest system in history for wealth creation. Nothing comes close to it. The freedom and human flourishing it has provided is mesmerising – just look at the progress of humanity over the past two centuries. But capitalism is built on institutions, and those institutions are largely built on values such as honesty, freedom, responsibility and vitality. The attack on capitalism at present is both at the level of values and institutions. The pillars are crumbling.
>
> Further, it's not at all clear what else is on offer other than more statist solutions to state-created problems. There may be utopian dreams, but they're a nonsense. As Martin Wolf has written: 'Those who condemn the immorality of liberal capitalism do so in comparison to a society of saints that has never existed and never will.'
>
> Our consumerist, materialist society does appear excessive, but remember that it emerges from the free expression of tastes and preferences you and I have chosen. If we don't like it, we're free to choose something else. That's the whole point.
>
> (www.cityam.com/1403122339/free-economies-will-crumble-if-we-fail-make-moral-case-capitalism)

What's Wrong with Capitalism?

Anti-capitalists note that far from being competitive our economy is dominated by mega-corporations who have scant interest in 'market forces'. They also suggest the bloody, chaotic and unjust origins of capitalism are removed from neo-liberal version of history. Slavery, land enclosure, forced labour, colonialism and most of the accompanying rape and pillage is ignored. Capitalism did not evolve gently but emerged covered in blood in a violent process termed 'primitive accumulation'. Climate change, declining fish stocks, the rise of the automobile and the prevalence of low-level nuclear waste suggest that statistics indicating a cleaner environment need questioning. Sadly in 2015, free marketeers often deny that climate change is influenced by burning fossil fuels, as discussed in Chris Mooney's book *The Republican War on Science* (2005).

Challenging the neo-liberal orthodoxy, anti-capitalists point to a range of problems that have grown with globalisation. Inequality is perhaps the most obvious. Thomas Piketty, in *Capital in the Twenty-First Century* (2014), has argued that, with the exception of one period in the twentieth century, inequality has tended to increase. This is, essentially, because those who own assets tend to see their income rise at a faster rate than those who don't. Piketty feels that this has negative consequences, and that policy makers should find ways of reversing or at least blunting this trend. Ideally, he would like to see a global tax to redistribute wealth.

In 2014, it was reported that the UK's richest one thousand people had doubled their wealth in the preceding five years, while the number of those living in poverty and resorting to food banks had sharply risen. The Equality Trust found the richest 1% of Britons had the same wealth as 54% of the rest of the UK population (www.theguardian.com/politics/2014/jul/24/green-party-calls-wealth-tax-assets-multimillionaires). Research by the charity Oxfam showed that the 85 richest people on the planet were as wealthy as 50 per cent of the world's population (www.oxfam.org.uk/blogs/2014/01/rigged-rules-mean-economic-growth-is-increasingly-winner-takes-all-for-rich-elites). In *The Spirit Level* (2010), a study of the negative results of economic inequality, Richard Wilkinson and Kate Pickett argue that inequality leads to societies run by, and for, the hyper-rich:

> Economists sometimes suggest that the market is like a democratic voting system: our expenditure pattern is, in effect, our vote on how productive resources should be allocated between competing demands. If this is true, someone with 20 times the income of another in effect gets 20 times as many votes. As a result, inequality gravely distorts the ability of economies to provide for human needs: because the poor cannot afford better housing,

their demand for it is 'ineffective', yet the spending of the rich ensures scarce productive assets are devoted instead to the production of luxuries.

(www.newstatesman.com/society/2010/11/inequality-social-health-essay)

In the former Soviet Union, the creation of a market economy led to catastrophe. In an article subtitled 'Russia appears to be committing suicide', noted that 'since 1989 the population of the former Soviet states has plunged by several million and is projected to fall from 147 million today [2004] to 120 million in 2030' (*The Economist*, 20 May 2004). Declining fertility, violence, sexually transmitted diseases, tuberculosis and alcoholism were symptoms 'of the long, dark night of the Russian soul ushered in by the disorienting collapse of communism'.

There are a number of explanations as to why globalisation paradoxically boosts GNP rates and at the same time pushes up poverty. Globalisation allows companies to move easily from country to country, enabling them to pay far less tax to governments, which leads to less redistribution. Equally, the monopoly power of drug firms was a major factor in pushing down life expectancy in Africa during the 1990s. Christian Aid cites Mara Rossi, head of the AIDS department of the Catholic Diocese of Ndola, Zambia, who noted:

> The availability of drugs to treat HIV/AIDS is an example of how capitalism fails to benefit some of the world's poorest and most needy people. Because of the monopoly of multinational pharmaceutical companies, drugs are not available to the majority of HIV infected people in Asia and Africa. These drugs must be made accessible in countries such as Zambia. It's no good promising loans to buy anti-retroviral drugs that in the end will increase foreign debt. The majority of AIDS patients in Africa need clean water and food as well as drugs to treat their illness. (Christian Aid 2000)

Neo-liberalism encourages governments to cut welfare programmes globally, in both the South and the North. Subsidies for cheap food have largely vanished. Privatisation has made it more expensive for the poorest to afford basic utility services such as clean water. Welfare benefits have been reduced or abolished in parts of the globe including the US. Capitalist globalisation makes it difficult for trade unions to protect workers' pay and conditions. Multinationals can keep moving to countries with ever lower wages, making it difficult for workers in developed countries to maintain employment and for those in poor countries to improve conditions.

Democracy is another area of concern for the anti-capitalists. While the number of states with nominally democratic systems has increased, globalisation has robbed voters of much of their influence over governments. The World Trade Organization's rules tend to reduce the sovereignty of local and national government by ruling that much of the legislation produced by states is protectionist and therefore illegitimate. Multinationals, which often are wealthier than nations, can effectively force countries to reject legislation that may damage corporate interests. Even supporters of capitalism sometimes admit the essentially undemocratic nature of the market. For example, Thomas Friedman, author of *The Lexus and the Olive Tree* (1999a), a lengthy hymn to market-based globalisation, has argued:

> For globalism to work, America can't be afraid to act like the almighty superpower that it is ... The hidden hand of the market will never work without a hidden fist – McDonald's cannot flourish without McDonnell Douglas, the designer of the F-15. And the hidden fist that keeps the world safe for Silicon Valley's technologies is called the United States Army, Air Force, Navy and Marine Corps. (Friedman 1999b)

Poverty is increased and democracy eroded by a process of social dumping or levelling down, driven by both the WTO and the multinationals. Countries that reduce governmental controls, taxes and public expenditure attract more investment by international corporations. In the desperate race to attract foreign investment, countries have a huge incentive to sweep away forms of social protection such as trade union rights, maximum working hours and an adequate minimum wage. Despite an ageing population, fewer and fewer workers can gain access to adequate pensions from their employers. Countries such as China and the Philippines have created blandly named 'Export Processing Zones' (EPZs), where manufacturers can ignore legislation protecting workers, so as to drive pay and conditions down, lowering average total costs.

Anti-capitalists believe that the process of neo-liberal globalisation has concentrated wealth and power into the hands of an ever-diminishing minority. This minority remains US-based and uses global institutions to cement its dominance. Thus, the existence of the US as the world's hyper-power is seen as increasingly damaging, allowing a tiny minority of North Americans to shape the world to serve their own interests. The growth of capitalism is based on the exploitation of the working class, small farmers and peasants, and it largely excludes women from meaningful participation in political and economic decision making. Racism is part of the process. All but a tiny minority are defined as 'the other' and seen as a means of creating wealth rather than as human beings with their own aspirations: creative, social, cultural and ecological. Anti-capitalists also challenge the ethos of capitalism, where local diversity in the arts, cuisine and other aspects of life are driven out, creating a homogenised global culture. Everywhere, individuals drink Coca-Cola, wear Nike and eat McDonald's. The sociologist George Ritzer created the concept of the 'McDonaldization' of society to explain how mass production is creating a world of increasing modular uniformity (Ritzer 1995). Such a capitalist culture breeds alienation, a feeling of homelessness in a world dominated by accountancy, which degrades even those who benefit in material terms from the rule of capital.

Ever-increasing capitalist accumulation damages the environment by lowering standards of protection and by locking us into an escalating system of waste. The world circles to destruction around a mountain of decaying trainers and trashed soft drink cans. The drive for endlessly growing international trade means that goods are transported ever-increasing distances, driving up fuel consumption and, consequently the C02 emissions which contribute to climate change. Higher agricultural exports encourage farmers to exploit ecologically sensitive and essential areas, such as the mangrove swamps and rainforests in Asia and Latin America. Capitalist growth for the whole planet would demand, according to some critics, the resources of four planet Earths, if everyone attained the average American standard of living, and such resources would have to grow to maintain the capitalist system into the future (Wilson 2002).

Products could be made to last longer, shared or made easier to repair. A central argument of this book is that we could have more access to the things we need, more real prosperity, without wasting resources. Yet sustainable prosperity challenges capitalism: the term 'planned obsolescence' is instructive. If goods are designed to fall apart so new products can be sold, profits can grow. It's argued that Apple make it difficult for customers to replace batteries on Macs, encouraging customers to buy new machines rather than replace them. Bad for customers, bad for the environment, good for profit: 'It's a form of planned obsolescence,' says Wiens. 'General Motors invented planned obsolescence in the 1920s. Apple is doing the same thing' (www.cultofmac.com/77814/is-apple-guilty-of-planned-obsolescence).

Neo-liberals argue that the world is getting cleaner, resources are growing rather than shrinking, poverty is disappearing and democracy is on the rise. The evidence is against them on all these counts.

Diversity or Chaos: Cataloguing Different Anti-capitalisms

It is possible to disentangle a series of different, although to some extent overlapping, anti-capitalisms. One group whose work underpins the protest can be termed 'anti-capitalist capitalists' (see Chapter 2). As establishment figures who have participated in global economic institutions, they cannot easily be dismissed by advocates of neo-liberal globalisation. George Soros and Joseph Stiglitz are excellent examples. Soros, an international financier who has made millions of dollars from playing the money markets, has come to argue that unrestrained free market forces erode democracy and create social chaos.

Stiglitz, who won the Nobel Prize (strictly speaking, the Swedish Bank prize) for economics for his development of microeconomic theory, echoes many of Soros's concerns, and is a prominent economist who headed the World Bank (Stiglitz 2002, 2003).

Others focus on the role of multinational corporations, arguing that footloose international companies drive down wages, hypnotise us into destructive consumerism and lower environmental standards. Naomi Klein, in *No Logo* (2000a), sees globalisation as leading to a race to the bottom, where countries struggle to lower standards so as to attract inward investment. Multinationals selling brands outsource production to companies that use the cheapest labour. David Korten, author of *When Corporations Ruled the World* (2001), argues that large corporations should be removed and replaced with a local market based on family and community-run businesses.

Green Parties and movements have argued that free trade lowers protection for workers and the environment and that unrestrained economic growth is unsustainable. While green economics overlaps with other schools of thought, the emphasis on ecological problems and the green critique of economic growth are especially significant. Chapter 4 deals with green critics of our current economic system.

Other anti-capitalists focus on money, banking and debt. The 2008 financial crisis made such critiques more cogent and accepted. Those who see finance as an evil and advocate the creation of debt-free money, along with less radical opponents of finance capital are discussed in Chapter 5.

Marxists, other socialists and trade unionists have long challenged the market. Chapter 6 introduces Marxist accounts of modern capitalism and neo-liberal globalisation. Chapter 7 deals with anarchism and autonomist Marxism, focusing on the work of Michael Hardt and Toni Negri. In *Empire* (2001a), Hardt and Negri argue that a militant movement – the multitude – can overthrow capitalism and create a new kind of society. Autonomism is placed in a historical tradition of anarchist economic thought, ranging from Kropotkin to the workers' communes of the Spanish Civil War. The Marxist and post-modern influences on militant autonomism are also outlined in Chapter 7, with an emphasis on *Empire* and the Occupy protests.

Chapter 8 examines the case for ecosocialism, which suggests the insights of both Marx and the Greens need to be combined if capitalism is to be understood and resisted. For ecosocialists, the basic atoms and molecules of capitalist production conjure up debt, multinational corporations, the dislocations of 'free' trade and all the rest. The idea that capitalism must continue to grow and dominate the planet is terrifying.

Chapter 9 looks at feminist economics, also a diverse field, with pro-market feminists, reformist feminists such as Amartya Sen, together with ecofeminists, radical feminists, Marxist and autonomist feminists. While rarely using the label 'feminist', the ideas of Elinor Ostrom, the first and thus far the only woman to win the Nobel Prize for economics, are also introduced. Finally, Chapter 10 concludes with a discussion of how an anti-capitalist economy can be built and sustained.

Debating Apocalypse

Even a brief survey of the main currents of anti-capitalism throws up a number of difficult debates that demand attention. First is the issue of what can be crudely termed 'conspiracy' or 'concept'? Are economic concepts mere window dressing to help legitimise the power of one group over another? While conventional market economists, the media and most politicians argue that there are enduring economic ground rules that provide a guide to constructing a prosperous future, many anti-capitalists suggest that economics is almost entirely irrelevant as an explanation for the workings of the system. The monetary reformers often argue that bankers control the politicians, so as to maintain power over the monetary system. Many of those concerned with trade, whether localists who want more protection or fair traders who want less, believe that bodies like the WTO are motivated not by a concern with comparative advantage and other economic principles, but simply by a wish to benefit the rich and powerful.

Conspiracies make life easy to explain and provide enemies – the bankers, the capitalists, the US – that are easy to attack. There is little doubt that many of our problems result from those with power exploiting those without. Unfortunately, conspiracy does not explain everything. While conspiracies exist, activists should also be critical of concepts and should beware of stereotyping that delivers an enemy who is satisfyingly easy to label, condemn and attack.

The blame game can also shade into a form of pseudo or not-so-pseudo racism, where entire groups are scapegoated for economic ills (Chua 2003). In the United States, politician Pat Buchanan has campaigned against the WTO, arguing along with other far-right nationalists that a one-world conspiracy exists to limit local diversity. Banking and capitalism are seen as creating a new world order that benefits only rootless cosmopolitans and wrecks nation states. The far right unites with the far left in its choice of conspiracy enemies (Rupert 2000). Martin Walker, in his study of the far-right British political party, the National Front, described a racist anti-globalism:

Chesterton [the founder of the National Front] combined his anti-Semitism, his anti-Communism, his anti-Americanism and his fervent patriotism and concluded that Jewish Wall Street capitalism was the same thing as Russian Communism. Jewish capital had funded the Bolshevik Revolution of 1917, he believed, and Jewish capital had funded the development and technological base of Soviet Russia. The Moscow-Wall Street axis had as its major objective the ruin of the British Empire, the mongrelization of the British race, and eventual world government. The United Nations, NATO and Jewish people were all to be regarded with the deepest suspicion as agents of 'the money power'. (Walker 1977: 29)

A second key issue is ecological sustainability. Many anti-capitalists would like to see the economy grow, essentially, forever. Yet for other anti-capitalists inspired by the green critique, such as ecosocialists, economic growth, however measured in a capitalist society, will destroy scarce resources, devastate global ecology and impoverish us in a whole range of ways subtle and not so subtle. The debate about growth throws up profound difficulties; it seems wrong to say that developing countries should not grow, yet capitalist growth for a minority already looks unsustainable given problems such as the greenhouse effect. What would the planet look like if car ownership was as high in Morocco or Mongolia as it is today in New Jersey? Perhaps ways can be found of enjoying life and meeting needs without producing more and more forever and ever?

A third area concerns strategy. Can the global economic system be changed by gentle reform plans, or are the problems identified so profound as to demand sudden and even violent change? Is it possible or desirable to describe a utopia, to paint a picture of a world without capitalism? How can a new kind of society be built that delivers prosperity without creating unsustainable environmental damage or crippling injustice? Changing apparently fixed tracks to the future is not going to be easy. Should anti-capitalists build alternatives or focus on blocking what exists and is cancerous?

These issues run through the entirety of this book and must run beyond it. Suffice to say, we need to take history by the scruff of the neck and debate alternatives that genuinely benefit humanity and other species. The literary theorist Terry Eagleton has argued cogently that the most bizarre utopians are those who predict that capitalism can feed the world and continue into the distant future. The soothsayer 'with his head buried most obdurately in the sand, is the hard-nosed pragmatist who imagines the future will be pretty much like the present only more so ... Our children are likely to live in interesting times' (*Red Pepper*, February 2004). While Marx famously taught us to doubt everything, we can be certain that another world is both possible and necessary. Getting there remains the question.

2

VACCINATING AGAINST ANTI-CAPITALISM: STIGLITZ, SOROS AND FRIENDS

> Interestingly, the state's share of GNP has not declined perceptibly. What has happened instead is that the taxes on capital and employment have come down while other forms of taxation particularly on consumption have kept increasing. In other words, the burden of taxation has shifted from capital to citizens. That is not exactly what had been promised, but one cannot even speak of unintended consequences because the outcome was exactly as the free-marketers intended. (Soros 1998: 112)

Some surprisingly sober and suited figures have been prepared to criticise neo-liberalism and the unfettered free market. Joseph Stiglitz, former chief economist of the World Bank, and George Soros, perhaps the world's best-known financier, are the most important. Other 'establishment' figures have echoed their assumptions that the capitalist market needs careful national and international regulation to function sustainably. During the 1990s, the late Sir James Goldsmith, the corporate asset-stripper once condemned as personifying capitalism at its worst, attacked free trade and took on GATT, before it was fashionable to do so (Goldsmith 1994). James Tobin, the economist who argues that speculative flows of capital should be taxed, also springs to mind. The example of John Gray, a former Thatcherite and contributor to the free market Institute of Economic Affairs, is instructive. His detailed and passionate attack on globalisation from the right is difficult for conservatives to answer (Gray 2002). Drawing upon the radical social thinker Karl Polanyi, he argues that neo-liberalism leads to social chaos, smashing the bonds of family and community necessary for a stable human order.

These critics argue that US-style capitalism is far less efficient than European or Asian variants. They believe that the Washington Consensus of unlimited free trade, privatisation and strong deflationary policies actually prevents capitalism from growing and developing countries from becoming financially secure. They echo the key assumption of the economist John Maynard Keynes, whose policies helped rescue the post-war global economy from recession and mass unemployment, that government intervention actually makes markets work more effectively. Their critique is not dissimilar to that of Paul Hirst and Graeme Thompson, who argue from a social democratic perspective that capitalism can (and should) be reined in by the nation state (Hirst and Thompson 1999). Long before the 2008 financial crash, they argued that deregulation would lead to catastrophe. Austerity has been attacked by them as leading to disaster. This chapter examines Stiglitz's and Soros's challenge to economic orthodoxy and shows how their ideas are derived from Keynes's reformist interventionist economic approach developed in the 1930s.

Stiglitz and Soros

Joseph Stiglitz became chief economist of the World Bank in 1997. He was also one of President Clinton's key economic advisers and chaired the US Council of Economic Advisers. His ground-breaking academic work on asymmetric information – the idea that markets may fail because consumers and producers have imperfect knowledge – won him a Nobel Prize in 2001 (*Guardian*, 11 October 2001). In 1999, he resigned from the World Bank because he felt that the more powerful International Monetary Fund (IMF) was blocking its agenda of reform. In 2001, he published *Globalization and its Discontents*, arguing that neo-liberal globalisation had led to poverty for millions of people and would fail unless thoughtfully reformed. The title echoes Freud's *Civilisation and its Discontents*, an explosive tome that shows how apparent rationality is based upon repression. Stiglitz observed, 'For decades, people in the developing world have rioted when the austerity programs imposed on their countries proved to be too harsh … what is new is the wave of protest in developed countries' (Stiglitz 2002: 3). While the prophets of capitalism ignore or ridicule most of their opponents, they hate Stiglitz with a corrosive passion:

> Mr Stiglitz's prose reads like a draft dictated to a secretary whose mind was apt to wander: readers too will be drifting off a lot. Also, the narrative conveys a whining self-righteousness that is always tiresome and sometimes downright repellent. (*The Economist*, 6 June 2002)

George Soros was raised in poverty, made a fortune and is now best known for using his wealth for ambitious political and social projects. Born in Hungary, his family hid their Jewish origins to avoid extermination by the Nazis and their anti-Semitic puppets. In the post-war years, Soros found his way to Switzerland, then moved to the UK to study at the London School of Economics (LSE). In 1956, he left for the United States where he managed to make a massive investment fortune. He specialised in arbitrage, the art of skimming off the differential change in value from dealing, especially dealing in currency. He was an early practitioner in the high-risk hedge fund market, an 'investment of $100,000 in Soros's Quantum Fund in 1969 was worth $300 million by 1996' (Hertz 2001: 137). In 1992, he bought billions of dollars' worth of foreign currency being sold by the British government to prop up demand for sterling. As the pound slid in value, his currency worth accelerated upwards. Britain was forced out of the European exchange rate mechanism and Soros as a result became even wealthier.

Fiercely hostile to the totalitarianism of both Hitler and Stalin, he embraced the free market philosophy of the Austrian philosopher Karl Popper. Soros established the Open Society Institute, his philanthropic foundation, in 1979, 'to help open up closed societies, help make open societies more viable, and foster a critical mode of thinking' (Soros 1998: 69). Popper argued that socialism led to a closed totalitarian society ruled by experts. Marx, for Popper, is prefigured by Plato who believed in a utopia governed by an elite of philosopher kings. Yet by 1995, Soros had come to believe that unfettered capitalism rather than socialist totalitarianism had become the main threat to freedom. Such sentiments are summed up in the title of his 1998 book, *The Crisis of Global Capitalism: Open Society Endangered*, which sees globalisation as a force that must be tamed if a market-based society is to be sustained.

Soros has advanced his ideas practically by funding a range of charitable projects and political campaigns. He allegedly helped to topple the president of Georgia in 2004 and poured dollars into anti-Bush campaigning:

> [He] gives away $400m a year through his Foundation and thus subsidizes many of the activist groups, luminaries and publications of the American left, probably dwarfing the sums that once trickled out of Langley or Moscow ... his monetary influence is one of those hushed secrets inside the left usually dismissed as conspiracy-thinking. (Sheasby 2003)

That a self-made capitalist, who has clawed his way to unimaginable wealth using the most abstract and advanced tools of unproductive finance such as derivatives and currency deals, is an opponent of the IMF and undiluted capitalism, should give apologists for 'business as usual' pause for critical thought.

Stiglitz and Soros on Financial Crisis, Recession and Austerity

Stiglitz and Soros were in a position to say 'I told you so' when it came to the 2008–09 financial crisis and resulting global recession. They have been strong critics of the austerity response of politicians like George Osborne, arguing that austerity was bound to make matter worse. The financial sector, by indulging in risky behaviour, had triggered the crisis and demands to cut government spending made it difficult to come out of recession. Stiglitz has argued that the power of financial institutions needs to be reduced and bankers should go to jail if they act in manipulative and disruptive ways: 'Banks and others have engaged in rent seeking, creating inequality, ripping off other people, and none of them have gone to jail' (<www.independent.co.uk/news/business/analysis-and-features/joseph-stiglitz-man-who-ran-world-bank-calls-for-bankers-to-face-the-music-7902920.html>).

Stiglitz addressed the Occupy camp in New York City and supported many of their demands; he has argued that the wealthy increasingly engineer the economic and social system to retain and enhance their power:

> Every economy needs lots of public investments – roads, technology, education … In a democracy you're going to get more of those investments if you have more equity. Because as societies get divided, the rich worry that you will use the power of the state to redistribute. They therefore want to restrict the power of the state so you wind up with weaker states, weaker public investments and weaker growth.
>
> (<www.independent.co.uk/news/business/analysis-and-features/joseph-stiglitz-man-who-ran-world-bank-calls-for-bankers-to-face-the-music-7902920.html>)

Soros has ridiculed attempts to reboot the global economy by cutting government spending during the recession, focusing on the British Conservative government of 2010–15, he noted, 'that austerity has resulted in a decline is not surprising. What is surprising is that anyone would be surprised by it' (www.telegraph.co.uk/finance/9828591/Soros-hits-out-at-Osbornes-austerity-programme.html). Soros and Stiglitz have criticised free market economics for several decades, arguing that the attempt to solve financial chaos and recession with more deregulation is dangerous. They have been consistent critics of the Washington Consensus and neo-liberalism.

From Keynes to Bretton Woods

Soros, Stiglitz and other establishment critics of neo-liberalism draw upon the work of John Maynard Keynes, who believed in the necessity of managing capitalism, both to provide a fair society and to maintain a capitalist system. During the 1930s, Europe and North America were plunged into recession. Economies shrank and unemployment figures mushroomed to millions. The resulting turmoil fuelled the political chaos that led to the Second World

War. The conventional 'liberal' or 'classical' free market economists believed that the economy worked best without government controls and tended to automatically correct any disequilibria. If demand for goods fell, prices would fall too and eventually shoppers would increase demand as they snapped up bargains. If individuals were unwilling to borrow money, interest rates (the price of money) would fall, and if rates fell low enough, demand for loans would pick up, rescuing the economy. Furthermore, if workers became unemployed, they could cut their wages until firms found them cheap enough to employ. These market advocates believed that apparently humane attempts to deal with poverty and unemployment, such as state welfare benefits, would simply make the recession deeper by discouraging wage-setting. Even socialist politicians, such as Rudolf Hilferding in Germany and Philip Snowden in Britain, came to accept this orthodoxy. As the years went by and liberal policies of non-intervention were accompanied by deeper recession, conventional economics became increasingly discredited. The only economies that seemed to work were to be found in Hitler's Germany and Stalin's Russia.

By the late 1930s, the western economies were slowly pulling out of the slump and demand rose with employment, as war led to large factory orders for guns, planes and assorted military paraphernalia. Nonetheless, by the 1940s and 1950s, the economic orthodoxy was largely abandoned for Keynesianism. Keynes suggested that economics has a psychological element: that if confidence is low, so too is consumption and growth. Prices, wages and interest rates may be 'sticky', by which Keynes meant they would not fall easily, because firms, banks and workers may be reluctant to lower them if they feel that they will still suffer when demand is low. Keynes argued that if people think bad economic news is on the horizon, they spend less and the bad economic news becomes a recessionary reality. Business people are edgy and suffer from a herd mentality, cutting investment when they fear bad economic news. Like deranged beasts, they stampede towards slump. The answer is for governments to inject spending into the economy when recession looks likely. In turn, if excessive spending threatens the economy, governments can control it by raising taxes and cutting expenditure.

In July 1944, Keynes acted as the British government's representative to the Bretton Woods Conference in New Hampshire, in the US. Bretton Woods aimed to create a new financial architecture and new global institutions to restore economic stability and remove the threat of world recession, after the war had been ended. The conference called for the creation of three key institutions. During the 1940s, the General Agreement on Tariffs and Trade (GATT), now known as the WTO, was established to sweep away barriers to trade in order to promote faster economic growth. The International Bank for Reconstruction and Development, commonly known as the World Bank, was set up to lend money to countries, initially for restoration of infrastructures that had decayed during recession and ultimately wrecked by war. Over time, the World Bank's role has increasingly shifted towards funding development projects in the South of the globe. Finally, the IMF was created to help countries faced with severe debt problems or balance of payments deficits. Stiglitz sees all three institutions as essentially Keynesian – examples of government intervention – aimed at making the market work and capitalism expand.

Against Washington

In the same way that revolutionary socialists argue that Stalin betrayed Lenin or Marx, moderate advocates of capitalism like Soros and Stiglitz argue that the IMF et al. have abandoned Keynes's original vision. It isn't that capitalism doesn't work; it is more the case that it hasn't been tried. According to Stiglitz:

> In its original conception, the IMF was based on a recognition that markets often did not work well – that they could result in massive unemployment and might fail to make needed funds available to countries to help restore their economies. The IMF was based on the belief that there was a need for collective action at the global level for economic stability ... Keynes would be rolling over in his grave if he could see what has happened to his child. (*Independent on Sunday*, 9 November 2003)

Since the 1980s, the IMF, WTO and World Bank have advocated the so-called Washington Consensus of fiscal austerity (government spending cuts), privatisation and market liberalisation. Swept along by the neo-liberal counter-revolution against Keynesian economics, the consensus argues that for development to occur, barriers to the market should be swept away. The policies that failed in 1930s Europe have been exported to almost the entire globe. Advocates of the Washington Consensus argued that the poorest countries in the world should cut government spending and increase taxes to reduce indebtedness. The tax burden should, of course, fall on ordinary citizens; taxes on profits would discourage investment and enterprise. State assets should be privatised as thoroughly as possible, while barriers to free trade should be swept away. Export-led growth is also advocated along with the removal of controls on capital. Multinational corporations are to be welcomed and government regulation slashed to the minimum.

While Soros and Stiglitz are by no means naturally hostile to the US, given their close links with previous American governments, they believe that the Washington Consensus, rather than being based purely on market ideology, is also inspired by the interests of an essentially US corporate elite. The Bretton

Woods institutions have massive power to impose their free market medicine: if they refuse to give a country a clean bill of health, foreign capital exits, leading to economic chaos. If a country rejects free market approaches, cash floods out of that country, forcing a rethink. By insisting that barriers to the movement of financial capital are removed, the Bretton Woods institutions make it difficult for countries to act independently and they become more closely tied to the whims of global financial markets. Indebted countries that reject the consensus are refused financial stabilisation deals by the IMF and aid from the World Bank. Even countries that are independent of IMF financial aid are influenced by the institution's prescriptions. Typically, British chancellors of the exchequer and Japanese finance ministers take close interest in the IMF's annual report of their countries' financial health.

Stiglitz believes that the emphasis on fighting inflation and reducing debt advocated by the IMF can be appropriate in some circumstances. He suggests that some Latin American countries during the 1980s attempted to print money to spend their way out of crisis, with predictable results in terms of high inflation: 'Countries cannot persistently run large deficits; and sustained growth is not possible with hyperinflation. Some level of fiscal discipline is required.' Neither does he reject all privatisation: 'Most countries would be better off with governments focusing on providing essential public services rather than running enterprises that would arguably perform better in the private sector, and so privitization often makes sense.' Equally, 'When trade liberalization – the lowering of tariffs and elimination of other protectionist measures – is done in the right way', so that inefficient sectors of the economy are removed and replaced with more competitive ones, there can be 'significant efficiency gains' (Stiglitz 2002: 53). Soros argues that in an 'ideal world' the complete removal of capital controls would be beneficial, noting that restrictions to prevent money moving across national borders create 'evasion, corruption and the abuse of power' (Soros 1998: 192). Suggesting that the collapse of the Soviet economy demanded significant change, including major privatisation, Soros notes: 'The fact that radical reforms are often radically misconceived does not obviate the need for radical reforms' (ibid.: 226).

However, both he and Stiglitz claim that these radical market-based policies have been applied in an inflexible and inappropriate way. Stiglitz argues that the Washington Consensus's obsession with reducing inflation is particularly damaging because it means that some of the poorest countries in the world must cut spending to prevent prices rising, when problems of joblessness and low growth are likely to be far more damaging. In Indonesia, to pick one example, Stiglitz notes how IMF-inspired cuts to food and fuel subsidies for the poor led to rioting (*Independent on Sunday*, 9 November 2003).

Privatisation breeds corruption when assets are sold off. Even when clean, privatisation often enriches an elite of corporate fat cats. Privatisation during a debt crisis when an economy is in chaos can mean that assets are sold at knock-down prices, which may simply mean that they can be bought up by US corporations which become stronger at the expense of developing countries. In Russia, according to Stiglitz, the swift privatisation of state assets led to their purchase by a criminal class who thereby gained massive political power.

Capital liberalisation has reinforced the tendency for democratic decision making to become subordinated to the demands of financial markets. Soros notes that tax burdens have been shifted from firms and financial operators to citizens, increasing inequality (Soros 1998: 112).

A country implementing policies that the financial markets find distasteful may find that the markets take their hot money and emerging share market portfolio funds elsewhere, causing slump and currency collapse. As well as tying developing countries to the free market agenda of the Washington Consensus, capital liberalisation means that such states are more susceptible to movements in global currency markets, which can cause sudden shocks to fragile economies:

> It has become an article of faith that capital controls should be abolished and the financial markets of individual countries, including banking, opened up to international competition. The IMF has even proposed amending its charter to make these goals more explicit. Yet the experience of the Asian crisis ought to make us pause. The countries that kept their financial markets closed weathered the storm better than those that were open. India was less affected than the Southeast Asian countries; China was better insulated than Korea. (Ibid.: 192)

Free trade is theoretically beneficial, but opening up an underdeveloped economy to trade has several major drawbacks. It may force down the price of commodities such as sugar or coffee, wrecking the livelihoods of peasant farmers who have little possibility of alternative employment. It can also destroy 'infant industries', that is, new industries that have yet to mature and become efficient, and will be killed by unprotected exposure to foreign competition. Stiglitz notes that to achieve growth the successful Asian economies such as Hong Kong, Japan and South Korea initially used selective protectionism to allow their industries to take off.

Soros and Stiglitz feel that the advocates of the Washington Consensus are remote from the problems of the developing world, act arrogantly and are consistently biased to the needs of the rich:

... modern high-tech warfare is designed to remove physical contact: dropping bombs from 50,000 feet ensures that one does not 'feel' what one does. Modern economic management is similar: from one's luxury hotel, one can callously impose policies about which one would think twice if one knew the people whose lives one was destroying. (Stiglitz 2002: 24)

The institutions promoting the Washington Consensus act as if they continue to bear the '[w]hite man's burden', persisting, according to Stiglitz, with the notion that they always know what is best (ibid.: 25). Stiglitz and Soros argue that the arrogance of the Washington institutions means that developing countries have little say in their own economic development and policies are imposed from above. Such arrogance inevitably breeds discontent, and even where globalisation has the potential to bring benefits, the Washington Consensus has fuelled a hostile counter-movement. Discontent is met by repression: rubber bullets against starving rioters. As Stiglitz observes:

A common characteristic is: We know best, and the developing countries should do what we tell them to ... They really see themselves as a harsh doctor, giving them the cod liver oil they need, even if they don't want it. The problem, of course, is that quite often the medicine ... kills the patient. (*Independent on Sunday*, 9 November 2003)

It is difficult to think of a single example of a country that has gained from the IMF model of structural adjustment. Botswana is often mentioned, but despite enjoying one of the globe's fastest economic growth rates, the Washington Consensus has not delivered sustainable prosperity:

The richest twenty per cent of the population earned more than twenty-five times as much as the poorest twenty per cent ... Botswana, at twenty-two per cent [population in work], has the world's sixth highest unemployment rate ... One of the few products of Botswana's increased economic activity which has been widely shared by its poorer inhabitants is AIDS. Women driven into prostitution by poverty are purchased by the truck drivers delivering goods to the elite. (Monbiot 2003b: 214)

In 2012, former World Bank Vice President Obiageli Katryn Ezekwesili noted that Botswana's income inequalities are amongst the worst in the world (www.botswanaguardian.co.bw/news/522-high-income-inequality-hampers-economic-growth).

Argentina, the Washington Consensus exemplar from South America, plunged into severe recession after following the model rigorously, with resulting mass unemployment, poverty and chaos, between 1998 and 2000. In recent years, Soros and Stiglitz have also, as noted, bitterly attacked austerity policies in developed countries, policies that have heaped tax increases on the poorest and cut services for those in most need.

Asymmetric Information and Reflexivity

While a number of critics wish to maintain a reformed capitalism, Soros and Stiglitz are particularly interesting because they challenge not only the excesses of global neo-liberalism, but also some of the foundations of economics. Economists, even many Keynesians, assume that markets generally work, with the actions of consumers and producers leading to efficient outcomes at a micro level. Stiglitz and Soros accept the principle of a market-based society but doubt that the market automatically delivers efficiency. Their critique, based on notions of reflexivity and asymmetric information, is similar to that of Keynes.

Economists since Alfred Marshall in the nineteenth century have argued that human beings are 'rational' in that they seek to maximise their personal benefits and minimise the costs of any transaction. Consumers aim to maximise 'utility', and producers profit. Both groups calculate the best course of action during millions of transactions. The actions of millions of producers and consumers functions as an 'invisible hand' creating choice, prosperity and even justice. The liberalisation suggested by the Washington Consensus is founded on assumptions of rationality, calculation and maximising behaviour. Given these foundations, it is safe to assume that the market should be extended as far as possible because it generates efficient outcomes.

Typically, we might argue that if a country removes capital controls, its entry into a global money market will bring benefits. If a country has sound economic policies, money will flow in as investors 'buy' its currency so as to make gains. If a country is running a trade deficit, demand for its currency will fall, because foreigners will demand less of it to buy the country's goods and services. Because demand falls, the value of the currency will fall; in turn, its exports will become cheaper and its imports more expensive. As more of its exports are sold and fewer imports are bought the deficit will be magicked away. The market is a structural device, a mechanism, for restoring 'equilibrium' or balance.

Yet, as Soros and Stiglitz argue, this notion of the market bears little resemblance to the conditions and complexities of modern economic reality. The money traded for goods is a tiny percentage of speculative currency flows, meaning that currencies are little affected by trade balances and therefore unlikely to float downwards to restore imbalance. With capital liberalisation, billions of dollars' worth of currencies flow in and out of economies in seconds. Such flows create waves of chaos rather than restoring equilibrium.

Shares, it is assumed, are bought for profit, so potentially profitable, well-managed companies will enjoy increased demand followed by rising share values. Rising share values will make it easier for such companies to expand. In reality, share values can reach mountainous heights before crashing back, as the dot.com bubble of the 1990s illustrated. Share values are often unrelated to company performance. Soros, who has made a billion-dollar fortune from such movements, particularly currency movements, argues that the market is shaped by reflexivity. Economic rationality increasingly depends on our ability to successfully guess the behaviour of other economic actors. Such reflexivity, where individuals reflect on what they think will happen in markets and change their behaviour accordingly, leads to an increasingly abstract and exaggerated economic system. If shareholders think others are likely to sell their stocks, shareholders sell, anticipating that prices will fall – such action leads to a stampede to sell and market instability. Even if a company has little value, the belief that others will buy pushes up share values into a bubble of inflated stock market value. Soros's appreciation of the potentially negative consequences of a market based not on rationality but predictions of mass and often hysterical behaviour is profound:

> The prevailing doctrine on how financial markets operate has not changed. It is assumed that with perfect information markets can take care of themselves; therefore the main task is to make the necessary information available and to avoid any interference with the market mechanism. Imposing market discipline remains the goal.
> We need to broaden the debate. It is time to recognize that financial markets are inherently unstable. Imposing market discipline means imposing instability, and how much instability can society take? (Soros 1998: 175–6)

To understand such instability, Soros uses the concept of reflexivity which he traces from Greek drama to the introduction of intersubjectivity into sociology by Alfred Schutz:

> The concept of reflexivity is so basic that it would be hard to believe that I was the first to discover it. The fact is, I am not. Reflexivity is merely a new label for the two-way interaction between thinking and reality that is deeply ingrained in our common sense. (Ibid.: 10)

Keynes was one of the few academic economists to make large amounts of money from commodity markets! The fact that he, like Soros, had a sharp understanding of reflexivity should be instructive to those who seek to play the markets. Keynes put the concept at the centre of his theoretical system:

[Economics] deals with motives, expectations, psychological uncertainties. One has to be constantly on one's guard against treating the material as constant and homogeneous. It is as though the fall of the apple to the ground depended on the apple's motives, on whether it is worthwhile falling to the ground, and whether the ground wants the apple to fall, and on mistaken calculations on the part of the apple as to how far it was from the centre of the earth. (Quoted in Moggridge 1976: 27)

Keynes feared the effect of capital liberalisation as a means of shifting investment from productive activity to a form of gambling:

The social object of skilled investment should be to defeat the dark forces of time and ignorance which envelop our future. The actual, private object of the most skilled investment to-day is 'to beat the gun', as the Americans so well express it, to outwit the crowd, and to pass the bad, or depreciating, half-crown to the other fellow. (Keynes 1960: 155)

Keynes, while no anti-capitalist, believed that extending the market meant extending uncertainties to new areas of human existence with destabilising and potentially damaging consequences. In the third millennium, see-sawing currency and share values mean that jobs may be swept away with one spin of the economic roulette wheel.

Stiglitz specifically examines asymmetric information as a form of market failure. He suggests that in the real world information is always imperfect to a lesser or greater extent. Such asymmetry means that markets may not work efficiently and if some actors have access to greater information than others, there is the potential for injustice. Assumptions of reflexivity and asymmetric information, ignored by the Washington Consensus, powerfully shape the operation of real markets and have important consequences. The financial crisis of 2008 shows the power of Soros's account.

1001 Uses for a Dead Karl Polanyi

Many of the critics of neo-liberalism examined in this text make some use of the ideas of Karl Polanyi outlined in his book *The Great Transformation*, first published in 1944. Typically Soros observes in his acknowledgements his thanks to 'John Gray [who] made me re-read Karl Polanyi's *Great Transformation*' (Soros 1998: v). Stiglitz provided the foreword for a new edition of *The Great Transformation* (Stiglitz 2001). An exiled Hungarian, writing in the 1940s and 1950s, Polanyi argues that far from being natural, markets are of secondary importance in explaining how goods and services are produced and distributed

(Dale 2010). He suggests that the role played by markets 'was insignificant up to recent times' (Polanyi 1957: 44). Much more important is a notion of human society within which the economy is embedded.

Social factors that glue communities together make the market and other forms of economic activity possible. Without an array of social, rather than state or market institutions, neither the state nor the market could function. We don't generally dump our grandmothers on the streets. Parents feed their children but rarely ask for payment, and examples can be multiplied. For Polanyi, the market is based on an a-historical myth, it is portrayed as universal and inevitable either for ideological reasons or from a failure of imagination. The market is embedded within a host of complex social institutions and practices. Indeed, the move towards a society where the market is dominant, *The Great Transformation* of Polanyi's title tends to erode the social institutions that the market depends upon. The ultimate extension of the market threatens the market, destroying the conditions upon which it depends. Childcare and socialisation, household maintenance including cooking and cleaning, and a host of other domestic tasks traditionally undertaken by women help to maintain economic activity, as do a range of social obligations such as the activities of postal workers or milkmen/ women who look in on the elderly. Soros, utilising Polanyi, argues:

> ... it seems clear that morality is based on a sense of belonging to a community, be it family, friends, tribe, nation, or humanity. But a market economy does not constitute a community, especially when it operates on a global scale; being employed by a corporation is not the same as belonging to a community. (Soros 1998: 91)

Polanyi's insights suggest that unlimited marketisation is unsustainable. Gray uses Polanyi to sustain an essentially conservative critique of globalisation in his book *False Dawn*. The fruits of globalisation for Gray are family breakdown, drug addiction, debt and an epidemic of alcoholism:

> The Utopia of the global free market has not incurred a human cost in the way that communism did. Yet over time it may come to rival it in the suffering that it inflicts. Already it has resulted in over a hundred million peasants becoming migrant labourers in China, the exclusion from work and participation in society of tens of millions in the advanced societies, a condition of near-anarchy and rule by organized crime in parts of the post-communist world, and further devastation of the environment. (Gray 2002: 3)

Radical use of Polanyi is made by autonomist and ecosocialist critics of globalisation, such as Hardt and Negri and Kovel, examined in later chapters. Polanyi's approach suggests that the market is merely one way of dealing with the economic problem and in historical terms a minor one – an insight that, if true, scuppers the ideological pretensions of those who advocate extending the market to virtually every area of human society. Polanyi suggests that economic alternatives to the market are far from absurd, whereas the introduction of the market is a violent process in at least two ways. First, it involves a battle between social classes: he notes that new Poor Laws were introduced in Britain in the eighteenth century as part of a battle to replace notions of a 'moral economy' with those of an extended market. Second, such processes are physically violent, with peasants being thrown off the land by processes of enclosure. In this sense, the Washington Consensus can be seen as a process not of development but violent expropriation, whereby communal resources and informal forms of economic activity are privatised. Armies of migrants facing deprivation provide cheap labour to fuel global corporate profit seeking.

Soros and Stiglitz, along with other advocates of a gentler capitalist globalisation, use Polanyi's insights to sustain a less fundamentalist vision of the market. They note that the imperfections of the market, including the fact that it is by necessity embedded in non-economic institutions and practices, demand that globalisation should be introduced gradually, should remain incomplete and should be cemented with a measure of global Keynesianism. Soros and Stiglitz both suggest that a swift march from state planning to a full market economy is likely to be costly because it wrecks social institutions without providing enough time for alternatives to mature. Stiglitz in particular suggests that the gradualist approach to economic reform in China has been more successful than the shock therapy that has left the Russian economy in chaos. He argues that the IMF

... tried to create a shortcut to capitalism, without creating the underlying institutions ... the Russian middle class has been devastated, a system of crony and Mafia capitalism has been created, and the one achievement, the creation of democracy and a free press, seem very fragile. (*Independent on Sunday*, 9 November 2003)

Anti-Empire

Given the insights of market imperfection outlined above, Stiglitz has suggested that politicians need to behave 'more like scholars' (Stiglitz 2002: x) but observes that 'the opposite happens too often.' Stiglitz and Soros since 2003 increasingly focused on the fact that economics has either been used to legitimate American interests or simply junked when it gets in the way of self-interested politicians:

They talk a free-market ideology but, if you look at their politics in terms of bailouts and protectionism, it is not a free-market policy; if you look at their procurement agenda and what they did with Bechtel in Iraq, it doesn't even look like a fair competition agenda. So you have to sort of suspect an element of ideology but more an element of particular groups seizing control. (*Observer*, 18 May 2003)

Soros and Stiglitz increasingly came to see neo-liberalism, especially under Republican presidents, as an ideological force driven not by market economics but by US demands for hegemony, with the economics of the market providing a gloss of legitimacy to the pursuit of naked power. Typically, Stiglitz notes that for many, globalisation appears to be 'triumphant capitalism, American style' (Stiglitz 2002: 5).

This said, Soros notes that European countries are far from immune when it comes to economic imperialism:

> ... the French government, for instance, has an even stronger tradition of pushing business interests through political means. The president of an Eastern European country I know was shocked when in a meeting with President Jacques Chirac the French president spent most of their time together pushing him to favour a French buyer in a privatization sale. I shall not even mention arms sales. (Soros 1998: 204)

Soros and Stiglitz believe that the Bretton Woods institutions must be reformed and also support the introduction of the Tobin Tax, named after the economist James Tobin, on capital flows. A percentage tax on capital transactions could raise billions of dollars for development projects and reduce the instability of markets. It is unlikely that universal backing for such a tax would be forthcoming, but studies have shown that even if only a minority of currency transactions were covered it would bring benefits. Tobin believes that his tax could also be levied on share transactions and administered by the IMF to make it stick (Henwood 1998: 319). Henwood, a keen Tobinist who, like Keynes, knows that financial markets are more about gambling or playing 'snap' than productivity, argues gleefully:

> Few things, aside from the threat of direct appropriation of their property, make Wall Streeters scream more loudly than the assertion that their pursuits are pointless or malignant, and that their activities should be taxed like noxious effluent. Listening to those screams would be another positive benefit of a transactions tax. (Ibid.: 319)

Tobin suggested a modest 0.5 per cent tax, and the networks campaigning for its introduction call for a levy as low as 0.2 per cent (see Chapter 5). Soros also advocates the creation of new global credits to finance debt. Stiglitz suggests that the IMF's structural adjustment programs be linked to social inclusive policies. Above all, the Washington institutions should act in a transparent way and engage in dialogue. Soros and Stiglitz have in recent years stressed Keynesian spending programmes as a way of escaping from low growth and have been highly critical of austerity. Stiglitz's 2010 book *Freefall* outlines his analysis of the financial crisis of 2008 and resulting recession. His most recent book, *The Price of Inequality* (2013), shows how the accelerating gap between the world's billionaires and the rest of humanity is a threat to the future.

Vaccinating Against Anti-Capitalism

Soros, Stiglitz and associates provide a penetrating critique of the Washington Consensus that is driving globalisation. They show how some of the axioms of conventional market economics are flawed, arguing that such concepts, consciously or otherwise, are used to legitimate increasing wealth and power for a corporate elite. Soros summarises, stating: 'the system is deeply flawed. As long as capitalism remains triumphant, the pursuit of money overrides all other social considerations' (1998: 102). Soros and Stiglitz recognise that market failure is a problem and suggest practical ways of dealing with it. However, their vision of an economic alternative to neo-liberalism is capitalism managed a little to make it fairer and more stable.

Given their Keynesian roots, this approach is hardly surprising. Keynes has been seen as an economic radical because he strenuously criticised many of the assumptions of market-based economics. He also showed an awareness of the subjective human costs of a capitalist economic system:

> The love of money as a possession – as distinguished from the love of money as a means to the enjoyments and realities of life – will be recognised for what it is, a somewhat disgusting morbidity, one of those semi-criminal, semi-pathological propensities which one hands over with a shudder to the specialists in mental disease. All kinds of social customs and economic practices, affecting the distribution of wealth and of economic rewards and penalties, which we now maintain at all costs, however distasteful and unjust they may be in themselves, because they are tremendously useful in promoting the accumulation of capital, we shall then be free, at last, to discard. (Keynes 1972: 329)

He also stated:

> For at least another hundred years we must pretend to ourselves and to everyone that fair is foul and foul is fair; for foul is useful and fair is not.

Avarice and usury and precaution must be our gods for a little longer still. For only they can lead us out of the tunnel of economic necessity into daylight. (Ibid.: 331)

The Economist noted cynically: 'So prolix was Keynes ... that he is thought to have said everything at least once' (9 October 2003). Keynes was indeed quite happy to promote luxury and waste as ways of sustaining economic growth. He believed that thrift was dysfunctional, but greed was good if it boosted demand and prevented recession:

> Keynes celebrated booms in a manner that would do a Texas populist proud. Shakespeare, said Keynes, died rich, and his days were 'the palmy days of profit' – one of the greatest 'bull' movements ever known until modern days in the United States ... the greater proportion of the world's greatest writers and artists have flourished in the atmosphere of buoyancy ... The Shakespeares of the era of junk finance have yet to be discovered, unless Bret Easton Ellis qualifies. (Henwood 1998: 195)

Keynesianism is an ideology that apparently sanctifies shopping and sees reduced consumption as a sin. The pioneering green economist E.F. Schumacher, author of *Small is Beautiful*, bitterly complained:

> Maybe we do not even have to wait for another sixty years until universal plenty will be attained. In any case, the Keynesian message is clear enough: Beware! Ethical considerations are not merely irrelevant, they are an actual hinderance, 'for foul is useful and fair is not'. The time for fairness is not yet. The road to heaven is paved with bad intentions. (Schumacher 1978: 22)

Keynes was well aware of Marx's critique of capitalism. Perhaps more surprisingly he was sympathetic to the monetary reformers like Major Douglas and Gesell (discussed in Chapter 5). Yet Keynes sought not to destroy capitalism or to move beyond it, but to sustain it. Indeed, he explicitly argued that in the class war he was on the side of the bourgeois. He developed, using his insights into macroeconomic market failure, a theoretical understanding of how capitalism, that appeared so weak in the 1930s, could be strengthened by selective government intervention. Stiglitz and Soros are in this sense neo-Keynesians, while their criticisms of neo-liberal globalisation are telling, like Keynes, it is inaccurate to describe them as anti-capitalists.

Stiglitz is a neo-Keynesian, trying in his academic work to shore up Keynesian macroeconomic analysis, which looks at national economies, with firm microeconomic principles that deal with the basic building blocks of an economy such as the behaviour of firms and consumers. Stiglitz is equally

Keynesian in his project to create a more stable and faster growing capitalism. Like many other centre-ground critics, the point is not to halt globalisation but to heal it, so it can be sustained and grow. In recent years, he has commented in some detail on the challenge of climate change but in doing so, places it very much in a Keynesian growth-based perspective. In 2013, listing a number of challenges, Stiglitz argued:

> The most serious is global warming. While the global economy's weak performance has led to a corresponding slowdown in the increase in carbon emissions, it amounts to only a short respite. And we are far behind the curve: because we have been so slow to respond to climate change achieving the targeted limit of a 2C rise in global temperature will require sharp reductions in emissions in the future.
>
> Some suggest that, given the economic slowdown, we should put global warming on the backburner. On the contrary, retrofitting the global economy for climate change would help to restore aggregate demand and growth.
>
> (www.theguardian.com/business/2013/jan/07/climate-change-poverty-inequality)

The solutions of such mainstream critics of globalisation such as transparency and the Tobin Tax appear to be modest, realistic and just. These capitalist critics of globalisation fear that if the market is extended too quickly or too completely it will collapse. They do not, despite their lip service to Polanyi and talk of asymmetry and reflexivity, follow their doubts and challenge the market in essence. More radical opponents of neo-liberalism, by contrast, suggest that markets are innately undemocratic, that indefinite economic growth is ecologically unsustainable and that the market based system is tyrannical because it reduces human life to a narrow pursuit of quantitative advantage. As Bob Dylan observed, money doesn't talk, it swears.

By attacking the most obviously repellent features of neo-liberal globalisation, Soros, Stiglitz and friends seek to show how capitalism can be maintained and to channel more radical sentiments into support for a supposedly 'nicer' form of globalisation. They act as a vaccine against the virus of anti-capitalist protest.

3

WHITE COLLAR GLOBAL CRIME SYNDICATE: KORTEN, KLEIN AND OTHER ANTI-CORPORATISTS

To the anti-globalisers, the corporation is a devilish instrument of environmental destruction, class oppression and imperial conquest. But is it also pathologically insane?

That is the provocative conclusion of an award-winning documentary, called 'The Corporation', coming soon to a cinema near you. People on both sides of the globalisation debate should pay attention. Unlike much of the soggy thinking peddled by many *anti*-globalisers, 'The Corporation' is a surprisingly rational and coherent attack on capitalism's most important institution.

Like all psychopaths, the firm is singularly self-interested: its purpose is to create wealth for its shareholders. And, like all psychopaths, the firm is irresponsible, because it puts others at risk to satisfy its profit-maximising goal, harming employees and customers, and damaging the environment. The corporation manipulates everything. It is grandiose, always insisting that it is the best, or number one. It has no empathy, refuses to accept responsibility for its actions and feels no remorse. It relates to others only superficially, via make-believe versions of itself manufactured by public-relations consultants and marketing men. In short, if the metaphor of the firm is a valid one, then the corporation is clinically insane. (*The Economist*, 6 May 2004)

Corporations have been described as the number one force driving globalisation by a number of authors and many activists. David Korten and Naomi Klein have sold hundreds of thousands of copies of their anti-corporate manifestos *When Corporations Rule the World* (Korten 2001) and *No Logo* (Klein 2001a). Korten came from the right:

I was born in 1937 into a conservative, white, upper-middle-class family and grew up in Longview, Washington, a small timber-industry town of some 25,000 ... [In 1959 as] a very conservative Young Republican, I was deeply fearful of the spread of communism and the threat it posed to the American way of life I held so dear. This fear drew me to take a course on modern revolutions the world over. In one of those rare, deeply life-changing moments, I made a decision. I would devote my life to countering this threat by bringing the knowledge of modern business management and entrepreneurship to those who had not yet benefited from it. (Korten 2001: 13)

Korten, who also served as a captain in the US Air Force in Vietnam, is another example of an individual wedded to conservative values who has been radicalised. He argues that globalisation is designed and driven by the corporations who seek the removal of national barriers to trade. This allows companies to sell to new markets and 'outsource' buying inputs from low-cost, low-wage producers in the poorest countries.

Klein, in contrast, gives the impression of being the prodigal daughter to generations of radicals. A spoilt 'mall brat' at high school, she returned to the fold as a student activist campaigning against sexism, racism and homophobia. She increasingly came to see capitalism rather than political incorrectness as the premier cause of oppression. Klein combines sophisticated cultural politics with a forensic study of marketing behaviour. Klein suggests that the creation of the brand drives outsourcing and leads to the manipulation of consumers. In a post-modern switch, she argues that they sell 'signs', not products. The Nike flash and McDonald's golden arches have huge symbolic value. This chapter examines the criticisms made of corporations by anti-capitalists, before critically examining Korten, Klein and other anti-corporatists.

The Rise of the Corporate Criminal

Korten and Klein are perhaps the best known of many other anti-corporate anti-capitalists who point to the growing power of giant corporations

Mega-corporations, according to Korten and Klein, create a uniform world of fast food outlets, ugly hotel towers, universal brands of margarine and coffee, monoculture computer software, homogeneous Hollywood entertainment and uniformly moulded pop stars. Cultural desiccation, animal abuse, poverty and global warming are all symptoms of a planet run by banal corporate bodies. Others, such as the journalist Greg Palast, note more sinister accusations. Pharmaceutical corporations have, on occasions, been happy to kill a few of their customers if the cost-benefit calculations warrant such action. Pfizer, a New York-based multinational, manufactured the Bjork-Shiley heart valve:

> At Pfizer's factory in the Caribbean, company inspectors found inferior equipment, which made poor welds. Rather than toss out the bad valves,

Pfizer management ordered the defects ground down, weakening the valves further but making them look smooth and perfect …

When the valve's struts break and the heart contracts, it explodes. Two-thirds of the victims die, usually in minutes. (Palast 2003: 228)

It is estimated that five hundred individuals died as a result before the US Justice Department took action against the company in 1994. Cigarette firms have long known that they sell a product that kills. False accountancy and stock market manipulation have been also widely practiced by transnationals. The collapse of the Enron Corporation is instructive. Enron, an energy corporation with reported revenues of $101 million made from selling privatised electricity, used opaque accountancy tricks to make its finances appear stronger than they really were: by rewriting its balances so they looked robust, for example, more funds could be generated from selling new equities to gullible shareholders to maintain expansion. Arthur Andersen, the auditors who checked their fraudulent accounts and passed them despite Enron's numerous instances of financial cheating, collapsed with Enron:

Enron's accounting trick was to record the value of the sale today of, say, gas, for delivery next year as *revenue* today, but not what it would have to spend to buy the gas. Revenues without costs generate huge profits! Of course, eventually Enron would have to record a cost for the purchase of the electricity. One can in fact continually blow up one's income this way, so long as one is growing; for each year, sales exceed purchase. It is a classic Ponzi scheme, like the chain letter of the past. Such schemes still occasionally occur: people who make money by selling franchises to others, who sell it on to others and on and on. But all such Ponzi schemes eventually come to an end. (Stiglitz 2003: 245)

Enron also created fictitious companies that it sold make-believe gas to. These non-existent sales were recorded as additions to its assets without any balancing liability (ibid.).

False accounting, the use of complex financial instruments, political manipulation and smart legal footwork are all instruments used to sustain profit. Dumping is another example; a supermarket will set up in town and sell bread for a fraction of the price of local bakeries. Almost inevitably, such dumping will wipe out the bakeries and a monopoly will result. Bread prices will rise.

Government officials are bribed to give planning permission or look away from pollution and safety abuses. Profits are deposited in offshore bank accounts to avoid paying tax. Employees may be spied on and their emails read to prevent whistleblowing. Both Klein and Korten note that in some parts of the world death squads are used to break strikes. Crimes may take on a political dimension: German corporations and even some North American players bankrolled Hitler (Guérin 1973), while IBM is one of many corporations that made money out of the Holocaust (Black 2001).

While crime is the everyday informal practice of the corporation, the relationship cuts both ways:

> Banks and big business are keen to get their hands on the proceeds – laundered – of organised crime. Apart from the traditional activities of drugs, racketeering, kidnappings, gambling, procuring (women and children), smuggling (alcohol, tobacco, medicines), armed robbery, counterfeiting and bogus invoicing, tax evasion and misappropriation of public funds, new markets are also flourishing. These include smuggling illegal labour and refugees, computer piracy, trafficking in works of art and antiquities, in stolen cars and parts, in protected species and human organs, forgery, trafficking in arms, toxic waste and nuclear products, etc. (de Brie 2000)

The Hidden History of Humanity

Rather than simply acting as global grocers or very large versions of the corner shop, Klein, Korten and other critics argue that corporations have real political influence. In the hidden history of humanity, corporations are driving events in their fight for new markets and cheaper sources of raw materials. North America was colonised by corporations such as the Plymouth and Virginia companies, whose existence long precedes the creation of the United States of America. In 1602, the Dutch monarchy provided a charter to the United East India Company for a monopoly over all Dutch trade from South Africa, across the Pacific to South America. The company made treaties, controlled territories and used its own armed forces to maintain dominance. Korten notes that the company used economic and legal manipulation to enslave producers, for example, banning non-Dutch producers in Indonesia for growing cloves, forcing peasants into poverty and dependence on over-produced rice sold by the company (2001: 60). The British East India Company colonised India and administered the country until 1858. An entire subcontinent became an instrument for producing profit for one corporation. In the early nineteenth century, the company bought tea from China using opium for exchange. The Chinese, resisting the chaos created by hard drug use, confiscated opium from company warehouses in Canton, leading to the Opium Wars of 1839–42. The British won. The price of victory allowed them to established the right to 'free trade', compensatory payments from the Chinese government and the entitlement of British citizens accused of crimes in China to be tried by British courts (Korten 2001: 61).

Countries become the instruments of corporations. There are numerous examples of national governments intervening, often outright invading, other states at the bidding of transnationals. In 1954, for instance, US-backed rebels invaded the Central American republic of Guatemala, on behalf of United Fruit Co. The Guatemalan President Guzmán, elected in 1950 had started to redistribute land to impoverished peasants. United Fruit were asked to surrender some of their estates and were offered compensation based on 'the value set on the property in 1952 for tax purposes "by the owner himself"' (Pearce 1976: 103). Colonel Carlos Castillo Armas, leader of the Guatemalan exiles who undertook the subsequent coup, was trained at the US Command and General Staff School at Fort Leavenworth, Texas. The whole operation was financed, armed and organised by the CIA. The then US Secretary of State John Foster Dulles was a major stockholder in United Fruit. Some have quipped that Iraq would not have been invaded if it had grown carrots, but Guatemala was assaulted for oranges rather than oil.

Salvador Allende's Chilean government was destroyed in a 1973 coup, after it had come into conflict with the ITT communications corporation. The coup was again organised by the CIA, who initiated a truck drivers' strike to destabilise the country. Suspected leftists were massacred in football stadiums, torture was rife and the 'Chicago boys', a group of 'free market' economists loyal to the monetarist Professor Milton Friedman, re-engineered the economy (Petras and Morley 1975).

Foreign policy remains driven by corporate needs into the third millennium, events since the publication of Klein's and Korten's key texts have strengthened their analysis. The Second Gulf War was influenced by corporations such as Halliburton and oil giant Exxon, which had strong links with the US administration of President George W. Bush. Corporations like Exxon have a strong interest in breaking the power of the Organisation of Petroleum Exporting Countries (OPEC), which controls the supply of oil and keeps the price that corporations like Exxon pay relatively high. A non-OPEC Iraq selling cheap oil would help the oil corporations to buy cheaper supplies and push up their profits. Examples of foreign policy as a corporate instrument, from the US, UK and Holland, or even from Spain, Japan, or Australia, could be multiplied.

Unnatural Monopolies

Criminal activities and coups may be, perhaps, the exception rather than the rule, but there is evidence that the day-to-day activities of multinationals exploit consumers, workers and the environment. Economists have generally assumed that strong competition between firms is beneficial. If there are many different banks, the ones that provide the best deal for customers will survive and the rest will be driven out of existence as savers shift accounts. If there are many producers of chocolate bars, consumers will buy from those that provide the highest quality confectionery at the lowest possible price. Workers can choose the best company with the highest wage, nicest boss and longest tea breaks. Healthy competition maximises the most efficient use of resources because inefficient firms will not be able to sustain the normal profit needed to keep wages sufficiently high to attract skilled workers and prices sufficiently low to maintain customer loyalty. The market tends to create the optimum economic conditions and the market works best when it draws close to a condition of 'perfect competition', marked by low barriers to entry for new firms and a large number of existing producers who compete sharply on price.

Monopoly, where a single firm sells a good, or monopsony, when one firm or consumer buys a product, are seen within traditional economics as situations that may lead to exploitation and inefficiency. The UK Competition Commission defines a potential monopoly as a firm with 25 per cent of market share. Such firms may have the potential to push up prices for consumers and push down the price of raw materials they buy from suppliers. Different sectors of the economy are increasingly being monopolised:

Small farmers are forced to cut prices to sell to commodity giants like Cargill. The growth of monopsonistic commodity brokers and huge agribusiness farmers has tended to squeeze out other farmers. According to Korten, between 1935 and 1989, the number of US farmers fell from 6.8 million to under 2.1 million. Small businesses serving local farmers, such as tractor and tool dealers, have gone out of business, causing entire rural communities to disappear (2001: 208). The top ten 'farms' in the US are now agricultural corporations:

> Three companies – Iowa Beef Processors (IBP), Cargill and ConAgra – slaughter nearly 80 percent of U.S. beef. One company – Campbell's – controls nearly 70 percent of the U.S. soup market. Four companies – Kelloggs, General Mills, Philip Morris, and Quaker Oats – control nearly 85 percent of the U.S. cold cereal market. Four companies – ConAgra, ADM Milling, Cargill, and Pillsbury – mill nearly 60 percent of U.S. flour. (Ibid.)

The retail market, which sells food to consumers, used to be a forest of small high street shops but is increasingly an arena of monopoly. In the UK, four supermarkets dominate the market and are able to push up prices for consumers and exploit farmers.

While it is rare for a single firm to control a market totally, unofficial cartels, where firms get together to fix prices rather than indulge in unprofitable competition, are both common and hard to detect. Korten uses the term 'managed competition', arguing that transnational corporations increasingly construct alliances and deals that make it difficult to distinguish one company from another. He notes that General Motors owns '37.5 percent of the Japanese auto manufacturer Isuzu'. During the 1990s, he also notes how IBM, Apple and Motorola put together an interfirm alliance to develop computer operation systems. Consumers are given an illusion of competition, when the reality is cooperation to raise profit. Consumer durables such as fridges, freezers, cookers and televisions are produced by five major corporations who control 70 per cent of the world market (ibid.: 207). 'Perfect competition', if it ever existed, is now dead.

Global Government Inc.

Korten suggests that modern corporations are the 'dominant governance institution on the planet' (1998: 60). From the power wielded by Russian oligarchs to the participation of Korean *cheabols* (corporations), big company influence on national governments, makes a global mockery of democracy. Leslie Sklair, a sociologist based at the London School of Economics, has identified the phenomenon of globalising politicians, who work for corporate interests by removing national barriers on trade and investment to benefit the transnationals. These politicians, often trained at neo-liberal university economics departments such as Chicago, Harvard or the Massachusetts Institute of Technology, believe that economic prosperity can only be created or maintained by making life easier for transnationals. Representative democracy has effectively become a system of elite pluralism, where rival elite corporations may compete for influence but where others, such as trade unionists, environmentalists, ordinary party members or the public, have little or no say in the debate. Politics becomes more like business and opposition to capitalism or even the worst excesses of corporate greed becomes impossible to voice (Sklair 2001).

Korten argues that corporations govern the globe and have created institutions such as the WTO to secure their power. Essentially, there is a shadow global government based upon hidden groups such as the Trilateral Commission and the Bilderberg Group who bring politicians, corporate heads, influential academics and journalists together (Korten 2001: 135; Sklair 1980). 'Free trade' is also, according to Sklair and Korten, driven by corporations. The WTO and trading blocs such as NAFTA (North American Free Trade Agreement) give large corporations access to new markets where they can sell goods to new sets of consumers. In turn, they can relocate production to countries where wages are low, and they export without facing barriers such as import taxes (tariffs). It might be thought that nationally based firms would be resistant to allowing access to foreign competitors. Indeed, one potential weakness of anti-corporate accounts of globalisation is the fact that different businesses may have opposing economic/political objectives. Thus in the US, law firms might benefit from stronger rules on corporate behaviour and have therefore been more likely to support the mildly reformist Democrats, who could be prepared to clamp down on the worst excesses of destructive corporations. Chemical and oil corporations have tended to favour the Republicans, who are more likely to reduce regulation. However, while disputes may exist, causing the state to act as a committee for corporations or an umpire between corporate interests, Sklair has found that corporations have an almost universal interest in 'free trade'. He notes how the pro-NAFTA lobby included the US Chamber of Commerce, the National Association of Manufacturers, the National Foreign Trade Council, the US Council for International Business, the National Retail Federation, the Business Roundtable and the American Farm Bureau Federation. In 1993, in the run-up to a Congressional vote on NAFTA, the US Chamber of Commerce phoned every congressional representative daily. 'No stone was left unturned. Even Miss Mexico spoke out for NAFTA as she was being crowned Miss Universe!' (Sklair 2001: 102).

The General Agreement on Trade in Services (GATS) extends free trade to 160 areas in the service sector and means that in principle WTO members must allow foreign companies to compete in the provision of postal services, tele-communications and healthcare. In preparation for competitive postal services, European Union postal services are being forced to cut costs and raise charges to bring in profit. In the UK, postal deliveries were cut to once a day (previously, in urban areas, there were two deliveries daily) and in 2013, the Royal Mail was privatised. In the rush to privatise, the shares were woefully underpriced. Six months after the sell-off, share price had risen by nearly 60 per cent, with most of the profit going to pension and hedge funds.

Privatisation leads to 'insourcing', where cheap, often illegal, migrant labour is used to cut costs even further. The market is aided by the fact that workers are 'illegalised' when they migrate, so their fear of discovery by the authorities means that they are unlikely to join unions or complain about poor pay. Right-wing media sources, in turn, demonise refugees rather than identify corporations as a source of low pay and social instability.

Globalising politicians have been keen to bring in private finance initiatives (PFIs). PFIs involve private companies both providing and paying for infrastructure projects such as new hospitals, schools and roads. PFIs were essentially an accountancy trick deployed by the UK government to make government debt appear to be lower that it really is. Private companies build the projects and then rent them to the governments at vastly inflated rates. PFIs have turned out to be far more expensive than state provision and have become mired in scandal.

In her book *No Logo*, Naomi Klein writes about how firms have been keen to move into new areas of public life to strengthen their brands and exploit new markets. She notes, for example, how education has become corporate-dominated. Schools may be sponsored by transnationals, textbooks may contain adverts and university research is ever more dependent on corporate grants. Corporate control of areas of life that were provided by the state or local community has reached absurd lengths. When, in 1998, Coca-Cola ran a competition for schools to design a marketing plan for their product, Greenbriar High School, in Evans, Georgia, suspended a 19-year-old student for wearing a Pepsi T-shirt to the official 'Coke-day' celebrations (Klein 2001b: 95).

Corporations are territorially expansive, globally seeking control over more and more local markets. Their ambitions are also intensive, even totalitarian, as they seek to dominate almost every area of social life. Bus shelters and road signs are branded. Sporting events, such as the Olympics, are marketing bonanzas for the merchants of fast food and fizz. Sklair believes that the power of corporations has created a new transnational capitalist class. He divides this class into four factions, including (1) transnational corporate executives and their local affiliates, (2) globalising bureaucrats and politicians, (3) globalising professionals, and (4) retailers and media communities. All are committed to creating a single, world corporate, paradise.

Klein notes that while corporations enjoy a governing role, they are reluctant to pay the taxes necessary for the state to support their position. Transnationals negotiate to move production to free trade zones where they can enjoy tax 'holidays'. Corporate welfare (where governments tax citizens and subsidise companies) is common, especially in the US and within the free trade zones.

Outsourcing

Klein suggests that corporations have become increasingly virtual, that is, selling not actual goods, but a brand image. Designer labels have become ever more important in the clothing industry and in food retailing. Advertising has been used to encourage consumers to buy goods and services that previously they didn't think they needed, as well as allowing firms to raise their prices. Klein argues with many post-modernists that the economy is increasingly based on symbolic values rather than material qualities. Firms seek to sell symbols of cultural value, to be consumed by individuals keen to assert their value in society through lifestyle consumption. Marketing is used to build brands. As Hector Liang, ex-chair of United Biscuits, observed, 'Machines wear out. Cars rust. People die. But what lives on are brands' (Klein 2001a: 196).

Klein never forgets that goods still must be made, by factory workers. Factory production, though, has been increasingly outsourced. Outsourcing is a process whereby corporations act as consumers rather than producers, buying goods from the cheapest supplier and reselling them. Outsourcing has accelerated the creation of ultra-low-wage Export Processing Zones (EPZs), where companies rather than states have jurisdiction and costs can be further reduced through use of sweatshop employees. Corporations are reducing their employment of industrial workers; instead, they buy the services of smaller localised manufacturers who compete to push wages and other costs down. Klein notes how Disney spokesman Ken Green responded to questions from the *Catholic Register* about the pay and conditions of the workers who made clothes for the company: 'We don't employ anyone in Haiti ... With the newsprint you use, do you have any idea of the labour conditions involved to produce it?' (Klein 2001a: 198)

Conditions within the EPZs are grim: workers work long hours for low pay, whilst unions are banned and safety is lax. Workers, often young women, have no job security and may be housed in barracks. Police or armed forces may help to maintain discipline. According to Klein, approximately a thousand EPZs existed in 70 countries and employed 27 million workers. The Philippines, Sri Lanka and Mexico are major centres of EPZs, but all are outstripped by China, where some of the worst abuses are apparent. Chinese EPZ workers are estimated to work for around 16 hours a day and are paid an average of only 87 cents an hour:

A 1998 study of brand-name manufacturing in the Chinese special economic zones found that Wal-Mart, Ralph Lauren, Ann Taylor, Esprit, Liz Claiborne, Kmart, Nike, Adidas, J.C. Penney and the Limited were only paying a fraction of that miserable 87 cents – some were paying as little as 13 cents an hour. (Klein 2001a: 212)

Countries that attempt to raise standards may lose business. Economic forces let loose by corporate globalisation maintain poverty. WTO rules make it illegal for states to refuse goods that have been produced by what is virtually slave labour. Klein notes the powerful example of the closure of the only unionised clothing factory in the whole of Guatemala in December 1998. The factory had been unionised after a long and bitter dispute, with wages rising from $56 a week to $71 (ibid.: 214). This victory became defeat when the factory was closed and production moved elsewhere. Political violence goes hand in hand with the discipline of the free market. States that resist the corporate agenda face invasion and sanctions, from Chinese opposition to free trade in the nineteenth century, or reforming governments in Central or South America more recently. Brutality remains a feature of the workplace:

In 1993, a Sri Lankan zone worker by the name of Ranjith Mudiyanselage was killed ... [after] complaining about a faulty machine that had sliced off a co-worker's finger. Mudiyanselage was abducted on his way out of an inquiry into the incident. His body was found beaten and burning on a pile of old tires outside a local church. The man's legal advisor, who had accompanied him to the inquiry, was murdered in the same way. (Klein 2001a: 214–15)

Outsourcing has led to EPZ-style labour standards in the North of the globe. European food producers, forced by supermarket monopolists to push down their costs, often turn to illegal foreign labour. Illegal immigrants are in no position to complain about poor conditions, potential injury and long hours. In February 2004, 19 illegal Chinese workers were drowned as they were gathering shellfish in Morecambe Bay in the north of England (*Guardian,* 9 February 2004).

Such exploitation of labour has helped to create a hyper-wealthy elite. Korten notes how the $20 million received by basketball star Michael Jordan in 1992 for promoting Nike trainers was more than the entire annual payroll of the Indonesian factory that manufactured the shoes (Korten 2001: 115). The highest executive package in 1993 was $203.1 million for Disney chair Michael Eisner. Executives are part of Sklair's transnational corporate class that travels by Lear jet, eats in the best restaurants and moves between gated villages, guarded apartments and country dachas:

> Of the many countries I have visited, Pakistan most starkly exemplifies the experience of elites living in enclaves detached from local roots. The country's three modern cities ... feature enclaves of five-star hotels, modern shopping malls, and posh residential areas ... My hosts [felt] as much at home in New York or London as in Karachi, Lahore, or Islamabad.
>
> Particularly striking, however, was the extent to which – in contrast to their knowledge of or interest in the rest of the world – they had little knowledge of or interest in what was happening in their own country beyond the borders of their enclave cities. It was as though the rest of Pakistan were an inconsequential foreign country not worthy of notice or mention. (Ibid.: 117–18)

The environmental ill-effects of corporate rule are perhaps too obvious to discuss. If environmental regulation is reduced, so are average costs, outsourced manufacturers are under unrelenting pressure to cut costs, which means cutting environmental corners. The race for profit can have some surprisingly sinister and unusual effects. Geographer Andrew Goudie blames the replacement of camels with Toyota's four-wheel-drive land cruisers as desert transportation for the dust storms that are disrupting the world's weather: 'I am quite serious, you should look at deserts from the air, scarred all over by wheel tracks, people driving indiscriminately over the surface breaking it up. Toyotarisation is a major cause of dust storms' (*Guardian,* 20 August 2004). This dust has even been found in the polar icecaps, darkening the earth's surface and absorbing light, which leads to accelerated melting and subsequent rise in sea levels.

Klein's book, *The Shock Doctrine* (2008), argued that economic, environmental and social crises were often exploited to introduce a market economy. She noted the 2003 Iraq War was used to provide economic niches for companies like Halliburton. The US-backed 1973 coup in Chile was followed by a free market experiment. Her latest book, *This Changes Everything* (2014), argues that the climate crisis is created by capitalism and we need a new post-capitalist economic system to protect our future.

Adam Smith's Ecotopia

Some variants of anti-capitalist economics are complex and subtle. In contrast, anti-corporate anti-capitalism is easily understood. However, Sklair draws on social theory, and Klein's ideas closely parallel post-modern accounts that suggest that large-scale Fordist production has been replaced by diverse and decentralised manufacture. Post-modernists also argue that culture in the form of the 'brand' has become more important than the physical properties of a good. People buy alternative lifestyles rather than sausages.

Klein is influenced by a tradition of cultural politics, derived in part from western Marxists such as Gramsci and Marcuse. Gramsci argued that the ruling class ruled through the creation of ideological hegemony or common sense. Such common sense prevented rebellion. Marcuse argued in, for example, *One-Dimensional Man* that consumer capitalism dulled workers into submission with television and commodities (1964). None of this is so far from Aldous Huxley's prophetic novel *Brave New World*, first published in 1932, which depicted a physical form of cinema, the 'feelies', and a drug, 'soma', used to pacify workers. Both Huxley and the Frankfurt School at their worst tended to cultural pessimism, fearing that all aspects of commercial culture were inferior to traditional high culture. Frankfurt philosopher Theodor Adorno, to give an extreme example, believed that jazz music was degenerate compared to Mozart and his peers (Jay 1973: 185). The Frankfurters also believed that a totalitarian society had been created that left little or no room for opposition. In contrast, the post-modern variant of cultural theory has tended to celebrate the subversive nature of all popular culture. Both the Frankfurt School and post-modernists have tended to shift political struggle to the symbolic realm, which is where Klein met their descendants. She notes how she and other young radicals became partisans in the 'culture wars' beginning in the 1990s, arguing that language and access were essential to liberation. Linguistic issues around representation in terms of sexuality, sexual orientation and ethnicity, became the key arena of struggle between left and right. She acknowledges that during the culture wars, the need to challenge corporate globalisation was largely forgotten, making it easier for companies to cut workers' pay and shape our subjective desires with confidence.

In *No Logo*, Klein shows that far from living in a totalitarian society, activists can battle the brands and sometimes even win. She is less pessimistic than the Frankfurters but more politically committed in her analysis than the post-modernists. Symbolic politics links to campaigns for better pay and conditions, when, for example, consumers boycott the Nike flash, to fight against the outsourced sweatshops that pay the workers only pennies for a pair of new trainers. Klein is refreshingly modest, she explicitly examines recent developments in corporate growth and makes no pretensions to producing a total critique. Her aim in *No Logo* is to catalogue opposition to corporate globalisation.

Korten claims that a change in consciousness will sweep away capitalism. He argues that western society is based on a dull, quantitative form of materialism, which worships technology. A new age will see social values based on spirituality with 'Millions of people' awakening 'as if from a deep trance, to the beauty, joy, and meaning of life' (Korten 2001: 340). While social change may require a revolution in ethics, new practices and a critique of many aspects of technology, Korten's strategic assumptions seem both optimistic and incomplete.

Korten has been termed a 'neo-Smithian' because, surprisingly or not, he is inspired by Adam Smith, often seen as the founding father of free market economics (Kovel 2002: 162). Smith, far from stating that greed was good, was a moral philosopher, with a distrust of concentrated power. He believed that both the state *and* corporations tend to abuse their authority and should be replaced by competitive producers. Indeed, both he and the historical record show that rather than being antagonistic, the strong state and the powerful corporations are friends. Corporations have their origin in grants of monopoly power from the state. He felt that the market would take power from both and hand it back to small producers, workers and consumers. McNally argues that both left and right used Smith's ideas and nineteenth-century radicals like William Cobbett might even be termed 'Smithian socialists' (McNally 1993). Korten states that the market is a useful and essentially fair device for producing and distributing goods and services. By popular action to localise production, the free market can be restored and mighty corporations made low. He believes that the early American economy based on small firms rooted in local communities provides an economic alternative to globalisation. He argues simply and passionately that capitalism has the same relation to the free market that cancer has to a healthy human body. It might be suggested instead that the relationship between markets and capitalism is rather closer to that of a chicken and an egg, than a cancer and a healthy body. Markets seem to have a built-in tendency to grow and grow. This tendency leads to the invasion of buying and selling into ever more areas of life, to concentrations of power and wealth, to injustice and ecological destruction. Markets tend to be the little acorns of great corporate oaks. They are the fiscal equivalent of plutonium, best avoided or at least contained, if life is to be preserved.

There is evidence that market economies are never fair. Property, as Proudhon famously argued, is theft, and private property is necessary to the market. Usually the act of enclosure that created the property is so distant in history as to be forgotten. This is not the case in North America. In the US, communal land was simply stolen from Native Americans. There was never a utopia in New England.

Korten is also a populist. Populists in general, whether of the right or left, claim to represent the 'people' against the dominant elite who exploit them (Canovan 1981). Populism is often linked to producerism, which stresses the rights of those who produce goods such as workers, farmers and small businesspeople over the unproductive sections of society who consume their goods. Big business and the banks are favourite targets. Right-wing populists often link in an elite conspiracy to the creation of a communist totalitarian state (Berlet and Lyons 2000).

The nineteenth century saw the emergence of populist parties and movements in the US, some of whose key demands were taken up by Democratic and Progressive politicians, resulting in anti-trust laws aimed at destroying monopolies (Ritter 1997). Individuals such as Ralph Nader and the film-maker Michael Moore have continued the populist anti-corporate tradition into the twenty-first century. Populism can, in the hands of Nader and Moore, be a relatively radical force. In any form, though, it tends to replace economic analysis with a focus on the misdeeds of an elite in a world of good guys and bad guys.

Korten's approach, like most populism, is both attractive and a little under-nourishing – a kind of fast-food alternative economics. Other anti-corporatists such as Klein and Sklair do a more convincing job, with perspectives based on stronger evidence and detailed consideration of cultural and sociological factors; however, there is more to anti-capitalism than hatred of corporations.

4

SMALL IS BEAUTIFUL: GREEN ECONOMICS

A few years ago I was eating at a St. Paul, Minnesota, restaurant. After lunch, I picked up a toothpick wrapped in plastic. On the plastic was printed the word *Japan*. Japan has little wood and no oil; nevertheless, it has become efficient enough in our global economy to bring little pieces of wood and barrels of oil to Japan, to wrap the one in the other, and send the manufactured product to Minnesota. This toothpick may have travelled 50,000 miles. But never fear, we are now retaliating in kind. A Hibbing, Minnesota, factory now produces one billion disposable chopsticks a year for sale in Japan. In my mind's eye, I see two ships passing one another in the northern Pacific. One carries little pieces of Minnesota wood bound for Japan; the other carries little pieces of Japanese wood bound for Minnesota. Such is the logic of free trade. (Morris 1996: 222)

'I am not a trade barrier', squeaks the dolphin on an anti-WTO flag carried by green activists at Seattle. Green parties, green direct action networks like Earth First!, environmental pressure groups like Greenpeace and Friends of the Earth have all challenged aspects of the current capitalist economy on ecological and social grounds. The International Forum on Globalisation (IFG), a body established by the late Edward Goldsmith, founding editor of the *Ecologist* magazine, did much of the intellectual groundwork for a wider mobilisation against free trade during the early years of this century. Goldsmith, a pioneer of green thought since the late 1960s, has developed a devastating critique of economic growth, free trade and conventional development strategies (Goldsmith 1988). Caroline Lucas, a leading member of the Green Party, and the first Member of Parliament for the party in the UK, attacked capitalism from a localist slant as ecocidal, exploitative and centralised in her book *Green Alternatives to Globalisation*, written with the late Mike Woodin (Woodin and Lucas 2004).

By the 1980s, ecological political parties had constructed an agenda which was well summarised by the four values espoused by the German Greens when they entered parliament in 1983: ecology, social justice, grassroots democracy and peace (German Green Party 1983). The German, French and Austrian Greens originated in social movements against nuclear power and nuclear weapons (Poguntke 1993). As Green parties have grown, they have been able to win seats in parliaments and local councils in ever larger numbers. One of the reasons for their success, especially in Europe, has been the movement to the right of traditional socialist parties like the German Social Democrats and British Labour Party. The socialist parties have come to adopt variants of a 'Third Way' ideology, which has committed them to the market because they perceive globalisation to be an inevitable process demanding ever greater competitiveness. The resulting wage cuts, bouts of privatisation and loss of services have meant that some trade union activists have been drawn to the Greens. Greens also include members of direct action campaigns like the anti-fracking movement and radical ecologists Earth First! as well as some green NGOs (Wall 1999). Green economics, like the other variants of anti-capitalist and indeed capitalist thought discussed here, swims in the sea of history and cannot be seen as a set of pure moral principles or scientific axioms. Social forces have helped shape green ideology and the most radical Greens have had to challenge more centre-ground members in a series of ideological contests (Wall 1994). A minority of environmentalists, as opposed to political Greens, are supportive of globalisation, with figures such as Paul Hawken (Hawken et al. 1999) suggesting in his book, *Natural Capitalism*, that such an ideology is a possibility. In Europe, where several Green parties have recently participated in coalition government, mild reform rather than ecocentric revolution has been the norm. However, many anti-capitalists are Greens. Here, the economic ideas underpinning a radical green approach are explored.

Against Growth

Perhaps the most unusual element of green anti-capitalism is opposition to economic growth (Goldsmith 1972; Porritt 1984; Trainer 1985). In the early 1970s, scientists became concerned that ever increasing economic growth would damage the environment (Meadows 1974). The idea that human societies should produce more goods and services every year is, as we noted in Chapter 1, environmentally suspect. Scarce resources such as oil will eventually be exhausted, although it is difficult to calculate when. In the search for new resources, vital ecosystems are disrupted. To produce more goods, more energy must be generated, which leads to an increase in greenhouse gases, or, if the nuclear route is taken, to problems of radioactive waste. If we consume more goods this creates jobs and enhances profits, but leads to ever larger mountains of rubbish that have to be disposed of by dumping or poisonous incineration:

The more people consume, the better it is. It's not so much a question of consumer durables as of durable consumers. And in order to achieve this, consumers must be manipulated into the smoothest possible cycle of acquisition and disposal, into a uniform, superficial understanding of personal and social requirements. Consumption becomes an end in itself. Even when the market reaches saturation, the process doesn't stop; for the only way to beat a glut is to turn everybody into gluttons. (Porritt 1984: 47)

There are many arguments that can be marshalled to suggest that economic expansion can be ecologically sustainable. Growth can be decoupled from energy use and waste (Weizsacker et al. 1997). Conservation measures and the application of new technology mean that more goods can be produced per kilowatt. Indeed, in recent years GDP, the most common measure of economic output, has been growing faster than energy use. As societies become wealthier, more services rather than physical goods are consumed, a tendency which also has the potential to reduce pollution. Because of green and environmental movement pressure, more ecologically sustainable practices are being used to maintain growth. In Germany, in particular, the practice of ecological modernism, which uses high technology to try to sustain both the environment and economic expansion, has become important (Mol and Spaarrgaren 2000). Solar, wind and other low-pollution, low-impact renewable energy sources have been advancing (Elliot 2003). Recycling has become a necessity and there is now a strong zero-waste movement (Greenpeace 2001). More people in western societies eat organic food or are vegetarian, practices that reduce waste because they need less energy input without artificial fertilisers and pesticides. Many of the fears that Greens linked to economic growth seem to have been either exaggerated or are non-existent. Oil did not, as some commentators suggest, run out in 1979! The move to a high-tech information economy has also been seen as a way of increasing economic value without increasing the output of pollution.

Yet as we have noted, environmental problems are severe and remain linked to growth. The burning of fossil fuels is exacerbating climate change, which may already be causing problems in terms of species loss, the migration of diseases and pests to new areas of the world, desertification and extreme weather patterns (Firor and Jacobsen 2002). The sun may be shining outside my home as I write, with temperatures above those of my childhood in the 1970s. I may be happy to contemplate buying an olive tree, yet I fear damage from the ever stronger storms that hit my home with increasing frequency year on year.

The information-based economy may seem virtual but, as Naomi Klein exhaustively demonstrates, branded goods and computers still must be produced, made by exploited workers (2001a). Computer manufacture and disposal are sources of pollution and resource use. Some services may have little physical impact, but the huge global growth in tourism is accelerating air travel, which has become the fastest-growing source of greenhouse gases. Cars are far cleaner than their counterparts in the 1970s, but pollution from cars is rising because the number of miles they are driven is increasing sharply in many parts of the world. From a green point of view, the fundamental problem with globalisation is that it leads to ever greater economic activity. Such activity demands more production, more consumption and increasing waste. Edward Goldsmith provides an instructive apocryphal story of two friends who each inherit a 10,000-acre tract of forest. Friend one leaves his 10,000 acres in its pristine state. Friend two sells the trees to McMillan Bloedel Corporation who cuts them all down, sells the mineral rights and the topsoil, fills the resulting dank hole with toxic waste, and constructs a shopping mall and theme park. Friend one is labelled as a waster; friend two boosts GNP by millions of dollars, runs for office and becomes a senator (Mander and Goldsmith 1996: 15).

Woodin and Lucas pointed out that globalisation by accelerating growth is strengthening the greenhouse effect (Woodin and Lucas 2004: 33). Greenhouse gases have continued to increase and new dangers from CO_2 emissions, such as ocean acidification, have been identified (Klein 2014).

Economics as Alienation

Greens also argue that economic growth cheapens human existence. Areas of life that are not directly productive in an economic sense come to be valued less and less. Indeed, it is only what can be calculated, bought and sold that truly has worth:

> Economics ... suddenly becomes the most important subject of all. Economic policies absorb almost the entire attention of government, and at the same time become ever more impotent. The simplest things, which only fifty years ago one could do without difficulty, cannot get done any more. The richer a society, the more impossible it becomes to do worthwhile things without immediate pay-off. [Economics] tends to absorb the whole of ethics and take precedence over all other human considerations. Now, quite clearly, this is a pathological development. (Schumacher 1978: 67)

The pressure to be competitive individually or collectively, which is driven by globalisation is particularly damaging. Workers are expected to put in ever longer hours. Universities must concentrate on promoting skills that lead to further economic growth. Status is measured by wealth that drives even the 'haves' to spend longer working and consuming. Far from maximising 'utility' or benefit for individuals, neo-liberalism increases levels of personal stress (Toke

2000). Economic rationality based on quantitative measures treats anything that cannot easily be measured and sold with contempt.

All needs in a capitalist society are transformed into the need for commodities. To be a good parent, one should work long hours to afford more 'things' for their children. To be fulfilled sexually requires a huge and diverse industry. The body, created by unhealthy food and a sedentary car-based lifestyle, has become a new focus of capitalist growth with billions spent on new diets (Fromm 1979). As Ted Trainer notes in *Abandon Affluence!*: 'Acquiring things is important to many of us today because there is not much else that yields interest and a sense of progress and satisfaction in life' (quoted in Dobson 1991: 85).

Economic growth does not even remove poverty: the richest generally see the greatest gains, and the poorest are usually separated from resources to which they previously had access. In the nineteenth century, surveying the chaos created by the Industrial Revolution, Sismondi echoed the green critique of growth and wider economics. In 1819, he identified England as the home of economics, a nation obsessed with global competition where wealth paradoxically breeds poverty, dissatisfaction and crisis:

> England has given birth to the most celebrated Political Economists: the science is cultivated even at this time with increased ardour ... Universal competition or the effort always to produce more and always cheaper, has long been the system in England, a system which I have attacked as dangerous. This system has used production by manufacture to advance with gigantic steps, but it has from time to time precipitated the manufacturers into frightful distress ... In this astonishing country, which seems to be subject to a great experiment for the instruction of the rest of the world, I have seen production increasing, whilst enjoyments were diminishing. The mass of the nation here, no less than philosophers, seems to forget that the increase of wealth is not the end in political economy, but its instrument in procuring the happiness of all. I sought for this happiness in every class and I could nowhere find it ... Has not England, by forgetting men for things, sacrificed the end to the means. (quoted in Luxemburg 1971: 175–7)

Economists would argue that England after the disruption of industrialisation benefited from prosperity, yet they seem to suggest that disruption should constantly occur so as to fuel ever more prosperity. Such a system, as Sismondi observed, turns humanity (and nature) which are 'ends' merely into 'means' for an alien economic system. GNP, competitiveness and production are in the saddle and ride humanity.

The Victorian social critic John Ruskin, in a statement that rings true a century after he penned it, noted:

... the real science of political economy, which has yet to be distinguished from the bastard science, as medicine from witchcraft, and astronomy from astrology, is that which teaches nations to desire and labour for the things that lead to life: and which teaches them to scorn and destroy the things that lead to destruction. (quoted in Boyle 2002: 13)

Like Sismondi and Ruskin, Schumacher, in his green economics primer *Small is Beautiful*, stressed that economics should be a means of making human beings happier and serving ethical needs:

This is standing the truth on its head by considering goods as more important than people and consumption as more important than creative activity. It means shifting the emphasis from the worker to the product of work, that is, from the human to the sub-human, a surrender to the forces of evil. (Schumacher 1978: 54)

Bad Trade

Green campaigners have increasingly turned their attention to trade. Economists have argued that trade is beneficial because of gains from comparative advantage, competitive pressure, economics of scale and technology transfer. Competitive pressure means that by opening a country up to trade, domestic producers lose any monopoly status they may have had and are forced to become more cost efficient. Comparative advantage, a notion developed by Adam Smith and refined by Ricardo, occurs when countries specialise in the goods or services they are best at producing and exchange them for others. Economies of scale occur when increased production by a firm leads to lower average costs. A firm with a national market typically might sell to 30 million consumers, while with a continental market the firm gains access to 300 million, and with a global market perhaps more than a billion. Increased production allows expensive machinery to be used more efficiently, bulk buying of parts and raw materials can be enhanced and specialised staff recruited. These and a host of other savings lower costs. Trade should also create development via technology transfer from richer, more skilled nations to the rest of the planet.

Greens are sceptical:

Trade is rarely conducted between equal partners. In Smith and Ricardo's theory, trading nations are assumed to be equal partners making rational decisions based on objective assessments of the factors of production each has available to it through accidents of history, climate and geography. No weight is given to the power imbalances that exist between traders and producers and between different nations. Throughout the history of international trade, 'comparative advantages' have been created artificially and protected fiercely. Whether through gunboat 'diplomacy', colonisation, slavery, land enclosures, or protective subsidies, dominant trading nations have for centuries expropriated and jealously guarded the factors of production and market access they need to establish 'comparative advantages' over would-be competitors. (Woodin and Lucas 2004: 7)

Competition usually leads to a race to the bottom, with companies forced to cut wages, and degrade working conditions and environmental protection in order to minimise costs. Korten has noted how competition may ultimately lead to a contradictory state of monopoly, as global corporations emerge and domestic firms are eliminated (2001: 206–7). Global corporations can then raise prices and punish consumers, but are less interested in using their increasing profit margins to benefit workers or the environment.

WTO rules on patents are aimed at preventing poorer countries from copying products from Europe and North America, and as a result actually prevent technology transfer. Most notoriously, patent controls, relaxed only after huge international protest, were used to prevent South Africa developing cheap versions of the anti-AIDS/HIV drugs it needed. Technological transfers can, on the other hand, spread toxic or socially disabling practices from one part of the globe to another. Economies of scale may be significant but *dis*economies can also occur. As Schumacher noted:

I was brought up on the theory of 'economies of scale' – that with industries and firms, just as with nations, there is an irresistible trend, dictated by modern technology, for units to become ever bigger ... [Yet] Small scale organisation allows for greater flexibility and human communication, in short decentralised economic activity allows for 'the convenience, humanity, and manageability of smallness.' (1978: 62–3)

Trade, when successful in conventional terms, accelerates economic activity, which damages the environment:

By now, it should be clear that our environment is becoming ever less capable of sustaining the growing impact of our economic activities. Everywhere our forest are over logged, our agricultural lands over cropped, our grasslands over grazed, our wetlands over drained, our groundwater's over tapped, our seas over fished, and nearly all our terrestrial and marine environment is over polluted with chemical and radioactive poisons ... In such conditions, there can only be one way of maintaining the habitability of our planet, and that is to set out to reduce the impact. Unfortunately, the overriding goal of just about every government in the world is to maximise this impact through economic globalization. (Mander and Goldsmith 1996: 79)

Green Alternatives to Globalisation

Mike Woodin and Caroline Lucas argue that opposition to neo-liberal globalisation is not enough: coherent economic alternatives must be outlined, together with a series of measures to move from our present society to an alternative future. They build on the approach of Colin Hines, author of *Localization: A Global Manifesto* (2000). Globalisation for all three authors is largely politically driven. Drawing on the analysis presented by anti-corporate anti-capitalists (see Chapter 3), they suggest that globalisation has been advanced to meet the needs of an elite, that globalisation is not an irreversible or automatic process; it is politically driven and can be rolled back or radically transformed.

Globalisation is ecologically damaging and therefore the ecological crisis that centrally motivates Greens can only be solved by reversing it. Woodin and Lucas also note the links between globalisation, privatisation and poverty. They note how the IMF's Structural Adjustment Programmes (SAPs) insist that in order to be given financial aid, countries must sell off publicly owned resources, including power and water supplies, telecommunications and even transport infrastructure. The European Union's stability pact insists that countries in the euro currency area limit government spending. Even without these institutional pressures, the need for foreign direct investment from multinationals encourages states to cut spending on public spending and the environment, so as to reduce corporation tax and attract firms (Woodin and Lucas 2004: 58). Senegal, seen as an IMF success, slashed government spending and increased growth rates, but saw unemployment rise from 25 per cent to 44 per cent between 1991 and 1996 (ibid.: 57). Transnational corporations may dominate the globe, but they produce relatively few jobs given their desire to downsize and outsource. The two hundred largest global corporations employ just 0.75 per cent of the world's workforce (ibid.: 73).

The ecological ill-effects of globalisation are emphasised with reference to food production. Peasants are being squeezed out by 'free trade', local diversity in diet is eroded and in the great food swap, identical commodities move thousands of miles across the globe, wasting energy and pushing up the production of greenhouse gases. Supermarkets are damaging to farmers, consumers, workers and the environment (ibid.: 155–6). European, North American and Japanese agricultural production is protected, while southern countries are forced by global institutions to open up their markets, often with disastrous results:

... the IMF bulldozed Haiti into liberalising its rice markets. It was flooded with cheap US imports and local production collapsed, destroying tens of thousands of rural livelihoods. A decade ago Haiti was self-sufficient in rice; today it spends half of its export earnings importing rice from the US. (ibid.: 147)

Woodin and Lucas outlined the absurdity of trading like-for-like, which seems to make a nonsense of comparative advantage and specialisation:

In 1998, Britain imported 61,400 tonnes of poultry meat from the Netherlands and exported 33,100 tonnes of poultry meat to the Netherlands ... it imported 240,000 tonnes of pork and 125,000 tonnes of lamb, while it exported 195,000 tonnes of pork and 102,000 tonnes of lamb. In 1997, the UK imported 126m litres of milk and exported 270m litres of milk ... In 1999, the EU imported 44,000 tonnes of meat from Argentina, 11,000 tonnes from Botswana, 40,000 tonnes from Poland and over 70,000 tonnes from Brazil ... meat exports from the EU to the rest of the world totalled 874,211. (ibid.: 148)

The food industry promotes obesity and is often hugely abusive to animals, which are transported ever increasing distances and factory farmed under appalling conditions to push unit costs down.

Woodin and Lucas stress that change must occur, arguing that the present trajectory of the global economy damages its citizens, other species and the natural environment that sustains life. The solution is to introduce local currencies (a theme discussed critically in our next chapter) and to rewrite the multilateral rule book of institutions such as the WTO, the IMF, the World Bank and the EU to promote local economic development. Localisation does not mean complete self-sufficiency, or the outright rejection of trade if it brings real gains. However, social and environmental concerns mean that it is often better to produce goods locally rather than exporting them from many thousands of miles away. Hines concisely defines localisation:

The alternative is that everything that could be produced within a nation or region should be. Long-distance trade is then reduced to supplying what could not come from within one country or geographical groupings of countries. This would allow an increase in local control of the economy and the potential for it being shared out more fairly, locally. Technology and information would be encouraged to flow, when and where they could strengthen local economies. Under these circumstances, beggar-your-neighbour globalization gives way to the potentially more cooperative better-your-neighbour localization. (Hines 2000: viii)

The localists have been challenged by a number of writers, including the journalist and green supporter George Monbiot, who argues that localisation would prevent development and would put countries in the South at some disadvantage (2003b). Other commentators reflect the view that globalisation can be greened, or reformed. The German Greens argue for 'green globalisation' and believe that institutions such as the European Union can be used to limit the environmental consequences of globalisation. Monbiot argues that trade should be made fairer, that globalisation has both benefits and costs, but must be regulated. Monbiot believes that global institutions such as the IMF and WTO could be used to benefit the poorest, if they were made subordinate to a new global parliament with representatives elected from the entire world. The localists respond that they are not fundamentalists and believe that trade should occur where vital.

A Green New Deal

Caroline Lucas and other Greens have argued, in response to the 2008 economic crisis and rising CO2 levels, for a Green New Deal, which would kickstart the economy and create jobs by massive investment in renewable energy, public transport and home insulation. While this is often seen as 'Green Keynesianism' and part of a pro-growth agenda, a Green New Deal could seen as part of a transition to a new post-carbon economy. More temperate voices have watered down some of the most radical demands of the Green New Deal, while right-wing governments in this century have increasingly embraced climate change denial, for example, in 2014, Australian Prime Minister Tony Abbott's government abolished that country's quite modest carbon tax. More positively, trade unionists have also supported the Green New Deal, with the UK's Trade Union Congress (TUC) creating a one million green jobs plan.

This century has also seen the renewal of critiques of economic growth with the creation of the 'Degrowth' movement. The British government's Sustainable Development Commission developed a radical 'Prosperity without Growth' project, only to see their work terminated by the 2010 Conservative-Liberal Democrat coalition government. In turn, Latin American governments have stressed the notion of '*buen vivir*' or 'good living' economics, based partly on indigenous practices that reject 'extractivism'. In 2010, the International Degrowth Conference in Barcelona came up with a number of proposals to promote a post-growth, post-capitalist economy that meets human needs ecologically:

... including: facilitation of local currencies; gradual elimination of fiat money and reforms of interest; promotion of small-scale, self-managed not-for-profit companies; defense and expansion of local commons and establishment of new jurisdictions for global commons; establishment of integrated policies of reduced working hours (work-sharing) and introduction of a basic income; institutionalization of an income ceiling based on maximum-minimum ratios; discouragement of overconsumption of non-durable goods and under-use of durables by regulation, taxation or bottom-up approaches; abandonment of large-scale infrastructure such as nuclear plants, dams, incinerators, high-speed transportation; conversion of car-based infrastructure to walking, biking and open common spaces; taxation of excessive advertising and its prohibition from public spaces; support for environmental justice movements of the South that struggle against resource extraction; introduction of global extractive moratoria in areas with high biodiversity and cultural value, and compensation for leaving resources in the ground; denouncement of top-down population control measures and support of women's reproductive rights, conscious procreation and the right to free migration while welcoming a decrease in world birth rates; and de-commercialization of politics and enhancement of direct participation in decision-making.

(www.barcelona.degrowth.org/Barcelona-2010-Declaration.119.0.html)

Beyond Green Anti-capitalism

The green critique at its most radical goes further than anti-corporate anti-capitalism by stating that economics is a system that tends to dominate and distort human values. The Greens, especially at their most radical, unpick economics bit by bit. The basic definition of economics found in any textbook is that it is 'a study of how scarce resources are used to meet unlimited human wants', and is a definition that Greens find alarming. While resources may be limited and demand careful nurturing, the notion that human wants are infinite is seen as both unproven and a source of danger. Economists' concern with unlimited wants suggests that economic growth must continue. Greens would argue that instead, the economic system in its reliance on economic growth, makes us want more and more. A modern capitalist economy is based on the systematic construction of dissatisfaction through branding, advertising and a range of ever more imaginative marketing techniques. One thinks of the Tibetan Buddhist realm of the 'hungry ghosts', where dissatisfied spirits wander, trying unsuccessfully to satisfy their infinite appetites.

The green critique has been combined, by some, with socialist theory to create an ecosocialist alternative to neo-liberalism (see Chapter 8). Other Greens have turned to various forms of monetary reform, seeking to understand how money and especially the creation of debt fuels capitalism, economic growth and globalisation. Such money-centred anti-capitalism is the subject of our next chapter.

5

PLANET EARTH MONEY MARTYRED: SOCIAL CREDIT, POSITIVE MONEY AND MONETARY REFORM

Anti-globalists see the 'Washington consensus' as a conspiracy to enrich bankers. They are not entirely wrong. (*The Economist*, 26 September 2001)

Many activists agree that the 'finance industry lies at the heart of neo-liberal globalization' (Hutchinson et al. 2002: 5). The Washington Consensus examined in Chapter 2 is a banker's consensus, driven by the need to pay back debt at all costs. Free trade allows payments to bankers to be generated, government spending must be cut to reduce debt, while privatisation allows global financiers to pick up bargains. Capital liberalisation, which removes all barriers to currency circulation between countries, means that money can be sucked out of a country if it pursues radical policies or otherwise displeases the markets. Over 95 per cent of capital movements between countries are speculative. A mere 5 per cent or less of the dollars, yen, euros and other national currencies that cross borders do so to pay for trade or to fund physical investment in factories. The rest is exchanged at ever faster rates to make money out of money – selling, for example, yen to buy dollars in the hope of generating a profit. The rather abstract nature of finance has led to calls for reform. Debt drives environmental damage – peasants may be forced to cut down forests, to displace rare mountain gorillas and drain fish-filled lakes, so they can sell commodities to pay off interest. Monetary reformer Frances Hutchinson observes that the anti-globalisation and environmental movement did not start with Rachel Carson, still less with Seattle, and goes on to describe a pedigree flowing back to the eighteenth-century Scottish banker John Law, biblical notions of jubilee, US populism and Douglas Social Credit (Hutchinson et al. 2002). Monetary reformers argue that elite bankers who lend money and collect the interest essentially create money out of thin air. Debt is often described as the primary source of social injustice. The solution involves debt forgiveness and the creation of debt-free money by states or local communities. The financial crisis of 2008, which was the result of the manipulation and mismanagement of increasingly complex and dangerous financial instruments, has seemingly made radical critiques of banking more respectable. This chapter outlines the case against the World Bank and the IMF, outlines the nature of ATTAC and finally examines the radical message of monetary reform.

IMF Apocalypse

The IMF, which lends money to nations with severe debt problems, was created to maintain the stability of the global financial architecture as part of the Bretton Woods process in the 1940s. In return for economic assistance, as we noted in Chapter 2, it has insisted on controversial structural adjustment programmes (SAPs) that lead to increasing poverty. The Canadian economist Michel Chossudovsky has argued that both the IMF and the World Bank helped to create chaos in the former Yugoslavia, reduced Russia to 'Third World' status and contributed to devastating poverty in many nations, including Rwanda and Somalia (Chossudovsky 1997). While Stiglitz and Soros tend to argue that the Washington Consensus has been a product of economic dogmatism rather than malice, Chossudovsky is one of many critics who see it as a weapon used to maintain super-imperialism.

In return for debt help, the IMF insisted on a series of SAP 'conditionalities' which, in theory, are sets of sound economic principles that a debtor must follow to help resolve financial crisis, similar to an alcoholic agreeing to pour away the whisky in return for professional help. Some see SAPS as tough but fair, and economically sound. In fact, as Stiglitz and Soros remind us, they may worsen the patient's condition, creating poverty, that is likely to swell rather than subdue debt.

Chossudovsky argues that SAPs, by insisting that governments privatise large parts of their economies, allow largely US-based multinationals to increase their ownership of foreign assets. Export-led growth, demanded by the SAPs, creates oversupply of commodities such as coffee, which further depresses prices and benefits relatively rich consumer countries rather than producers. Spending cuts create political instability, and as in the case of Yugoslavia, allegedly lead to the disintegration of states (ibid.).

Among other 'conditionalities', SAPs have included the devaluation of national currencies to enable export-led growth, by reducing the price of products sold on the world market. Yet such devaluation has made it even cheaper for foreign corporations to buy up assets, at knockdown prices. Currency devaluation has made it prohibitively expensive for citizens to buy even basic foodstuffs and has fuelled inflation. As we noted in Chapter 2, inflation is the number one enemy for the Washington Consensus, whose proponents then insist on further cuts in government spending to keep prices from rising. IMF policies have led to the collapse of the Somalian economy, creating famine and vicious civil war. In particular, currency devaluation pushed down revenue from crops and pushed up prices for fuel, fertiliser and other farm inputs (ibid.: 102).

Chossudovsky provides many case study examples of his basic thesis that the IMF is an instrument of US foreign policy. In Vietnam, the US re-ran the war they lost militarily in the 1970s, gaining financial victory during the 1980s:

> The social consequences of structural adjustment applied in Vietnam since the mid-1980s are devastating. Health clinics and hospitals have closed down, local-level famines have erupted, affecting up to a quarter of the country's population, and three quarters of a million children have dropped out of the school system. There has been a resurgence of infectious diseases with a tripling of recorded malaria deaths during the first four years of the reforms. Five thousand (out of a total of 12,000) state enterprises have been driven into bankruptcy, more than a million workers and some 200,000 public employees, including tens of thousands of teachers and health workers, have been laid off.
>
> A secret agreement reached in Paris in 1993, which in many regards was tantamount to forcing Vietnam 'to compensate Washington' for the costs of the war, required Hanoi to recognise the debts of the defunct Saigon regime … as a condition for the granting of fresh credits … The achievements of past struggles and the aspirations of an entire nation are undone and erased. (Ibid.: 147)

A free market discourse is used to legitimate the policy goals of an elite. The IMF along with the World Bank are 'regulatory bodies' that intervene to control the global economy through 'a worldwide process of debt collection' (ibid.: 15).

Financing Enclosure and Ecocide

From 1997 through 2000, Joseph Stiglitz acted as vice president and chief economist for the International Bank for Reconstruction and Development, more commonly known as the World Bank. The World Bank aims to lend money to development projects across the globe to create economic growth in the poorest nations. However, it has been widely criticised for focusing on projects that wreck the environment and promote enclosure (Rich 1994). The bank has been targeted by environmentalists and social justice campaigners for funding huge dams and other projects that have dispossessed millions of people and devastated local ecosystems (Caulfield 1997; Rich 1994). Active in over a hundred countries, the Bank is an enormous force; it is the number one financier of the big dams that Roy and Shiva attack so vehemently (see Chapter 4). In its 60-year history, the bank has funded at least 552 dams, at a cost in 2004 currency of $86 billion (the Yacyret Dam, Argentina/Paraguay, alone involved $6 billion lost to corruption) and at least 10 million people evicted from their homes. It has also spent over $26.5 billion on fossil fuel projects such as coal- and oil-fired power stations since 1992 (www.irn.org/programs/finance).

In 1992, World Bank Chief Economist Larry Summers scandalised the world when he wrote that the developing world was under-polluted and it would make economic sense for African countries to receive more toxic waste, in a memo that was leaked by *The Economist*. His economic logic, in orthodox neo-liberal terms, was clear. Individuals in African states had a far lower income than those in wealthier parts of the world, so death or injury would be less costly in terms of lost income. In response, the *Financial Times*, a newspaper not known for its radical credentials, ran a piece under the title 'Save Planet Earth from Economists' (George and Sabelli 1994: 98–100). Summers later became director of the White House's United States National Economic Council, shaping President Obama's economic policy The World Bank has also been criticised for supporting dictatorships and colonial powers. One of its earliest loans in 1947 allowed the Dutch government to launch a war against Indonesian nationalists who were attempting to gain independence (Rich 1994: 69). Between 1976 and 1986, the bank lent Indonesia $630 million to resettle millions of their poor to Borneo, Irian Jaya (the occupied western half of Papua New Guinea) and Sumatra. Six million people were moved into areas that were often pristine rainforest. Deforestation proceeded at a rate of 10,000 square miles a year. Environmental problems ranged from acidification of soils to plagues of insects. The Indonesian military dictatorship massacred several million socialists in the 1970s and were keen to use resettlement as a means of reducing discontent by funnelling the poor into wild areas occupied by the state (ibid.: 37).

Protests have forced some change in the bank's policies. For example, in 2003 it cut funding to the Cambodian Forestry programme after it was found that the government had inflated the amount of rainforest left in the country, and allowed companies illegal logging access and barred conservationists (Bretton Woods Project, 16 January 2004). However, 2004 also saw the bank return to funding big dam projects and deciding to restart funding for Cambodia, despite a lack of progress over the country's forestry policy.

An endorsement from the World Bank encourages other lenders and donors to provide support. Credit-rating agencies such as Moody's or Standard & Poor assess the financial worth of entire countries, mainly based on IMF and World Bank data. Those states that break neo-liberalism's rules see their ratings plummet and cash flowing out. Development is based on enclosing the commons, enclosure that demands military force and repression. The World

Bank continues to finance globalisation in the third millennium, a process that seeks to integrate the poor violently into a market economy.

On the ATTAC

Without the Bretton Woods institutions, global financial forces would still, according to many commentators, threaten justice, ecology and democracy. Trillions of dollars of currency, as we have noted, at several points in this text flow at ever faster rates across the globe on a daily basis. While such cash is largely speculative (that is, used to make money out of money) rather than invested physically, outflows of 'hot money' can lead to falling exchange rates and potential economic collapse. Currency speculation provides an example of the basic economic law that there is an inverse relationship between one's contribution to society and monetary reward. In *The Bonfire of the Vanities*, Tom Wolfe's central character, a bond trader, is at a loss to explain his job to his daughter – for bonds we may read currency or shares or hedge funds or any other way of making money from buying and selling financial instruments to scrape off tiny, but incremental, margins of gain:

> 'Daddy, what is it that you do?' And the Master of the Universe is lost for words – how indeed would you describe bond dealing to a seven-year-old? And his wife jumps in and says, 'Well, darling, just imagine that a bond is a slice of cake, and you didn't bake the cake, but every time you hand somebody a slice of cake a tiny little bit comes off, like a little crumb, and you can keep that.' (Wolfe 1988: 260)

The growth of 'unproductive' speculative cashflows increasingly distorts the 'normal' workings of capitalism. Speculative flows have tended to intensify economic crises, for example, leading to the near-collapse of the Asian 'tiger' economies in 1997.

In response to the Asian crisis, the editor of *Le Monde Diplomatique* Ignacio Ramonet wrote an article entitled 'Disarm the Markets' and launched the Association for the Taxation of Transactions and for Aid to Citizens (ATTAC) in 1997 (Patomaki 2001: 180). His main demand is the creation of a Tobin Tax, named after the economist who introduced the idea, of a 0.5 per cent charge on all speculative currency transactions. This would reduce speculation and thus create greater currency stability, making the destruction of national economies less likely in times of economic instability. By discouraging speculation, the tax would make it easier for national economies to resist global market forces. The tax would also raise billions of dollars that could be used to relieve hunger, fund environmental protection and perhaps finance the United Nations, or other instruments or institutions capable of creating a more democratic form of global governance.

While there are a number of technical problems with the tax, it should be difficult for speculators to avoid it by shifting countries. After all, the bulk of transactions are made in four currencies: the dollar, the euro, the pound sterling and the yen, and most transactions take place in only ten key countries. The Finnish economist Heikki Patomaki, who has produced the most extensive and sophisticated account of the tax as a means of 'throwing sand in the wheels' of the global market, admits:

> Nobody should be led into the false belief that the Tobin tax – or another regulation mechanism for the financial system – would solve all the world's problems … More thorough reforms are needed to make the global economy socially responsible and democratic. (Ibid.: 221)

Monetary Reform

Rather than blaming merely the Washington Consensus or speculative flows of hot money, the most radical monetary reformers believe that the very existence of debt-creating banks is the source of global chaos. Canadian John McMurtry, author of *The Cancer Stage of Capitalism*, argues fiercely that:

> There is no fraud in history that remotely approaches the monopoly expropriation by private banks of the public powers of money creation and dissolution. Its invisible chains bind and imprison the lives and life economies of people across continents. (McMurtry 2002: 130)

McMurtry's vigorous attack on the banks is largely inspired by the work of Major Douglas, 'labelled as a "crank" by every newspaper that banks advertised in or lent to' (ibid.: 127). Major Clifford Douglas, an engineer, writing in the aftermath of the First World War, argued that debt-based money created by banks is the root of most evil. Critics of globalisation, including McMurtry, Herman Daly, Richard Douthwaite and David Korten, acknowledge the value of Douglas' social credit philosophy (Rowbotham 1998).

Most money, even in Douglas's day, was no longer created by governments but by private banks who then lent the money to governments who paid for it using taxation. Douglas saw money as socially constructed and of symbolic value only. Despite its lack of 'reality', money, rather than being a neutral fluid that allowed economic development to take place, could distort production, distribution and consumption. Banks created credit, increasing the money supply, to maintain economic activity. Yet credit created by bankers must be repaid, according to monetary reformers enslaving both producers and consumers with debt; 97 per cent of the money supply in the UK at present is made up of debt money that must be paid back with interest:

> Most people, when they are told this, dismiss the claims utterly and in their minds clearly regard you as politically disturbed person; a sad case of mental fixation, perhaps unable to cope with the demands and opportunities of the modern world. This is really quite understandable. The natural assumption is that there must be more to this matter. If banks and building societies do indeed create money, there must be a rationale behind the decision to leave the creation and supply of money to them. It defies belief that such an extraordinary arrangement should exist without there being a good reason for it, but it is true. (Ibid.: 5–6)

Banks create money and lend it to borrowers, who then spend it into circulation. The economist John Kenneth Galbraith noted that this is 'a method so simple the mind is repelled' (cited in ibid.: 10–11). Modern money is electronic and virtual, it only has value because we believe it has value.

Douglas believed that social credit, quite literally debt-free money, created by the community could be used to reward all citizens with an income. He believed that the real riches of society were based on cultural inheritance built up by society by generations of creativity. Such cultural inheritance was for Douglas a forgotten and all-important factor of production. Wealth is generated by ideas, which give rise to technological innovation. Rather than being the unique product of particular inventive individuals, such cultural wealth is produced by the community, which should be rewarded for its collective intellectual labour with a national dividend (Hutchinson and Burkitt 1997: 59–60).

Douglas was an economic utopian:

> The strength of the appeal, which Major Douglas makes to his followers, is that his theories promise something for nothing. Consumers are to receive credits; dividends are to be issued to all; taxation will become unnecessary and no one will be called upon to pay the cost. (Hiskett and Franklin 1939: 163)

Keynes famously described him as 'a private' rather than a general in an army of economic radicals challenging the bankrupt orthodoxy of liberal thought (Bell 1993: 163). Nonetheless, Keynes felt that he was a more important economic commentator than Marx, because he suggested that credit could be used to prevent recession. Douglas's social credit enjoyed some support and interest in the 1930s. A Social Credit Party was established in the Canadian province of Alberta and won a stunning victory in the 1935 provincial elections (Macpherson

1953; Stingel 2000). Social credit has also been politically significant in Australia and New Zealand. Indeed, the New Zealand Labour Party is said to have won a general election on a social credit programme (Hutchinson and Burkitt 1997: 147). Working-class activists in the Coventry League of the Unemployed and the Kibbo Kift Kin, a bizarrely named socialist scouting body, came together to found the Social Credit Greenshirts (Drakeford 1997).

Social creditors contend that ecologically destructive economic growth is explained by the creation of debt money, which forces us to produce and consume more and more. In the 1930s, Douglas noted that:

> Industry has run riot over the countryside. A population, which has been educated in the fixed idea that the chief, if not the only, objective of life is well named 'business,' whose politicians and preachers exhort their audiences to fresh efforts for the capture of markets and the provision of still more business, cannot be blamed if, as opportunity occurs, it still further sacrifices the amenities of the countryside to the building of more blast-furnaces and chemical works. (Douglas 1979: 107)

Douglas powerfully criticised the notion that human wants were unlimited and growth must therefore continue infinitely. He saw wants as constructed by forces of finance to maintain accumulation. He also believed that 'the genuine consumptive capacity of the individual is limited, [therefore] we must recognize that the world, whether consciously or not, is working towards the Leisure State' (ibid.: 110). In Douglas' alternative future, business

> ...would of necessity cease to be the major interest of life and would, as has happened to so many biological activities, be relegated to a position of minor importance, to be replaced, no doubt, by some form of activity of which we are not yet fully cognizant. (Ibid.: 110)

Supporters have argued that social credit produced by the community rather than banks could be used to fund expensive policies without massive tax rises. Alternative energy systems, home insulation, recycling schemes, land reclamation and measures to end poverty could be funded by debt-free money produced by the community (Price 1981).

Douglas and modern social creditors, such as Hutchinson, believe that a national dividend, a form of guaranteed income, could be introduced. This would decommodify labour, encouraging individuals to workshare and allowing unpaid creative and necessary social labour to be undertaken. Jobs that were unnecessary and ecologically destructive could be swept away, thus removing the opportunity cost of environmental destruction as the price of job preservation. The building blocks of conventional economics – infinite wants, scarce resources and opportunity cost – would be removed by the Douglas revolution. Scarcity is a particular target of Douglas's ire:

> The world is obsessed, or possessed, by a scarcity complex. While at the date of writing Great Britain is preparing for another war, she still has a million unemployed, farms going out of cultivation and agricultural products being destroyed because they cannot be sold, publicists still inform us on the one hand that the situation is due to over-production, and on the other hand that sacrifices must be made by everyone, that we must all work harder, consume less, and produce more. (Douglas 1979: 89).

Social credit, for advocates, seems an obvious solution to the global debt crisis and provides a way of tempering globalisation, which is seen as a product of demands for increased free trade as nations struggle to export surplus goods that are unsold because of the chronic loss of purchasing power (Rowbotham 2000).

Douglas, never an easy man, according to his biographers, seems to have become increasingly ill and embittered after the 1930s. His ideas became marginal even amongst those who challenged the economic orthodoxy. Depressingly, Douglas was, even for a rather intolerant age, astonishingly anti-Semitic. Prone to conspiracy thinking, he celebrated the 1940s by becoming an early advocate of Holocaust revisionism, suggesting that Jewish financial forces were behind the Second World War (Stingel 2000). The social credit movement shrank and split into various warring factions and it was not until the 1990s that his ideas re-emerged. Sadly, Douglas support groups have often functioned as a rather bizarre dating club where Greens and leftists have been able to partner neo-Nazis and anti-Semites (Wall 2003).

Of course, opposition to finance capitalism goes far wider than Douglas, indeed critics of usury look to Aristotle, the Bible and the Talmud. Frances Hutchinson, Mary Mellor and Wendy Olson flag up the importance of John Law, an eighteenth-century Scottish banker who fled to France after a legal scandal (Hutchinson et al. 2002: 57–60). He invented a form of paper money for the French government to help them overcome financial crisis. Regrettably, investors lost faith in paper and bankruptcy resulted. A very great range of monetary experiments accompanied the American Revolution. Way back in 1731, Benjamin Franklin, amongst his other hobbies, used to print money (Boyle 2002: 25). In the 1780s, Franklin and other American revolutionaries advocated not only taxation with representation, but believed that national sovereignty was based on the ability for states to create their own credit. There is a long pedigree of opposition to the banks by small farmers and workers in the US populist movement (Ritter 1997).

President Abraham Lincoln, finding that the banks would only lend his government funds to fight the Civil War at high interest rates, issued his own currency, the greenback. This was spent into existence, much to the annoyance of the bankers (Greco 2001: 43). Some argue that his assassination was part of a bankers' plot to preserve their power. Lincoln was, in the words of one populist pamphlet, 'money martyred' (Search 1977).

Monetary reform was significant at the birth of socialism. The utopian socialist Robert Owen, for example, advocated the creation of labour notes to replace bank money. The anarchist Proudhon in the 1840s saw banks as a source of injustice and backed the creation of labour credits to make way for a socialist system (McNally 1993). Arthur Kitson, an inventor and industrialist active in the early twentieth century, also campaigned on the injustice of debt money, which he claimed was produced by self-enriching bankers (Hutchinson et al. 2002: 158). Frederick Soddy, a Nobel Prize-winning chemist who wrote on ecological issues and feared the effects of economic growth, saw bankers as a force for evil because they, rather than productive groups, governed the economy. Silvio Gesell, a Swiss Austrian, called for the principle of demurrage – essentially a negative interest scheme, where money would progressively lose its value if not spent, and thus a principle designed to promote economic activity. Like Douglas, Keynes lavishly praised him (Boyle 2002: 233). There are perhaps hundreds of monetary reform theorists who agree that it is wrong for banks to hold a monopoly of credit (Boyle 2002; Lietaer 2001).

In 2014, the Green Party of England and Wales adopted the policy of Positive Money, a pressure group who wish to place money creation in public hands. Quantitative easing, where money was created and used to buy back government debt, put nearly £4 billion into the UK economy to prevent negative economic growth and deflation, during the recession from 2009 onwards. Inflationary in ordinary circumstances, in a state of austerity, this policy was used to keep the economy afloat. Tragically, rather than being used to fund renewable energy schemes, build schools, or even end poverty through a basic income scheme, the money was simply pumped into the banking system in the form of cheap credit. Monetary reformers argue that such money creation could be used to banish poverty and finance a sustainable future, rather than helping bankers.

Modern Monetary Theory (MMT) argues that the obsession with government debt used to promote austerity is misleading; currency can be created by the state and should not be used as an excuse to destroy services. MMT seems to provide a good basis for a more social justice approach to monetary economics: while it doesn't argue that all credit should be created by the state, it does suggest that states have alternatives to austerity. A good introduction to MMT is provided by the US economist Warren Mosler in works such as *Seven Deadly Innocent Frauds of Economic Policy* (2010).

Lets and Local Currencies

Monetary reform ideas were put into action in the small Austrian town of Wörgl in the 1930s, where the local mayor Michael Unterguggenberger created demurrage money to move his community out of recession (Boyle 2002: 236). Local factories had closed during the 1930s economic crisis and the local council had found it difficult to raise local tax. The council issued 30,000 Austrian schillings. These currency notes fell by 1 per cent every month, so recipients had an incentive to spend them as fast as possible. The currency was also known as 'stamp scrip', because unless it was stamped by the authorities to show the decline in value, it would not be accepted and would become worthless. The currency circulated quickly, taxes were raised, unemployment fell and Wörgl prospered until the Austrian National Bank stepped in to close the system down in 1933.

Inspired in part by such ideas, thousands of local monetary experiments have been launched around the globe. Micro-credit, where development networks allow local community enterprises to borrow on favourable terms, is another (Hulme and Mosley 1996). 'Time dollars' from Ithaca, New York allow citizens to swap labour and have been recognised by government agencies (Greco 2001). The fastest growing have been Local Exchange and Trading Systems (LETS), invented by the Canadian activist Michael Linton (Greco 2001: 89). Since the 1980s, they have become increasingly common, using computer software to construct local barter schemes where individuals trade services such as plumbing and babysitting (Douthwaite 2000). The New Economics Foundation has argued with some technical flourish that rather than being dependent on bankers and global finance, governments could create their own money and control their own economic destiny (Huber and Robertson 2000).

The former banker Bernard Lietaer has drawn attention to a variety of new locally created currencies, which he sees as the basis for a future of 'sustainable abundance'. He is particularly enthusiastic about the example of municipal rubbish-based currency in the Brazilian city of Curitiba. When a new mayor, Jaime Lerner, was elected in 1971, he found that the town was out of cash and the rubbish was piling up in the streets, so anyone who brought their glass, paper, plastics or vegetable waste for recycling was rewarded with a bus token. The tokens evolved into an alternative local currency and the town took off. The average citizen earns three times the Brazilian minimum wage and according to Lietaer, Curitiba has been able to 'join First World living standards within one generation' (2001: 201). Local currencies are seen as a way of encouraging local economic activity so as to act as a barrier to globalisation (Woodin and Lucas 2004: 194).

Positive Money

The ideas of monetary reformers with their schemes to print money and create a new economic order cannot be dismissed entirely. Money, far from being 'real', is clearly socially created. Making this point in an otherwise strongly critical account of Douglas social credit, Hiskett and Franklin note that:

> The attempt, which is sometimes made, by orthodox defenders of the banking system, to show that banks do no more than lend the money, which is deposited with them, is based on a specious argument, which tries to prove too much. The indisputable fact is that, by action of the banks, £1,000 of new cash, deposited with the banking system, is built up into a total of £10,000 deposits by the addition of £9,000 of credit money. (1939: 105)

Their account is slightly out of date. Today, banks feel little need to maintain reserves of currency and continue to build up mountains of debt-based cash. Yet although money is 'virtual', the message of the monetary reformers may not quite provide a panacea. Conventional critics of monetary reform argue that money creation can be ineffective or inflationary. More radical voices suggest that the development of debt-free money may not be as crucial to creating an ecologically sound and social justice economy as the reformers suggest.

One issue is 'neutrality'. Most conventional economists argue that money is neutral, which means that money should not be confused with real wealth. By producing more money, we cannot really make people richer. For example, if the Australian government doubled the amount of money in the economy this would not automatically double the quantity of goods and services in the Australian economy. Instead, the price of goods and services would tend to increase.

Keynes argued that money was not entirely neutral, if there were unemployed resources in an economy, for example, if workers were unemployed and land 'idle', an increase in the money supply might be accompanied by growth. However, he believed that consumer and especially business confidence were far greater influences on 'real' economic activity. Simply printing money does not create wealth, as some monetary reformers seem to suggest. Money, even if it is made in a debt-free form, will fuel either growth or inflation. If the community 'prints' more money and spare productive capacity is present, more goods will be produced, creating more economic growth which is potentially destructive from a green perspective.

Money is socially constructed and has no objective source of value other than collective sentiment. If banks simply produced unlimited amounts of money at the stroke of a pen, their legitimacy would fall and their deposits would cease to be seen as 'good'. If governments or the community were simply to supply more money, public confidence in the currency might fall. If confidence in a currency is low, it falls in value and may be unacceptable. This explains the value of the dollar. The political and military power of the US creates confidence in the dollar which is seen as a 'hard currency', so that in many parts of the world US currency rather than the local currency is used. Military and political stagnation with rising debt pushes the dollar down. Thus, socially constructed money is still likely to follow Gresham's law – that accepted credit will be pushed out by that with less perceived legitimacy, that is, good money is driven out by bad. To make money work appropriate rituals must be performed. Equally, bankers cannot be seen as the source of *all* evils, as wicked magicians who commit the evil of usury to gain dominance over creation. If people believe that money has value, then it has value! If authorities have power, money works perhaps to give them more power, but merely to construct money is not enough. Currently, only a minority use local currency and LETS schemes, and they are very much at the fringes of society. Bitcoins have had however a larger impact and it might be argued that all the anti-capitalist alternatives discussed in this volume are marginal and a hard struggle will be needed to take them centre stage.

Radicals, as well as defenders of the economic orthodoxy, also criticise the monetary approach. Monetary reformers argue that debt money is the root of all evil. Yet all forms of money have ill-effects on society. Money has long been a source of destruction and it's largely pointless to distinguish between good (debt-free) and bad (banker-created) cash (Buchan 1997). In a money-based economy, an individual must have money to exchange for goods and services to survive. This means that one must constantly find new ways of acquiring money, leading to waste and dissatisfaction. To survive, I need to sell more books. Therefore, if more people borrow my books from friends or libraries, I find it more difficult to profit from writing. Money discourages us from creating an economy based on what is useful and instead creates new needs. The need to constantly buy and sell to survive leads to human alienation and ecological destruction. The prophetic anarchist Fredy Perlman argued:

> As soon as men [*sic*] accept money as an equivalent for life, the sale of living activity becomes a condition for their physical and social survival. Life is exchanged for survival. Creation and production come to mean sold activity. A man's activity is 'productive,' useful to society, only when it is sold activity. And the man himself is a productive member of society only if the activities of his daily life are sold activities. As soon as people accept the terms of this exchange, daily activity takes the form of universal prostitution. (Perlman 1992: 36)

James Buchan, a former *Financial Times* journalist, argues that all money has destructive consequences because it promotes quantity over quality and makes everything, from emotional responses to wildlife, potentially purchasable. Hegel, Marx and the Romantic poets suggest that money is dangerous:

> ... the habit of calculating and making comparisons in money diminishes much that is strange and precious in creation, indeed abolishes quality itself as a mental category by which to understand reality; displaces trust in people by trust in money, and thus poisons the relations between human beings and atomises society; and submerges being in possessing. (Buchan 1997: 271)

Money is rather addictive, Buchan describes it as 'frozen desire', and it fuels addictive compulsive behaviour. Hegel famously stated that the spirit of money was the life of that which is dead moving within itself (*ein sich in sich bewegendes Leben des Toten*) (Avineri 1972: 35). Capitalism is about more than finance. As the Marxist geographer David Harvey, for example, argues, a capitalist economy tends towards crisis for a variety of reasons including the mismatch between consumption and investment (1999). He believes that credit creation allows firms to invest in factories and machinery, despite a lack of demand for their goods in the short run. Debt rather than driving the system instead functions to smooth out mismatches between supply and demand. Rather than being the 'heart' of the system, it is the 'liver' or 'kidney', an essential but not the essence of the economic body. While Harvey acknowledges that debt creation ultimately leads to greater potential for crisis, he suggests it should be seen as part of the system not its principle driving force.

The case for monetary reform has been enhanced by the 2008 financial crisis. Ever more complex financial instruments together with subprime mortgages, provided at high interest to poor householders in Florida, led to chaos. Criticism of the banking system has become mainstream. However, while part of the process of economic crisis, economists both mainstream and radical, argue that there were deeper causes. Changing finance is insufficient to achieve either a more stable capitalism or a post-capitalist economic alternative.

The Curibita example shows that local currency experiments can aid environmentally friendly rather than greed-centred economies, but Lietaer overstates his case. Monetary reformers argue that if banking was reformed, capitalism would no longer be destructive or perhaps would not exist at all. This seems a little simplistic both in terms of explaining the forces that drive capitalism and the forms of injustice it creates in the world. Marxists, in providing an alternative account of capitalism, have argued that the problems we face have rather deeper roots. Marxism, evaluated in the next chapter, has its own strengths and weaknesses in explaining the process of globalisation and looking to alternatives.

6

IMPERIALISM UNLIMITED: MARXISMS

The Times of November 1857 contains an utterly delightful cry of outrage on the part of a West Indian plantation owner. This advocate argues with great moral indignation – as a plea for the re-introduction of Negro slavery – how the *Quashees* (the free blacks of Jamaica) content themselves with producing only what is strictly necessary for their own consumption, and, alongside this 'use value,' regard loafing (indulgence and idleness) as the real luxury good; how they do not care a damn for the sugar and the fixed capital invested in the plantations, but rather observe the planters' impending bankruptcy with an ironic grin of malicious pleasure ... As far as they are concerned, capital does not exist as capital. (Marx 1973: 325–6)

Karl Marx is often seen as 'the anti-capitalist thinker'. All Marxists reject the idea that one aspect of capitalism, such as banking or corporations, can be reformed or removed to create a fairer society. Positive money does not negate a negative system: everything must go. Typically, Canadian Marxist David McNally notes:

It is the nature of capitalism to degrade, dehumanise, and oppress – to commodify everything and to exploit all but the tiny minority who control the world's wealth. Rather than accidental, a perverse distortion of an otherwise fair system, this drive to commodify and exploit is the very nature of the beast. (McNally 2002: 273)

Marx's ideas are difficult to understand for a number of reasons. First, however carefully one reads him, his ideas remain frustratingly unfinished. Much of what he wrote in the nineteenth century is surprisingly robust. Marx can be amusing, exciting to read, and is generally more subtle than many Marxists and critics admit. His core arguments – that capitalism is exploitative, tends to continue expanding, and leads to alienation and to the growth of monopoly – are at least clear. Yet some of the most important links *between* his ideas were never made; for instance, he argues that profits tend to fall and that capitalism is prone to recession, but he 'did not develop a complete theory of crisis' (Went 2000: 65).

Second, attempts to fill in the gaps and popularise Marx have often made matters worse. His co-author Engels tried to reconstruct much of what Marx wrote after his death in 1883. Scraps of paper and crossed-out paragraphs were put together to finish the volumes of *Capital*, his masterwork. One gets the impression that much of his *Theories of Surplus Value* was scratched onto cigar packets left under his bed. By attempting to present Marx's ideas in a way that they would appeal politically to the working class, Engels may have emphasized the elements of Marx's thought that suggested that capitalism was doomed and communism was inevitable. The Second International Marxism of the late nineteenth and early twentieth centuries enhanced the view that Marxism was a form of scientific socialism, a political version of physics, based on laws of historical progress:

> What distinguished Marxism in this context was its rare ability to link revolutionary fervour and desire for change with a historical perspective and a claim to be scientific. Almost inevitably, therefore, the inherited ideas were simplified, rigidified, ossified. Marxism became a matter of simple faith for its millions of adherents. (McLellan 1980a: 2)

Third, academic Marxism has become a minor industry, producing conference papers, books and doctoral theses. While there is nothing innately wrong with this and advances have been made, much theorising has been obscure and devoid of political implication. Some of the more obscure variants of Marxism with the least apparent connection to practice, such as the Japanese Uno School, are extremely important in providing detailed and sophisticated accounts of how modern capitalism works. While we may agree with Uno theorists that anti-capitalists 'must not shy away from using abstract theory to make sense of the world', there is a danger that academisation may hide the contributions Marxism can make to real-life struggle (Albritton 1999: 181).

Fourth, Marxism has become a tree with a thousand branches. Lenin invented the concept of the Communist Party, having split his Bolsheviks from the Mensheviks. Some pre-Leninist Marxist parties, such as the DeLeonists, exist as tiny political fossils in the twenty-first century. Trotsky split from Stalin to create the Fourth International; this has, in turn, splintered many times. Mao also separated from the Stalinist orthodoxy. Fidel Castro, while a leader of an 'orthodox' Leninist party once linked to Moscow, has combined guerrilla warfare strategy, Third World nationalism and, most recently, environmentalism in a distinctly Cuban version of Marxism. Euro-communism, an exception to revolutionary hostility to capitalism, has been a distinct strategy of Communist parties keen to prosper in parliamentary systems. Intellectual divisions include Western Marxism (a diverse and untidy tradition including the Frankfurt School), analytical Marxism, several varieties of post-Marxism, regulation theory, critical realist Marxist, and so on. Marxist doctrine as developed by Marxist parties has sometimes functioned as a tactical weapon against others on the far left, rather than a serious guide to action. Marxist parties may maintain their distinct identities in a small but crowded field through differences of ideology.

Finally, Marx's own, often splendid, deep and provocatively rude writings, have a rich and complex philosophical basis, making them difficult to understand fully. While it draws upon Hegel, Feuerbach, and Spinoza, Marx's approach often seems (although there are no direct links), to owe something to William Blake or Taoism (McLellan 1980: 101). Marx did read Kopel's biography of the Buddha, but his method was drawn more explicitly from European philosophy and the classics (Sheasby 2004). His PhD examined the philosophical differences between Democritus and Epicurus and he was a member of the Young Hegelian circle. Without appreciating the paradoxical feel of his ideas, little progress can be made in understanding them. Typically, the *Communist Manifesto* (co-written with Engels) contains statements that are, seemingly, both pro- and anti-capitalist. Thus some familiarity with Marx's broad method of thinking which draws upon contradiction to think creatively about society is necessary to understand his ideas.

For the reasons outlined above, any serious review of Marxist anti-capitalism will be both something of a roller-coaster ride and inevitably superficial. The Marxism that effortlessly linked exploitation, class struggle, capitalist crisis and communist victory is no more. Marx's ideas are best understood if one understands the man himself and his social context, an easy and pleasurable task which can be approached by reading any of several excellent biographies, especially Francis Wheen's amusing book (2000).

In this chapter, a summary of Marx's economic analysis and method is offered. Marxist accounts of imperialism are introduced, and more recent Marxist accounts of capitalism from the points of view of Fidel Castro, David Harvey and Hugo Chávez are discussed.

Marxist Economics: The Utter Basics

History is the history of class struggle, declare Marx and Engels in the *Communist Manifesto*, later arguing that capitalists exploit the labour power of workers. A worker makes, say, ten mopeds in a day and the capitalist takes seven of these. A worker produces, say, 100 DVD players in a day but receives only a fraction of their worth in wages, equivalent to perhaps the value of 30 DVD players. This, of course, oversimplifies Marx's case, because he saw economic activity as increasingly social. For Marx, the market economy was based upon cooperative not purely private individual production, after all it's difficult to build a bus on one's own. However, in his account of what we produce, only a fraction of the value is retained by us in the form of a wage; the rest of the value goes into profit, that is, to the capitalist owner of the company. To simplify, slightly, we have a system of economic theft. Workers can go on strike and use various means to achieve a 'fair day's pay for a fair day's work', but will always be exploited in a capitalist system because the capitalist will take some of what they produce and control how they work:

> People overwhelmingly prefer to cling to precarious conditions as farmers, fishers, hunters and the like rather than sell their human capacities to a buyer. It is only when there is literally no other way to survive – when, in short, all other economic options have been taken away from them – that people reluctantly accept a life as wage-labourers. (McNally 2002: 65)

Individuals must be forced to work for capitalists by separating them from their own means of production. If people have their own land to grow food or their own tools to produce goods, they will be reluctant to work for the capitalist. We must be forced to work through violent processes that generally involve taking away communal land and other shared resources. This process is discussed in more detail in the next chapter and has been noted by the subsistence Greens examined in Chapter 4.

Goods (and services) have both use value and exchange value. Use value is determined by the usefulness of a product, yet capitalists are not primarily motivated by use. Instead, they seek to increase exchange value. Exchange value is the amount of money (or goods/services) for which a product can be exchanged. The market is based on 'inherently unequal relations of exchange between large property owners and those who are property less. If the latter risk hunger and deprivation in the event that they cannot find a buyer for their labour, they are at a structural disadvantage' (ibid.: 61). Capitalists are compelled to maximise profit by exploiting labour power to multiple exchange values. Workers can be made to work harder or longer. Exchange values have to be 'realised' by selling goods and services so 'use' values cannot be entirely ignored, since consumers will be unwilling to buy useless objects. However, capitalism puts enormous energy into marketing, to make us find the 'useless' 'useful' in order to keep consumption levels up. The problem of how 'use' relates to 'exchange' is examined in Chapter 8.

The surplus value which capitalists extract from workers in exchange for wages is the basis of profit and such profit is extracted from the workers. Profit is reinvested in capital, that is, machines and other means of production to raise productivity. Capitalists may or may not be 'bad' people, but are forced by competition to increase profit levels by exploiting workers. This is because a company that does not invest in the most efficient machinery will find that its costs tend to be higher than rival firms. A firm must invest in order to survive turning money into capital and back again into money. The lazy or humane capitalist fails in the race and is put out of business.

The capitalist firm must keep on growing or it will die, because it will be overtaken by other businesses. While competition is unlikely to be eliminated, the advantage given by economies of scale means that smaller companies are likely to be replaced by larger ones. The development of global markets and the emergence of giant multinationals, which Schumacher condemns, are clearly explained by Marxist analysis:

> Constant efforts to cut costs are forced on capitalists by competition, the primary driving force in capitalism. Any new method of production which reduces costs (a technical improvement, or an 'improvement' in labour discipline) will bring extra profits to those who introduce it quickly, before the general price level has been forced down. Once it is generally adopted, competition forces prices down in line with costs, wiping out any remaining high cost producers. Marx assumed (in general rightly) that large-scale production is more efficient than small-scale. Competition therefore forces capitalists to accumulate and reinvest as much as possible in order to produce on a large scale. Marx called growth through reinvestment of profits, *concentration of capital*. Bigger firms will be better able to survive, especially in slumps, and will be able to buy out smaller firms. The growth of the scale of production by amalgamation of capitals is called *centralization of capital*. (Brewer 1990: 33)

Although Marx, like most economists of his day, thought in terms of private ownership by entrepreneurs, public ownership by shareowners will encourage even a monopoly to keep growing. Shareholders will demand high share values and/or higher dividends and will dump firms that do not grow. Marx, as David Harvey notes, provides a structural theory of accumulation: capitalists exploit the creativity of workers, skim off profits and reinvest in new capital, not because they believe in a particular set of values, as David Korten suggests, but simply to survive in business.

Economics is a field of conflict with workers fighting to improve pay and conditions and firms attempting to maximise profit. Technological, cultural and social changes are the only constants of capitalism. Capitalism is like a bicycle. A bicycle tends to fall over if one ceases pedalling; capitalism tends to collapse if it fails to grow. Although it might be said that capitalism demands, unlike a bicycle, that we pedal faster and faster forever. It can be distinguished from other forms of society 'by dynamism and by instability' (Callinicos 2003: 37). Thus capitalism is crisis-ridden. Marx argued that labour power is the source of exchange value and profit. Machines gradually replace workers and as the proportion of labour in the production process falls, so, other things being equal, does profit. In Marx's analysis, if all value comes from labour, then if less labour is used to produce goods, less value will be generated when such goods are sold. While this may seem a little obscure, simple supply-and-demand analysis gives us the same result. As workers are replaced by machines, oversupply pushes up the quantity of goods produced and leads to falling profit. Crisis is not fatal, at least not immediately. Marx identified a whole host of processes from selling more goods (small profit margins multiplied by greater sales maintain profit) to exploiting workers more intensively, which tend to conserve the capitalist 'mode of production'. While Marx, in several passages, stated that crises would intensify, careful study of his work suggests that this is not necessarily the case (Desai 2004).

Marxists have long argued as to the exact nature of the tendency for profit to fall and the crisis identified by Marx (Went 2000: 65). Many Marxists have argued for an under-consumptionist view, suggesting that consumption will fail to keep up with production, leading to falling prices, negative profits and killer slumps. Others stress over-accumulation, noting that supply will rise too fast to sustain profit. These two views are essentially one. Other contradictions include the possible mismatch between different 'departments' (more or less 'consumption' and 'investment' in machinery) of the economy; thus capital may increase faster than demand for goods and services, again feeding into slump. Autonomist Marxists stress the essential conflict between workers, who want to hold on to more of their labour power and capitalists who wish to steal it away (Cleaver 2000). For ecosocialists, the basic contradiction between use values and exchange values is the mother of all other contradictions and crises (Kovel 2002).

As capitalism develops, ways around contradictions tend to be found but they tend to lead to new contradictions. For example, the growth of vast financial markets producing credit, which horrifies social creditors, allows consumption to expand to maintain profitable demand. Accelerating debt expands consumption and allows exchange values to be realised. The mismatches in the economy can be bridged by borrowing (Harvey 1999). However, this leads to new contradictions. While the problems of capitalism cannot be blamed on the banks, debt creation certainly leads to new problems.

Contradictions and conflicts, whether class-based, environmental or economic, to the extent that they can be separated, lead to change. Marx argued that capitalism, by massively increasing the means of production and forging working-class opposition, tends to create communism. Marxist politics tries to activate these tendencies. Ultimately, accelerating change may lead to a communist society, where the market is replaced by conscious human planning. Abstract economic 'laws' and the 'needs' of an elite are replaced by a society based on human need. This process is a revolutionary one both because it is likely to demand violent change and because it leads to a break between one kind of society and another. Capitalism in its search for profits is the force that promotes globalisation but will mutate into communism.

Marx drew upon a rich heritage of thought, including Hegel, Kant and Spinoza, which is often forgotten by anti-capitalist activists today. From Feuerbach, he gained the notion of 'fetishism', a process where we give something invented by the human imagination, artificial but effective power over us. Gods and goddesses invented by human beings rule over us. Objects are given power and return to shape our desires. Commodities, goods we make, are given energy and become our masters. Capitalism is a process of 'fetishism' whereby an economic system constructed collectively by the actions of millions of human beings, comes to dominate human beings (Kolakowski 1988: 276). Desai notes how Marx's

> ... training in Hegelian philosophy equipped him [to deal with economic questions] at a level of depth and generality which was totally alien to the British way of doing political economy. He used the method of immanent criticism. This meant mastering the classical political economy completely, accepting its logic but then proposing a better political economy as a critique from within which to point up and resolve the internal contradictions. (Desai 2004: 55)

Hegel specifically equipped Marx with the concept of the dialectic, which came from the ancient Greeks and is akin to dialogue, the interplay between two forces that transforms both, like conversation, or cooking, or sex.

Reality is a process of constant revolution. Identity is relational: we have identity in relation to that which is different from us. Change occurs when relationships are rearranged. Phenomenon is a product of self-contradiction and such contradiction leads to change. Contradiction is all; Marx characteristically notes the contradiction between 'progress' and exploitation. Concepts enslave workers, machines crush their individuality in the pursuit of surplus value:

> ... all means for the development of production undergo a dialectical inversion so that they become means of domination and exploitation of the producers; they distort the worker into a fragment of a man, they degrade him to the level of an appendage of a machine, they destroy the actual content of his labour by turning it into a torment; they alienate from him the intellectual potentialities of the labour process in the same proportion as science is incorporated in it as an independent power; they deform the conditions under which he works, subject him during the labour process to a despotism the more hateful for its meanness; they transform his life-time

into working-time, and drag his wife and child beneath the wheels of the juggernaut of capital. (Marx 1979: 799)

Marxist Theories of Imperialism

Marx wrote little directly on processes of colonialism and he never even used the term 'imperialism', let alone 'globalisation' (Brewer 1990: 25). His main efforts in *Capital* went, despite much historical digression and polemic, into describing an abstract model of the 'pure' capitalist society. What he did write on the creation of global markets through foreign colonialism, is, unsurprisingly, contradictory. He argued that the British acted to oppress Ireland, that Ireland was Britain's first colony and efforts to bring capitalist development to Ireland had been deliberately aborted (Brewer 1990: 48). For Ireland, we could swap Iraq or Vietnam and no great theory would be required. Such analysis is based on nationalism as much as economic analysis and would reflect the very straightforward view that imperialism is based on the exploitation of the weak by the strong.

In contrast, Marx argued that British colonialism in India was progressive in the long term. The British brought capitalism to India, and this was a violent process, but one which created the preconditions for real economic growth and expansion. The dilemma with Marxist accounts from Marx onwards is that they provide a mixed message: imperialism, capitalism and globalisation are both good and bad. Marx noted that the British had transformed land ownership, created a free press and introduced the 'electric telegraph'. The British bourgeoisie (capitalist class) would ultimately have to be thrown out, but their attempt to draw the country into a global market was necessary:

Has the bourgeoisie ever done more? Has it ever effected a progress without dragging individuals and peoples through blood and dirt and misery and degradation? The Indians will not reap the fruits of the new elements of society scattered among them by the British bourgeoisie till in Great Britain itself the ruling classes shall have been supplanted by the industrial proletariat or till the Hindoos themselves shall have grown strong enough to throw off the English yoke. (quoted in Brewer 1990: 55)

Clearly, the view of a purely exploitative relationship would end the need for further speculation: what is the point of developing a sophisticated theoretical account of one group kicking another and stealing their stuff? The more theoretical account, in turn, puts Marxists, perhaps, in the pro-globalisation camp, stressing that the growth of global markets is a precondition for socialism (Desai 2004: 154). Marx is never straightforward and accounts that contradict this reading are also apparent; he was damning about the use of torture in British Victorian India, and wrote extensively of the damage wrought by the East India Company:

> We have here given but a brief and mildly-colored chapter from the real history of British rule in India. In view of such facts, dispassionate and thoughtful men may perhaps be led to ask whether a people are not justified in attempting to expel the foreign conquerors who have so abused their subjects. And if the English could do these things in cold blood, is it surprising that the insurgent Hindoos should be guilty, in the fury of revolt and conflict, of the crimes and cruelties alleged against them?

> (www.marxists.org/archive/marx/works/1857/09/17.htm)

The first Marxist to challenge and develop Marx's views on imperialism was Rosa Luxemburg. A Polish revolutionary, killed after the abortive Spartacist Uprising, she believed that capitalism suffered from a potential crisis of under-consumption. Exploitation of the working class meant that consumers, who derived their income mainly from work, did not have enough purchasing power to buy the products manufactured by capitalism. This mismatch between production and consumption could be overcome by selling to new markets outside the capitalist system. Imperialism used military force to gain control of territories outside of capitalism whose populations would buy excess goods. Her approach fits the facts of the Opium Wars, where Britain went to war to force the Chinese to accept imports of the drug. Her views parallel the accounts of social credit/monetary reformers who see excess production as a motive for enhanced trade. John Hobson, a non-Marxist critic of imperialism, held broadly similar views. Imperial expansion might also provide a source of cheap raw materials and labour. Luxemburg notes the importance of creating a reserve army of spare labour, a theme previously explored by Marx, to keep wages low in the capitalist heartlands (Luxemburg 1971).

Luxemburg, who bitterly attacked the processes leading to the enclosure of the commons and saw little of intrinsic value in capitalism, argued that the full creation of a global market would lead to the collapse of capitalism because it would cease to have outside markets in which to sell excess goods. Critics have suggested that excess production can be mopped up by capitalist investment in new means of production, by credit creation or state consumption, especially of military equipment. However, whatever other conclusions can be drawn from Luxemburg, expansion of capitalism globally is strongly motivated by demands for new markets, cheap raw materials and new sources of potential labour power.

The 'classic' Marxist account of imperialism was developed out of the insights of Hobson and Luxemburg by Hilferding, Bukharin and Lenin. Lenin's pamphlet

Imperialism: The Highest State of Capitalism (Lenin 1982) is the most readable description. All three argued that capitalism had shifted into a new epoch of imperialism. The union of financial interests and manufactures in finance capital marked this. Finance capital, a term coined by Hilferding, a German socialist, has nothing to do with monetary reform or a world run by bankers. Bankers and industrialists band together and cooperate in new corporations. Finance capital leads to monopolies that dominate their respective national economies. The monopolists, to cut a long story short, control governments and launch wars to capture new territories. Territorial expansion provides markets, raw materials and cheap labour. The First World War can be seen as an imperialist war, with the German, British and Russian empires competing for domination.

Imperialism was 'the highest state of capitalism', Lenin argued, because the 'anarchy' of the market was largely replaced by the planned decision making of huge corporations. Since the 'classic' account of imperialism, matters have become muddily confused for a number of reasons. Imperialism, as described by Lenin and co., did not lead to the replacement of capitalism by communism. Fordism and post-Fordism are generally seen as new stages of capitalism and there may be many more stages to go before socialism is achieved. The multi-imperialism of the European powers was replaced by a globe divided between the Cold War powers. After the Cold War, the US emerged as the global hyper-power, while in the twenty-first century, the growth of China has challenged US power.

In a loose sense, we can talk of American imperialism. There are many examples of US intervention in virtually every continent, interventions that are motivated by the needs of US corporations. Wars for oil are imperialist and the Gulf Wars pitted US imperialism against the needs and desires of French firms, like the Thompson Group (http://www.nydailynews.com/archives/news/france-iraq-link-cia-report-article-1.641550).

Imperialism in the everyday sense is exploitation. However, in Marxist accounts, including those of Bukharin, Lenin and Luxemburg, far from leading to poverty, it brings capitalism to new parts of the globe. While this is a violent process and may increase inequality, it raises the productive forces, which creates 'growth'. The idea that imperialism leads to *under*development is alien to the Marxist tradition. Continuing and even increasing poverty in the South of the globe cannot easily be explained by a Marxist approach. Imperialism has been analysed by a series of dependency theorists who argue that through processes of 'unfair' trade, such poverty will remain. These reverse the Marxist conception of imperialism, but this is generally forgotten. Likewise the view that the Americans dominate the world, so if we sweep away US power we can achieve a just world, is a view that is too crude to sustain and has little or nothing to do with Marxism. Dutch or Indonesian capitalism would still be capitalism.

Marxist Approaches to Globalisation

Some Marxists and writers influenced by a Marxist tradition argue that the creation of a global market is necessary for the creation of a Communist society. This approach can be justified by examining Marx's work, particularly the *Communist Manifesto*. In the 1980s, Bill Warren's book *Imperialism – Pioneer of Socialism* inspired controversy with this view (Warren 1980).

The *Communist Manifesto* contains several passages endorsing the revolutionary effect of capitalism in sweeping away traditional local economies:

The bourgeoisie has, through its exploitation of the world market, given a cosmopolitan character to production and consumption in every country. To the great chagrin of reactionaries, it has drawn from under the feet of industry the national ground on which it stood. All old-established national industries have been destroyed or are daily being destroyed. They are dislodged by new industries, whose introduction becomes a life and death question for all civilized nations, by industries that no longer work up indigenous raw material, but raw material drawn from the remotest zones; industries whose products are consumed, not only at home, but in every quarter of the globe. In place of the old wants, satisfied by the production of the country, we find new wants, requiring for their satisfaction the products of distant lands and climes. In place of the old local and national seclusion and self-sufficiency, we have in every direction, universal inter-dependence of nations. And as in material, so also in intellectual production. The intellectual creations of individual nations become common property. National one-sidedness and narrow-mindedness become more and more impossible, and from the numerous national and local literatures, there arises a world literature.

The bourgeoisie, by the rapid improvement of all instruments of production, by the immensely facilitated means of communication, draws all, even the most barbarian, nations into civilization. The cheap prices of commodities are the heavy artillery with which it batters down all Chinese walls, with which it forces the barbarians' intensely obstinate hatred of foreigners to capitulate. It compels all nations, on pain of extinction, to adopt the bourgeois mode of production …. (Marx and Engels 1985: 83–4)

This pro-globalisation strand of Marx's thought is often ignored by Marxists who seek to work with the anti-neo-liberal globalisation movement; it would be difficult to sell socialist newspapers to demonstrators with banner headlines of 'Defend the WTO – forward to Socialism'. One common theme from Marxists in the movement is the idea that globalisation has not really occurred or is only a cover for imperialism, defined as a political process closely linking economic and military power.

James Petras and Henry Veltmeyer in *Globalisation Unmasked* (2001) argue that the capitalist world, far from entering a new era, is essentially the same. They specifically enumerate a range of groups who can be brought together to fight neo-liberalism. As well as the traditional working class, the unemployed and indigenous people are also important. Globalisation is an ideological excuse for maintaining a market economic system and strengthening US control. Chris Harman argues that the world is far less economically integrated than is often thought, but the capitalist economic system has long made it difficult for national governments to pursue truly independent policies. For example, in the 1930s, the British Labour government was forced to drop radical redistributive policies because of the perceived need to retain the Gold Standard. The Gold Standard fixed the value of the pound to gold and was thought necessary to maintain Britain's economic standing in a global system. Today, imperialism remains and such imperialism is largely American (Harman 2000a; Wood 2003b).

Castro on Globalisation

Other Marxists have given more thought to practical change and have stressed the ecological dimensions of opposition to globalisation. Former Cuban President Fidel Castro, for example, has examined the contradictory nature of Marxist accounts of globalisation.

Castro argues that while US imperialism directly threatens Cuba, globalisation cannot be reduced to the needs of specifically US corporations. He believes that globalisation is a cultural phenomenon with language, literature and music becoming worldwide in scale. There is even existing *socialist* globalisation, with Cuba sending doctors and teachers to Africa, South America and other parts of the globe. Technological development is another reason why globalisation is in principle beneficial and cannot be reversed. Castro also rejects the view that globalisation is a product of a plot by a small elite; instead, the *Communist Manifesto* indicates that it is born out of a broad historical process (Castro 2003: 9). However, Castro then notes the world is dominated by a particular form of neo-liberal globalisation, which even capitalists admit is destructive. He is particularly amused that a capitalist multi-millionaire like Soros is so critical of neo-liberalism:

> ... neo-liberal globalization wants to turn all countries, especially all our countries, into private property ... They want to turn the world into a huge free-trade zone, it might be more clearly understood this way because, what is a free-trade zone? It is a place with special characteristics where taxes are not paid; where raw materials, spare parts and components are brought in and assembled or various goods produced, especially in labour intensive

sectors. At times, they pay not more than 5 per cent of the salary they must pay in their own countries and the only thing they leave us with are these meagre salaries. (Ibid.: 13)

Progress, Castro argues (echoing Marx's dialectical account), creates its own discontents:

Labour productivity and the most sophisticated equipment born out of human talent multiply material wealth as well as poverty and layoffs, what good are they to mankind[?] Perhaps to help reduce working hours, have more time for resting, leisure, sports, cultural and scientific upgrading? That is impossible because the sacred market laws and competition patterns – increasingly more imaginary than real – in a world of transnationals and megamergers do not allow it all. Anyway, who are competing and against whom? Monopoly- and merger-orientated giants against giants. (Ibid.: 15)

While nearly all Marxists now pay lip service to environmental sustainability, Castro is explicit in his suggestion that unlimited economic growth is unacceptable. Rather than seeking to raise the productive forces in crudely quantitative ways, Castro argues that there are ecological limits to growth. He echoes the approach of Greens, stating that needs must be met for people on a planetary basis rather than providing luxury goods. Castro's ideology in the 2000s combines organic agriculture with *Capital*:

By creating unsustainable consumer patterns in industrialized countries and sowing impossible dreams throughout the rest of the world, the developed capitalist system has caused great injury to mankind. It has poisoned the atmosphere and depleted its enormous non-renewable natural resources, which mankind will need in the future. Please, do not believe that I am thinking of an idealistic, impossible, absurd world; I am merely trying to imagine what a real world and a happier person could be like. (Ibid.: 18)

Castro has been leader of a state that has survived constant attacks from the US since he first came to power in 1959 and has managed to make considerable progress in health care and education. Castro is extremely proud of the fact that Cuba has a high level of Olympic gold medal winners per capita and that literacy levels and infant mortality figures are better than parts of the US. Cuba has also made major progress in moving to organic agriculture. The British NHS has sought to learn from Cuban medical care. Cuba has benefited in many ways from relative isolation, a case study in the real advantages of 'localisation'. Although desperately poor in comparison to western countries, Cuba is relatively prosperous compared to neighbouring Haiti. However, Cuba remains a one-party state (although of course the record of the US as a two-party system is hardly an ideal model of a liberal democracy) and civil liberties, while better than many Caribbean states, are hardly stunning. The relative success of Cuban anti-capitalism demands support, but does not necessarily provide a model that can be exported on a global scale. The recent thawing of US/Cuban relations in 2015 suggests Cuba may move in a more market-based direction similar to China, or it may continue to create an alternative to neo-liberalism.

David Harvey's Seventeen Contradictions of Capitalism

David Harvey's book *Seventeen Contradictions and the End of Capitalism* (2014) renews Marx's economic analysis for the twenty-first century. Harvey, whose video lectures and other recent books are useful tools to help us read *Capital* and understand Marx's work, argues that the crises of capitalism are multiple. Contradictions drive capitalism, and a contradiction in one area tends to be displaced to another rather than being 'solved' in a fundamental way. Harvey identifies what he terms 'foundational' contradictions, 'moving' contradictions and 'dangerous' contradictions. As we have noted, capitalists like to cut costs by reducing wages, replacing workers with machines and increasing productivity, but this means supply can rise faster than demand, suppressing the wages needed to buy the goods produced. Other contradictions include the need for a capitalist state to maintain discipline and keep workers educated and healthy enough to work, which clashes with the corporate demand to cut taxes. Technological innovation helps capitalists produce, but drives up unemployment. Unemployment pushes wages down by creating a reserve army of labour, but can reduce consumption and threaten growth. Capitalism creates inequality, yet such inequality erodes the support for the status quo. Harvey's dangerous contradictions include the endless compound growth that capitalism demands, its destructive relationship with nature and the revolt of human nature against the alienation of capitalism. Harvey notes that 'Crises are essential to the reproduction of capitalism. It is in the course of crises that the instabilities of capitalism are confronted, reshaped and re-engineered to create a new version of what capitalism is about' (Harvey 2014: ix). The desire for human beings to be in control of their own destiny, for Harvey, is a major source of resistance, but he is aware that the powers of capital are strong:

> Oligarchic capitalist class privilege and power are taking the world in a similar direction almost everywhere. Political power backed by intensifying surveillance, policing and militarised violence is being used to attack the well-being of whole populations deemed expendable and disposable. We are daily witnessing the systematic dehumanisation of disposable people.

Ruthless oligarchic power is now being exercised through a totalitarian democracy directed to immediately disrupt, fragment and suppress any coherent anti-wealth political movement (such as Occupy). (Ibid.: 292)

Harvey discusses how we can work as associated producers to overthrow capitalism and create a cooperative economy. The failure of the left, including the Marxist left, to either overcome capitalism or create a successful economic alternative, makes these tasks seem difficult. One area of the world where the left have been advancing is Latin America. The survival of Cuba, and the victories of left parties from El Salvador to Chile and Uruguay but perhaps most significantly in Venezuela, Ecuador and Bolivia, has inspired Marxists and other anti-capitalists.

Marx in Caracas

Marx died in 1883, and Marxism seemingly expired in 1989 with the demolition of the Berlin Wall, and later the collapse of the Soviet Union. However, the election of Hugo Chávez as president of Venezuela helped place Marxist ideas back on the agenda. A former army education officer, who led a coup against a previous president who had repressed anti-austerity protests, Chávez only became an anti-capitalist after being elected. The history of Venezuela is difficult to summarise, but during the twentieth century, the country was dominated by a small political and economic elite, many people lived in extreme poverty in the barrios, the economy was almost totally dependent on oil, corruption was endemic, crime high, government weak and political power and influence networks utterly in the pockets of the US. Wilpert (2007), Bruce (2008) and Gott (2005) provide good accounts of recent Venezuelan history and Chávez's period in office. In short, it is a difficult country in which to try to create a sustainable socialist system, and every day since 1999 when Chávez was elected, to date, as I write in 2014, Venezuela's anti-capitalist experiment has been under threat. However, Chávez's victory produced the first new country in decades to attempt to move from capitalism to socialism.

Chávez promised to challenge elite rule, poverty and corruption. At first he was inspired by Tony Blair's vision of the 'third way', seeking an inclusive, people-friendly capitalism. Chávez was a product of mass grass-roots politics; long-term struggle, liberation theology, the legacy of Latin America's liberator Simon Bolivar and the participatory values of Paulo Freire also went into the mix. Challenging the elite led to media pressure to remove him from office, and with the covert support of the US government, he was removed from office in a coup in 2002. However, after mass protests by the Venezuelan population, he was swiftly returned to power. The US has spent millions funding opposition groups in Venezuela and the world's media has been hostile to Chávez and his successor, former bus driver Nicolás Maduro.

After the coup, Chávez moved left and argued for the creation of a socialist system. He rejected the Soviet model of a centrally planned economy, calling for socialist property rights, as opposed to a raising of the means of production, as key. He advocated an ecological and grass-roots socialist system that would deepen over time. His triangle of socialism included social but not state ownership, because only with the creation of communal property rights was socialism possible. Workers' control and participation were promoted, because collective ownership, without democratic management, led to centralisation and disillusionment. The third side of the triangle was an ethic of common good and sharing, the creation of a socialist rather than a capitalist culture. Michael Lebowitz links Chávez's triangle of socialism, to Marx's perspectives in the *Grundrisse*, Marx's notebook for *Capital* (Lebowitz 2010).

Socialist activists Peter McLaren and Mike Cole note that there have been some successes:

> Venezuela's creation of more than 100,000 worker-owned co-operatives consisting of more than 1.5 million workers, and these include both agricultural co-operatives and manufacturing co-operatives. Accompanying this success has been the creation of more than 16,000 communal councils that facilitate the development of infrastructure projects advanced by community participants. But it is also important to note that Venezuela has done much to address gender inequities (Leech, 2012). In accordance with the Venezuelan constitution (Article 88), the Venezuelan government pays women for housework they perform in their homes. Approximately 100,000 poverty-stricken housewives receive 80 percent of the national minimum wage (Leech, 2012). Furthermore, programs have been created to provide education and training to women who are living in poverty. In 2008, Venezuela surpassed Chile and Costa Rica to become the country with the second-lowest level of inequality in Latin America (Cuba has the lowest level).
>
> (http://venezuelanalysis.com/analysis/10740)

But there have been failures as well. Corruption remains a problem, the country is socially polarised and Venezuela is still economically dependent on oil. In 2015, with plunging oil prices, the country faced hard times. In turn, the inspiration of Venezuela has meant that Chávez, who died in 2013, and his successor have been unrelentingly attacked by a global media which defends neo-liberalism. The election of other left governments in the region and the creation of ALBA, a fair rather than free trade group of nations has been another success. Marx would have argued that utopian experiments are impossible, citing the difficulty of building socialism in one oil-dependent country, and Marx was very hostile to Simon Bolivar. However, Marx would have loved the Venezuelan people's work in placing an anti-capitalist alternative on the agenda for the twenty-first century.

Marx Beyond Marx

New kinds of Marxism have evolved that seek to go beyond Marx, or to emphasize a greener and more anarchic bearded prophet, for example, ecosocialism, influenced by Marxism and green politics, which is examined in Chapter 8. In turn, autonomist Marxists have cross-fertilised anarchist and socialist ideas. Harry Cleaver, a leading US autonomist, noted that 'several generations of Marxists have given us the habit of perceiving the mechanism of domination. What we need now is to use Marx to help us discover the mechanisms of liberation' (Cleaver 1991: xx). Autonomism, particularly in the form presented in Hardt and Negri's *Empire*, has also attempted to develop a sophisticated understanding of global sovereignty. Autonomism, described in the next chapter, has also fed into Occupy and other new protest movements that have emerged since the beginning of this century.

7

THE TRIBE OF MOLES: AUTONOMISM, ANARCHISM AND EMPIRE

Old Mick was a veteran squatter, rebel and thief. His most successful heist was the reclaiming of his life from those bosses and jailers who think they own us. For decades he lived in the gaps. No one made him into a wageslave. No dropout, he fought. He was no saint, but if ever there was a temporary autonomous zone, Mick was it.

His funeral was one of the best 'actions' I have ever been on. Mick wanted to burn in Lyminge Forest, a larger part of which was saved from destruction by direct action. Funeral pyres are illegal, death rights have to be sanctioned by the state. Mick wasn't going to take that, neither were his mates ... Ten foot the pyre of 'stolen' wood rose, Mick's coffin astride. Night came. Fireworks shot into the sky. Crackling fire, we saw Mick's bones burn, back to the earth. For hours he burnt. (Anon. 2003: 100)

Anti-capitalists are as likely to label themselves as anarchists as well as socialists or greens. Anarchism, far from merely being about bad attitude, draws on a rich intellectual tradition. In the nineteenth century, anarchist movements inspired by the writings of Mikhail Bakunin, Peter Kropotkin and Emma Goldman dominated radical politics in much of Spain, Italy and southern France (Woodcock 1963). Paradoxically, perhaps, one of the primary intellectual sources for today's anarchists is autonomism, a body of theory that claims to be 'communist' and which is informed by Marxist theory. The anti-capitalist magazine *Aufheben* noted:

For many of those dissatisfied with the versions of Marxism and anarchism available to them in the UK, the notions of 'autonomy' and 'autonomist' have positive associations ... 'anti-capitalist' mobilizations of J18 and Seattle both drew on themes and language associated with *autonomia*, such as autonomous struggles and diversity. (www.geocities.com/Aufheben2/auf_11_operaismo.html)

Autonomism, which developed in Italy during the 1960s and 1970s, starts from the principle that the working class should resist capitalism independently, that is, autonomously from political parties and trade unions (Dyer-Witheford 1999; Wright 2002). *Empire*, written by Michael Hardt, a US literary theorist, and Toni Negri, a former political prisoner/Italian philosopher, provides a detailed explanation of capitalist globalisation from a broadly autonomist perspective (Hardt and Negri 2001a). The book has been a minor literary sensation, although it is probably, given the complexity of its ideas, more bought than read. Nonetheless, *Empire*, and the autonomism that it draws upon, are important strains of anti-capitalist thought. For autonomists, the working class consists not only of factory workers but of all who serve and are exploited by capital. Society has become the social factory; housework helps support capitalism; students by developing the power of intellectual labour are also part of the working class, and so on (Wright 2002: 37). So although autonomism originated as a form of 'workerism', it has perhaps been the current of anti-capitalist theory that is happiest to see social movements and counter-cultures as the cutting edge of resistance. The expression 'tribe of moles' was coined to identify the varied subversives who fight capitalism from the margins of the social factory. Such diverse forms of militant resistance from DIY culture to squatting and wildcat strikes, are generated by members of the tribe:

> One early characterization of this new subjectivity (which is actually seen as a diversity of subjectivities) was given by Sergio Bologna in the 1970s who identified a new 'tribe of moles' – a loose tribe of highly mobile drop-outs, part-time workers, part-time students, participants in the underground economy, creators of temporary and ever-changing autonomous zones of social life that force a fragmentation of and crisis in the mass-worker organisation of the social factory. (Cleaver 2003: 49)

Marx identified the international working class with the mole: emerging into open struggle when it could by digging subversively between bouts of open conflict. 'Well grubbed, old mole', he might shout from his desk after reading a *Times* account of strike or rebellion (Hardt and Negri 2001a: 57). The notion of moles and diverse protest fits in with Occupy and ongoing revolts against the 1% in 2015, but it has deep roots.

Autonomism originated when a group of socialist intellectuals and union activists established the journal *Quaderni Rossi* ('Red Notes') in October 1961. They drew hope from a wildcat (unofficial) strike at Fiat, which saw militant workers not only reject union advice but also march upon and occupy the offices of the UIL, one of the three big national unions (Fuller 2001: 65). *Quaderni Rossi* argued that the Communist Party and other far-left parties and unions had brokered a compromise between workers and capitalists that was preventing, temporarily at least, the construction of a socialist alternative. The Fiat action, in contrast, showed that the Italian working class could create its own political space outside of these institutions and build a culture of resistance.

Even at its strongest during the 1970s, *Autonomia Operaia* ('Workers' Autonomy') was never a party or a single organisation. Within a particular city, several autonomist cells might exist, often divided bitterly over matters of philosophy, strategy and political organisation (Wright 2002: 152; Dyer-Witheford 1999). The spring of 1977 saw a peak in factory-based protest and action in the universities by autonomists followed by shocking state repression. Although the Communist Party sought to create a historical compromise coalition government with the centre-right Christian Democrats (DC), during the last years of the 1970s, naked class warfare broke out in Italy. Aldo Moro, the DC leader, was kidnapped and murdered by the Red Brigade, a shadowy far-left terrorist group. The autonomists were attacked by the Italian state. Negri was arrested and accused of masterminding the kidnapping, and he later fled to France and accepted political asylum. During these years a 'shoot to kill' anti-terrorist law led to the deaths of 150 people, and in 1980, it was estimated that there were 3,500 political prisoners in Italy (Plant 1992: 129). The movement was shredded by repression (Bull 2003: 83).

In both Italy and France, autonomist-influenced gangs were dubbed 'metropolitan Indians' by the press because they painted their faces and wore feathers. The 'Indians' variously broke into shops and stole or 'expropriated' ostentatiously useless goods, dined in expensive restaurants without paying, blockaded leftist party congresses and indulged in other guerrilla tactics (Plant 1992: 129; Wright 2002: 197). In Denmark, Germany and Switzerland, the Autonomen, a loose network of radical squatters, anarchists and anti-fascists, influenced by autonomism, have been a feature of the political landscape since the 1970s (Katsiaficas 1997). Autonomists have long acted against neo-liberal institutions:

> September 1988, when the Autonomen prepared demonstrations against the conventions of the World Bank and the International Monetary Fund in Berlin. Thousands of militant demonstrators tried to stop the top finance ministers of 150 countries and over ten thousand world bankers from planning their future exploits ... For their part, the Green Party and its affiliates attempted to defuse the planned confrontation by calling for a convention of their own to discuss the possibility of an 'alternative world banking system'. Unlike the Greens, the radical Autonomen would have little to do with banks – alternative or not – or any kind of system. The type of world they seek to create and to live in is as far removed as possible from money, centralization, government, and ownership in all their forms. (Katsiaficas 1997: 12)

The Zapatista movement in Mexico shows autonomist affinities and has networked with autonomist figures such as Harry Cleaver, a Texan professor who wrote *Reading Capital Politically* (2000) (Hardt and Negri 2001a: 55; Holloway and Pelaez 1998). Autonomists have also fed into academic discourse, contributing to journals such as *Capital and Class* and *Rethinking Marxism*. Political shoplifting is one repertoire of action:

> A group of 200 leftwing protesters wearing balaclavas, carnival masks and bandanas over their faces, went on a 'proletariat shopping spree' in a Rome hypermarket at the weekend, carrying off goods and handing them out.
>
> They swarmed into the Panorama hypermarket on the outskirts of the Italian capital on Saturday shouting 'free shopping for all'.
>
> After failing to negotiate a 70% discount with the supermarket's manager, the group barged loaded trolleys past cashiers and distributed the goods to a crowd outside.
>
> Police chose not to intervene but later claimed to have identified 87 members of the group, who now face legal action.
>
> The 'proletariat shoppers', included a Communist town councillor, Nunzio d'Erme, and the spokesperson of I Disobbedienti (formerly the Tute Bianche), Luca Casarini, who led violent G8 anti-globalisation protests in Genova in 2001. (*Guardian*, 8 November 2004)

Autonomists are Marxists, but not exclusively so. Michael Hardt has suggested that drawing upon one thinker 'rather than a set of methods, principles, and ideas always runs the risk of precluding innovation and creating a new dogmatism' (Hardt 2004: 170). He and Negri prefer the label 'communist' to 'Marxist', arguing that 'Spinoza was a communist thinker long before Marx' (ibid.: 170). Autonomism fuses, roughly speaking, Marxism, anarchism and post-modernity. It stresses working-class resistance rather than structural laws, as the driving force of economic development. While Hardt and Negri refuse to be labelled as anarchists, it has been suggested that, 'their view of the state is recognizably an anarchist one' (Rustin 2003: 3). Finally, Hardt and Negri in particular look to a number of thinkers usually seen as post-modernists, such as Deleuze and Foucault (Callinicos 2001; Read 2003). The philosopher Spinoza provided Hardt and Negri with the concept of the multitude, their particular version of the revolutionary class. The power of the multitude is latinised as *potentia* (Ryan 1991: 216). These three sources of thought appear contradictory: what can anarchist, Marxist, post-modern theory be, other than mud? But all three fields of thought point towards a relatively simple and surprisingly coherent conception of economics. The innate creative energy of life fizzes through us all and this energy means that capitalism can be resisted, reshaped and ultimately abolished (Hardt and Negri 2001a: 358). The multitude is the angry and determined tribe of moles.

Anarchist Marxism

Autonomism grew, as we have seen, out of Marxism. Even *Empire*, as we shall discuss later, reads like an over-the-top post-modern version of *Capital*. Unlike most variants of Marxism, discussed in the last chapter, autonomism stresses the power of the working class rather than the workings of capitalism. Drawing upon the first chapter of Marx's *Capital*, autonomists argue that capitalism is driven by the need both to exploit and to control the working class (Cleaver 2000). Thus autonomism is a form of 'subjective' rather than 'objective' Marxism. Autonomists argue that ordinary people, rather than being the puppets of the capitalist system, jerked up and down by its mechanisms as it lurches through crisis, instead force capitalism to change. Such power is not the power that can only create a revolution in the future, when the productive forces are 'ripe', but is a power that workers exercise on a day-to-day basis. Tronti has noted:

> We too have worked with a concept that puts capitalist development first, and the workers second. This is a mistake. And now we have to turn the problem on its head, reverse the polarity, and start again from the beginning: and that beginning is the class struggle of the working class. (Dyer-Witheford 1999: 65)

Nearly everything planned by capitalists, who include both factory bosses and government ministers, is concerned with keeping the tribe of moles from grubbing up the foundations of the system. Technological change occurs because capitalism requires new ways of keeping workers under control. Government policies are introduced to prevent rebellion by ordinary people. Globalisation, as we shall see, is used as a weapon in the struggle against the powerful and ever adaptable tribe of moles. The autonomists are intoxicated by Marx's observation that it 'would be possible to write a whole history of the inventions made since 1830 for the sole purpose of providing capital with weapons against working class revolt' (ibid.: 3). Autonomists share with Harry Braverman, and perhaps Marx, given the previous quotation, the assumption that new technologies are introduced not directly to increase productivity, but to deskill the working class, so that they can be controlled more easily (Braverman 1974). As the working class finds new forms of resistance, the capitalists must develop new means of retaining control. Class struggle moves through cycles of class recomposition and decomposition. When the working class recomposes, it becomes stronger and more militant, ready to throw off its chains and cease to be a class at all.

Resistance to capitalism accompanies recomposition. To survive, capital needs to create class decomposition so as to disperse working-class power (Cleaver 2003).

The tendency for profits to fall is directly a product of working-class resistance, which raises wages and lowers working hours as militancy succeeds. The autonomist analysis is, ironically, similar to the supply-side economics of neo-liberals like Milton Friedman and right-wing politicians such as General Pinochet, Ronald Reagan and Margaret Thatcher. Every aspect of economic debate, from the existence of inflation to the movement of foreign direct investment, is a result of the conflict between workers and capital.

The struggle of Vietnamese peasants in their war against the US forced an increase in US military spending and virtually bankrupted the US in the early 1970s. The expansion in the US money supply fuelled inflation and wrecked the Bretton Woods system of currencies fixed to the dollar. Interestingly, the autonomists here ignore the role of the Vietcong, the Vietnamese Communist Party. As we have seen, the activities of Communist parties are seen by the autonomists as preventing the spontaneous struggle of the multitude.

In short, crisis is created by working-class action. At both the factory floor and the state level, new structures are created to prevent the collapse of capitalism. In explaining political economy, the autonomists draw upon the insights of regulation theory. Regulation theory, developed by French theorists, suggests that a particular form of management, associated with particular institutional forms, is needed within different states at different periods, to preserve capitalism. Autonomists argue that Keynesianism, as applied in western Europe and North America between the 1940s and 1973, provides a good example. Rather than being seen as an alternative form of economic analysis to free market classicalism, it was a political means of controlling working-class revolt. Because of the growth of working-class militancy, a welfare state had to be created to prevent all-out revolution and the collapse of capitalism. The working class, not Keynes, created Keynesian economics. When Keynesianism failed, new strategies had to be found. Monetarism is normally seen as an abstract economic theory that explains how increases in the money supply lead to rising inflation. Monetarist-inspired government spending cuts and attacks on union power were part of a political struggle. Alan Budd, one of Mrs Thatcher's advisers, stated that her economic policies were designed to weaken the working class: 'What was engineered in Marxist terms – was a crisis in capitalism which re-created a reserve army of labour, and has allowed the capitalist to make high profits ever since' (quoted in Harvey 1999: xv).

Autonomists argue that emerging capitalism first faced the professional worker. This worker is highly skilled and operates complex and sophisticated machinery; one thinks of print workers who set type by hand before the introduction of computer technology. Such workers are in a strong position to push up wages and conditions, and given their power may see no necessity for capitalist management.

To defeat the professional worker, new forms of machinery were introduced to mass produce individuals as well as products. The mass worker is created by this new state of capitalism. The mass worker is shorn of skills and can be more easily controlled as she or he is forced to work at the rhythm of the conveyor belt. Thus 'Fordism' is a response to the professional worker, which came to be linked to Keynesianism and a global economy based on the dollar:

> This meant that production-line type work was introduced, removing the need for many highly skilled workers or any direct connection to what was being produced. Productivity and production were increased by stepping up the exploitation of the workforce, allowing both wages and profits to rise, thus creating the demand to absorb the increase in production. Fordism was a system based upon mass production and mass consumption. It was premised on an implicit trade-off between increased alienation and boredom at work and increased consumption during 'leisure' or 'free' time – dissatisfaction turned into demand. The ever-increasing rate of exploitation, consequently, expanded the total amount of capital in circulation and made possible the growth of finance capital and the boom in credit and lending. (Anon. 1999b: 38)

Workers in the post-Second World War Fordist era accepted a 'social wage' in the form of a pension and other state benefits in return for higher productivity. However:

> Things start to come apart. In the inhuman conditions of the assembly-line factory, the productivity deal always rested on a delicate balancing of capitalist profits and worker anger ... Mass workers increasingly refuse to restrain wage demands within limits functional to capitalist growth or to tolerate conditions accepted by their unions. Management responds to wage pressures with attempts to intensify the pace and intensity of work, thereby precipitating further resistance. A wave of wildcat strikes, slowdowns, sabotage, and absenteeism – which the autonomists christen 'the refusal of work' – sweeps across Europe and North America, rendering factories from Detroit to Turin to Dagenham virtually unmanageable. (Dyer-Witheford 1999: 75)

Thus the deal broke down in the 1970s, causing economic and political crisis as strikes, sabotage and 'sickies' took their toll on productivity. The workers recomposed as a class, so capital had to promote class decomposition, a process that created a globalised, information-based, post-modern economy. Keynesian economics is replaced by free market substitutes, factories close in those areas of the globe with greater militancy and new technologies are used to make workers easier to dismiss and control.

In this post-Fordist era, the tendency for society to become a social factory, with profit generated in diverse locations, accelerates. Production becomes increasingly decentralised and virtual. Academic, communicative and caring professions become economically vital. By splitting workers away from the factories and reconstituting society on a for-profit basis, control is reasserted. Yet from student unrest to unofficial strikes in call centres, from anti-road protests to the on-street movement against globalisation, the working class/ multitude has shown its power (*potentia*) again.

Notions of the social factory have given rise to a distinctive feminist current in autonomist theory. Feminist autonomists have emphasised that capitalism has long depended on the unpaid domestic labour of women to support male factory workers, socialise children and to undertake other forms of 'affective' production to maintain the system. According to Maria Dalla Costa, women directly produce surplus value as housewives (Wright 2002: 134), and it was autonomist feminists who inspired the Wages for Housework campaign. However, neo-liberal globalisation has led to the increased use of women as poorly paid producers of goods in Export Processing Zones.

Negri, in his reading of Marx, associates such forms of exploitation with the notion of 'formal' and 'real' subsumption of labour. Formal subsumption occurs prior to the creation of capitalism and in its early stages. Marx links the early stages of formal subsumption to 'primitive accumulation', where individuals can survive outside of the market economy by growing food, using common land to graze animals and squatting. They don't want to work in the factories because they have their 'means of production' to keep them fed. They must be forced to become workers by separating them from their ability to be economically independent. The land is enclosed with fences and the peasants are turned into homeless wanderers, who can be incorporated into the factory system. Marx provides many examples of this process. For instance, in Scotland in the eighteenth century:

> ... the Gaels were both driven from the land and forbidden to emigrate, with a view to driving them forcibly to Glasgow and other manufacturing towns. As an example of the method used in the nineteenth century, the 'clearings' made by the Duchess of Sutherland will suffice here. This person, who had been well instructed in economics, resolved, when she succeeded to the headship of the clan, to undertake a radical economic cure, and to turn the whole county of Sutherland, the population of which had already been reduced to 15,000 by similar processes, into a sheep-walk. Between 1814 and 1820 these 15,000 inhabitants, about 3,000 families, were systematically

hunted and rooted out. All their villages were destroyed and burnt, all their fields turned into pasturage. British soldiers enforced this mass of evictions and came to blows with the inhabitants. One old woman was burnt to death in the flames of the hut she refused to leave. It was in this manner that this fine lady appropriated 794,000 acres of land which had belonged to the clan from time immemorial ... The remnant of the original inhabitants, who had been flung onto the sea-shore, tried to live by catching fish. They became amphibious, and live, as an English writer says, half on land and half on water. (Marx 1979: 890–92)

The Sutherlanders were then expelled from the seashore, which was rented out to London fishmongers by the Duchess. In formal subsumption, the newly created workers are disciplined by placing them within particular locations of control, such as factories, schools, prisons and mental hospitals. Such discipline is direct: the factory is a form of prison and so is the school (Read 2003). No doubt the working class swept from the Highlands into the city, recomposed as professional workers on Red Clydeside and other industrial parts of Scotland, only to be decomposed by factory closures ... and so on.

Real subsumption occurs when such relatively crude methods cease to be necessary and workers take on their role willingly because they see no alternative to waged work. Social norms – 'values' – keep them at work; they need to earn money for their families to consume, and fear of unemployment is used to maintain discipline with a lighter touch. The social factory produces not only commodities, but a capitalist society and capitalist subjectivities:

When capital reaches a high level of development, it no longer limits itself to guaranteeing collaboration of the workers ... something it so badly needs. At significant points it now makes a transition, to the point of expressing its objective needs through the subjective demands of the workers. (Fuller 2001: 66)

The anti-capitalist protest group Mayday Monopoly observed: 'Capitalist society requires a specific social structure and a precise form of "individual". A whole machine is geared to create such a set up' (London Mayday Collective 2001: 38). Our assumptions, beliefs, practices and personality are forged by the capitalist economy. The creation of capitalist subjectivities is never totally complete. In part, this is because different institutions and practices within capitalism may have contradictory demands and produce contradictory effects:

A somewhat simplistic example of this would be the conflict of the demands of consumption and production – the demand to consume as much as possible – necessary for the realization of surplus value and the demand to live frugally in order to be productive, which is necessary for the production of surplus value ... The dissonance produces possibilities and conditions for subversion. (Read 2003: 143)

Even though education, the media, advertising and other aspects of the social factory work to create a capitalist personality, workers still resist. This belief in resistance, despite a system that seeks to engineer our souls, is an important bridge between autonomism and a larger, older, anarchist anti-capitalism. Formal subsumption and discipline are never entirely replaced, as Naomi Klein has shown in her accounts of the prison-like conditions of the Export Processing Zones (2001a: 215). The commons is constantly re-enclosed to maintain capitalism (de Angelis 2001).

The autonomist analysis takes us a long way from the approach of Soros and Stiglitz. Autonomists might suggest that as representatives of capital Soros and Stiglitz believe that the Washington Consensus provides an unworkable means of controlling the multitude. What we have is not a debate about economics, but a discussion between those who would punch us with an iron fist, or greet us with a welcoming hand when opening the prison door. Autonomists like Cleaver, perhaps, substitute economics with politics and arguably turn Marx into a bearded anarchist, happier smashing up the street than theorising in his study.

Marxist Anarchism

While Hardt and Negri reject the anarchist label, other autonomists like Cleaver note the importance of anarchist thinkers such as Emma Goldman and Peter Kropotkin within a broadly communist tradition (Cleaver 2000: 14). Anarchists generally see politics as taking precedence over economics, and stress the power of the state rather than the activities of corporations alone. Like the autonomists, they see the state as instrument of oppression. Anarchists argue that human beings are cooperative and resourceful. Bursting with potential, they don't need the state to instruct them to do work which is necessary or to channel their creativity. A minority, particularly in the US, are supporters of the market – seeing it, especially in its Smithian original form of small local firms, as a force for liberation. From Rothbard onwards, the libertarian market-based anarchists provide much food for thought, but as self-proclaimed *Radicals for Capitalism* demand discussion elsewhere (see Doherty 2007).

Numerous anarchist magazines, networks and quasi-political parties have fed into the anti-capitalist movements, often drawing inspiration (both positively and negatively) from Marxist sources.

The most extreme green anarchists, who reject civilisation and see a society rooted in the primitive, draw heavily upon the work of John Zerzan. Originally an autonomist, Zerzan has argued that even such institutions as written language and agriculture function as instruments of social control (Zerzan 1999). The great refusal demands that we re-create a primitive society. Although such theorising appears insanely extreme, primitivists point to studies such as Marshal Sahlins' *The Original Affluent Society* (1972) that argue for stone age prosperity, as well as archaeological evidence that prehistory may not have been as nasty and brutish as is usually supposed. Zerzan's call for humanity to be wild and free is promoted in journals such as *Green Anarchy*, *Green Anarchist* and *Fifth Estate*, which are often sold on anti-capitalist protests.

Other green anarchists draw upon the ideas of the US thinker and activist Murray Bookchin, who died in 2006. Bookchin argued that ecological destruction is produced by the state and capitalism. He believed that Athenian democracy and the late eighteenth-century township meetings that brought together American citizens to make decisions provide models for direct democracy. Bookchin sees direct democracy, which enables the community to take collective decisions, as an anarchist alternative to the state. He was hostile to primitivism, deep ecology and other currents that he dismissed as irrational. Bookchin, one of the most well-known anarchist thinkers of the twentieth century, has challenged Marxism in many ways, but based his understanding of economics largely on *Capital* (Bookchin 1974: 178). The Kurdish leader Abdullah Ocalan read Bookchin's work in prison and abandoned Marxist-Leninism for such self-organised ecological anarchism. The mainly Kurdish autonomous region of Syria known as Rojava, which translates as 'the West', along with Kurds in Turkey, have attempted to put these ideas into practice. As I write in 2015, the revolutionaries of the YPG (Community Defence Force) are locked in conflict with the so-called Islamic State, but it is clear that their work is a practical example of anti-capitalist, ecological and feminist alternatives. A report in 2014 noted:

Many people from the rank and file and from different backgrounds, including Kurdish, Arab, Muslim, Christian, Assyrian and Yazidis, have been involved. The first task was to establish a variety of groups, committees and communes on the streets in neighborhoods, villages, counties and small and big towns everywhere. The role of these groups was to become involved in all the issues facing society. Groups were set up to look at a number of issues including: women's, economic, environmental, education and health and care issues, support and solidarity, centers for the family martyrs, trade and business, diplomatic relations with foreign countries and many more. There are even groups established to reconcile disputes among different people or factions to try to avoid these disputes going to court unless these groups are incapable of resolving them.

(https://libcom.org/news/experiment-west-kurdistan-syrian-kurdistan-has-proved-people-can-make-changes-zaher-baher-2)

The 'classic' anarchists, writing and agitating, at the beginning of the twentieth century, often promoted green anti-capitalism. Typically, in 1906, writing in her journal *Mother Earth*, Goldman promoted an ecological perspective:

> Whoever severs himself [*sic*] from Mother Earth and her flowing sources of life goes into exile. A vast part of civilization has ceased to feel the deep relation with our mother ... Economic necessity causes such hateful pressure. Economic necessity? Why not economic stupidity? This seems a more appropriate name for it. (Goldman 1906: 2)

Peter Kropotkin (1842–1921) produced a guide for cooperative economies based on communal ownership. Kropotkin argued that many goods and services within the economy were already free, for example, books provided by libraries. Where goods remained in short supply, rationing could be introduced. In the end, money could be abolished. He further argued that only five hours' work a day would be necessary if more goods were used communally. And he believed that the desire to be creative and part of the community would tend to encourage work, despite the absence of monetary reward (Kropotkin 1972: 122–3). It must nevertheless be admitted that Kropotkin was more interested in gardening than providing a detailed analysis of trends within the global economy of the early twentieth century.

Autonomism is not the only movement which straddles the divide between Marxism and anarchism. The council communists who rejected Lenin's creation of a disciplined centralised party and supported workers' control equally combined Marxist theory with anarchist principles (Smart 1978). Anti-capitalist ideas are often a melange of council socialism, situationism, green anarchism and cultural theory. Situationism, which originated in France during the 1950s, argued for an autonomous society and challenged the society of the spectacle in which the media shaped and controlled desire. Influential during the student uprising of Paris in 1968, the situationists came up with a number of provocative and utopian slogans, along the lines of 'Be realistic, demand the impossible.' Many of their ideas were derived from Marx, particularly his *Paris Manuscripts*, which challenged the alienation created by capitalist work (Marx 1977). Such themes were combined with a rejection of parties and unions. Situationism was influenced by the libertarian group Socialisme ou Barbarie (Plant 1992). The journalist Paul Mason, describing student occupations and youth street protests in London in 2010, noted.

> Many students were familiar with Debord and his Situationist movement, for the simple reason that he is taught on every art course, and the big London art schools – Slade and Goldsmiths – were centres of militancy … some of the Situationist tactics that failed in May 1968 – basically, spreading out to create chaos – do not look so ludicrous if you own a Blackberry. (Mason 2013: 46–7)

Michael Albert, editor of *Z* magazine, has developed the concept of 'Parecon', shorthand for participatory economics, based loosely on council communist and anarchistic economics. Property is owned socially instead of by private individuals, and economic decisions are made by a process of dialogue, known as 'iteration', between worker and consumer councils. Albert describes his scheme in the following terms: 'Participatory economics as proposed in this book combines social ownership, participatory planning allocation, council structure, balanced job complexes, remuneration for effort and sacrifice, and participatory self-management with no class differentiation' (Albert 2004: 24). He has argued in some detail that a participatory economy would increase human welfare compared to the present state- and market-based economies (ibid.).

The lived anarchy of, say, autonomist squatters in South London or the Zapatistas or unemployed Argentinians organising after the virtual collapse of the formal economy during the 1990s also provides a model of what is possible. For example, the *piqueteros* in Argentina, a network of the unemployed who picket roads, demand subsidies from the government and self-organise their own economies:

> Carlos, an unemployed telephone technician in his fifties, is part of one of the most radical branches of the *piqueteros*, the MTD (Movement of Unemployed Workers). His group is transforming a huge, abandoned electronics factory into a self-managed organic farm, clinic, and media centre. He said that his most profound political moment since the December 2001 uprising was seeing three young *piqueteros* faint from hunger. 'Our main aim now is to have enough bread for each other … After that, we can concentrate on other things.' (Notes from Nowhere 2003: 394)

Believing in a 'solidarity economy', they get together twice a week, a group of 70-odd people in a circle, and make decisions about what to produce and how to go about it:

> We have a group building sewage systems, and another that helps people who only have tin roofs put proper roofs on their houses. There is a press group

that produces our newsletter and makes links with the outside media. We have the *Copa de Leche*, which provides a glass of milk to children and a free meal every day. We have a store that distributes second-hand clothes, two new bakeries, vegetable plots, and a library. (Ibid.: 394–5)

I have been at meetings of squatters in the UK with 20–30 individuals planning how to open up new flats, create a social centre, or collect fruit and veg thrown out of New Covent Garden market. These meetings may not go smoothly but they at least provide an experiment in an economy that seeks to move beyond market and state control. People can get together and make decisions.

During the Spanish Civil War in the 1930s, the country's huge anarchist movement fought against Franco's forces, which were eventually to impose a dictatorship. At the same time, they collectivised property and built local economies based on anarchist principles. Within industrialised towns and cities, CNT, the anarchist union, found it relatively easy to reorganise factory production based on a system of workers' control. In Alcoy, the second largest city in Alicante, 20,000 workers were organised into councils that ran everything from weapons production to hairdressers:

In spite of all the monumental difficulties, one big fact stands out: in Alcoy 20,000 workers organized in their syndicates administered production, coordinated economic activities, and proved that industry can be operated better in every respect than capitalism, while still assuring freedom and justice for all. (Leval 1990b: 106)

In Catalonia, anarchist workers produced millions of rounds of bullets, bombs and hand grenades to fight Franco's armies (Souchy 1990b: 96). In the countryside, peasants were more than happy to produce collectively in Spain, and even Marx admitted that peasant communism based on the traditional *mir* (the pre-Revolutionary Russian peasant commune) might have allowed Russia to move from feudalism to socialism in one leap (Desai 2004: 98). At one point, half of Spain's oranges were grown by anarchist farmers (Leval 1990c: 124). Many anarchist rural communities abolished money, produced what they felt was needed and redistributed goods from warehouses.

Anarchism almost vanished during the twentieth century, yet during the century's last decades, it revived to some extent. The anarchist approach suggests that protest need not be aimed at achieving minor changes in government policies, but may be seen as a way of trying to create a new society. Thus Reclaim the Streets, a key network that helped to kick off the new anti-capitalist movement during the 1990s, proclaimed:

Direct action enables people to develop a new sense of self-confidence and an awareness of their individual and collective power. Direct action is founded on the idea that people can develop the ability for self-rule only through practice, and proposes that all persons directly decide the important issues facing them. Direct action is not just a tactic, it is individuals asserting their ability to control their own lives and to participate in social life without the need for mediation or control by bureaucrats or professional politicians. Direct action encompasses a whole range of activities, from organising coops to engaging in resistance to authority. Direct action places moral commitment above positive law. Direct action is not a last resort when other methods have failed, but the preferred way of doing things. (RTS leaflet distributed July 1996)

Such an understanding of the anarchic power of grass-roots action is apparent in Hardt and Negri's *Empire*, with its emphasis on the actions of the multitude rather than that of limited policy change. Anarchist economic theorists have become significant in the anti-capitalist movement since 2001. The anarchist anthropologist David Graeber (2011) has argued that debt is a key form of exploitation. Long before capitalism, conquering states demand tribute, which lead to debt bondage. This mafia principle may go far back in history, but debt continues to be a threat. With the 2008 financial crisis, along with the operation of the IMF and similar institutions (see Chapter 5), we continue to see debt used to reinforce exploitative social relations:

The IMF (International Monetary Foundation) and what they did to countries in the Global South – which is, of course, exactly the same thing bankers are starting to do at home now – is just a modern version of this old story. That is, creditors and governments saying you're having a financial crisis, you owe money, obviously you must pay your debts. There's no question of forgiving debts. Therefore, people are going to have to stop eating so much. The money has to be extracted from the most vulnerable members of society. Lives are destroyed; millions of people die. People would never dream of supporting such a policy until you say, 'Well, they have to pay their debts.'

(http://brooklynrail.org/2011/09/express/world-of-debt)

The US anarchist economist Kevin Carson has built on insights from many anarchist thinkers and radicals, including Kropotkin and Ivan Illich, to develop a sophisticated account of a decentralised open-source alternative. He sees capitalism as state capitalism, with firms using the state to create market barriers, such as patents, to artificially raise their profits. Capitalism leads to over-accumulation, and neo-liberalism involves the state picking up the bill for such over investment. Carson's practical anarchism is based on his concept of the 'Home Brew Industrial Revolution': utilising decentralised and open-source alternatives we can three-D print, brew and build local community production. Carson's work cannot be captured or critiqued in a couple of paragraphs, but it points to an economics beyond the corporation and the state, which can be implemented and advanced to create an alternative. His work is online and free, so those interested can study in more detail here: https://homebrewindustrial-revolution.wordpress.com/.

Foucault on Rioting

Foucault, a thinker closely linked to anarchism, also influenced Hardt and Negri, along with other post-structuralist or post-modern theorists. Michael Ryan, an editor of Negri's *Marx Beyond Marx*, suggests that post-modernism is 'the philosophic equivalent of autonomy' and is most strongly associated with 'Deleuze, Derrida, Foucault and Lyotard' (Ryan 1991: 214). Indeed, Hardt and Negri draw heavily upon a number of post-modernist thinkers; especially Michel Foucault and Gilles Deleuze. Deleuze and Foucault, in turn, are largely inspired by a tradition of philosophy opposed to the grand theorising of Hegel. Given the autonomists' Marxist credentials, this is something of a paradox, as Hegel is often seen as Marx's most important philosophical source. Hegel is criticised for his determinism, which is seen as putting people in the service of a grand historical process, which finds spirit achieving its fulfilment in human society. According to post-modernists, Hegel limits human history to a series of laws.

Hardt and Negri draw upon thinkers normally seen as post-modern for an understanding of how power is produced. Foucault, Deleuze and Guattari argue that power develops on a small scale (the 'molecular' or 'micro') as much as on a large scale (the 'molar' or 'macro'), through the use of surveillance and language. Foucault suggests that power, more properly termed 'biopower', rather than being primarily exercised at a macro level by the state, works in socially sophisticated societies at a micro level, producing subjects. Foucault argues that society has become governed by the logic of the panoptikon, which means the 'all-(*pan*) seeing eye (*optikon*)'. He derived this metaphor from a prison design, where the guards could view prisoners from a tower situated in the centre of the structure. Discourse, a term equally key to Foucault's perspective, is normally understood as a form of socially situated speech such as the disempowering jargon of economists or the phraseology of priests (Foucault 1979, 1980, 1991). In a disciplinary society, Foucault suggests, repression is used to maintain domination by an elite; in a more advanced system of 'control' individual personalities are shaped so as to maintain rule (Foucault 1980). His argument

– that a disciplinary society has made way for one based upon control – is mirrored in Negri's work by Marx's distinction between the formal and the real subsumption of labour. Capitalism produces personalities, as well as laptops, pet food and exotic package holidays.

Gilles Deleuze supplies the authors of *Empire* with the concept of the multitude, which he borrowed along with the all-important distinction between power as domination and power as creativity from Spinoza. Indeed, Hardt and Negri claim that the two inspirations for their book are Marx's *Capital* and Deleuze and Guattari's *A Thousand Plateaus* (Hardt 2004: 169).

The assumption that we have moved to a post-Fordist economy is also shared with the post-Marxists and derived from post-modern thinkers. Such an economy is based on knowledge; physical factory production is less significant, as work is outsourced to distant parts of the globe and the traditional Western working class largely disappears. While for post-Marxists such as Laclau and Mouffe (1985) political opposition is based on the demands of new social movements which are no longer primarily concerned with economic need, for the autonomists, the whole of society becomes a factory and the demands of the social movements can only be met by destroying capitalism. The creation of a new post-modern economy, hinted at by authors such as Naomi Klein in *No Logo* (2001a), is explored in *Empire*.

The anti-capitalist movement at its most playful seems to draw upon notions that the distinction between culture and economics has been eroded in a post-Fordist economy. Brands are subverted through 'subvertising', which involves stencilling and graffiti on advertising hoardings and the like, to erode the codes of Nike and McDonald's. Deleuze and his co-author Guattari, in books such as their *Capitalism and Schizophrenia* (1988), advocate nomadic action based on marginal groups. The growth of social media and the World Wide Web has increased the importance of such assumptions since *Empire* was published in 2001. Paul Mason (2013) notes in his study of the protest movements of the twenty-first century such as Occupy that the influence of thinkers like Foucault, Deleuze and Guattari has led to a deeper understanding of power amongst anti-capitalist activists.

Empire as a Pure Model of Capital

Having outlined the sources of autonomist ideas, it is now tentatively possible to discuss some of the main themes presented within *Empire* and the broader autonomist approach to globalisation. First, working-class resistance explains globalisation as a force for promoting a new neo-liberal capitalism. Workers have pushed up pay and improved work conditions, so multinational corporations relocate or outsource so as to push wages back down. Firms exploit the low-cost conditions of Export Processing Zones where repression can be used to prevent wages rising. Globalisation is a product of working-class victory, rather than defeat. The Vietcong, the Fiat workers, the British miners and other working-class insurgents have propelled it. These forces wrecked the Keynesian system, which maintained economic peace by providing higher pay linked to productivity, a measure of state intervention in the market and the welfare state. When Keynesianism no longer worked, the empire evolved as an alternative form of global regulation (Hardt and Negri 2001a: 179). Cleaver notes: 'Capitalist imperialism, fleeing the obstacles created by class struggle at home, spreads its class antagonism across the globe. This is the moment of the world market, but also of the global factory and the international ruling class' (Cleaver 1991: xxv).

Rather than the old imperialism identified by Lenin, Luxemburg and Hobson (see Chapter 6), where various states fought each other for economic and political dominance, the new imperialism is based on one global entity. Empire has no country and exists globally. Nowhere is truly outside of Empire, it has run out of frontiers to cross and further colonisation in the geographical sense is impossible. The old imperialism was analogous to Foucault's notion of the disciplinary society, with gunboat diplomacy being used to extend and maintain exploitation. While the US *looks* as if it dominates the globe, domination has largely escaped from state control and now circulates on a global basis (Hardt and Negri 2001a: xiv). The WTO, the IMF and the UN act as judicial institutions of Empire; thus even the world's one superpower prefers to act in 'collaboration with others under the umbrella of the United Nations' (Hardt and Negri 2001a: 309).

Empire runs on fear of unemployment and poverty through the operation of global markets in finance and investment. A country that resists the market is consigned to the discipline created by falling share values, currency and investment. A truly national economic policy is impossible. Even the US is threatened by the sovereignty of Empire: if debt grows too high, for example, market forces make economic growth unsustainable for the country. As an article in *Do or Die!* noted:

> Speculation is directed at those countries whose domestic policies are in some way incompatible with global competitivity requirements, i.e. those who have not made sufficient attempts to subjugate or co-opt workers or who display any weakness by bowing to pressure over controlling public finance and social expenditure. Those countries which have begun a 'healthy restructuring' program are rewarded with currency stability and the loyalty of the speculators. (Anon. 1999b: 49)

Instead of using external territories to offload excess production that cannot be sold to domestic populations who lack purchasing power, as in Rosa

Luxemburg's analysis, exploitation has moved inwards. Thus as the price and profits generated from manufactured goods fall, capitalism commodifies new areas of life to maintain profit: 'Capital no longer looks outside but rather inside its domain and its expansion is thus intensive rather than extensive' (Hardt and Negri 2001a: 272). Instead of selling to new markets, within Empire, we are increasingly sold the services of personal trainers and encouraged to buy brands produced symbolically as well as physically.

The global sovereignty of Empire has been made possible both by deregulation (privatisation plus the removal of governmental controls on business) and the creation of new communication technologies, such as the Internet and World Wide Web. It has created a new global economy where the social factory rather than old-style mass production is key. Work is increasingly based not on production, but knowledge and caring:

> ... the role of industrial factory labor has been reduced and priority given instead to communicative, cooperative, and affective labor. In the postmodernization of the global economy, the creation of wealth tends ever more toward what we will call biopolitical production, the production of social life itself, in which the economic, the political, and the cultural increasingly overlap and invest in one another. (Hardt and Negri 2001a: xiii)

An economy based on intellectual and emotional work leads to the multitude. The multitude can produce because of their ability to manipulate knowledge and care. Empire generates resistance to itself in the form of highly skilled, highly mobile workers who have both grievances against the social factory and the ability to produce autonomously. The multitude are the new face of the international working class: indigenous people in Mexico networked via the web; squatters in Peckham who can exploit their law degrees to live a little longer without paying rent; old women who sit in the road to protest for pension rises; anarchists who climb buildings and break locks on government doors; call-centre operatives who know how to sabotage the phones without being caught; students who can operate pirate radio stations; cyclists who can use webcams to broadcast their actions against car culture on the Internet. The new anti-capitalism has no need of parties, NGOs, pressure groups, or leaders. It is energetic and endlessly mobile. The multitude 'is in fact the foundation of all social creativity' (Hardt 2004: 173). Cyber-capitalism creates a cyber-proletariat busy digging the grave of Empire.

Strategy

Autonomists do not believe in constructing a blueprint for a post-capitalist society, nor do Hardt and Negri develop a detailed strategy for getting there.

Alternatives, they believe, will emerge from the struggles of the multitude; it is foolish for writers to think that they can produce great plans that their readers will then translate smoothly into reality. Nonetheless, a number of assumptions about how neo-liberal globalisation can be challenged emerge from *Empire*. For Hardt and Negri, the resort to localism is impossible; globalisation must be accelerated, with workers migrating in waves and technologies speeding away. Instead of looking to past certainties because capitalism cannot be reined in, we must seek the security of an utterly mobile and constantly mutating world. Nation states, far from being better than global sovereignty, were equally repressive. The process of globalisation creates the multitude. The multitude has the power to create another world. Hardt and Negri insist time after time that nowhere is outside Empire, rejecting measures to create local economies insulated from the world market.

There is a tacit assumption that mobile (both socially and geographically) individuals are able to develop new social codes appropriate to a post-capitalist society. This notion of nomadism is drawn from Deleuze and reflects the title of Melucci's study of social movements *Nomads of the Present* (Melucci 1989). The nomads living on the margins create new ways of life; the squats and protest camps are high-pressure factories where experimenters can forge alternative ways of life. Negri notes in *Marx Beyond Marx*, 'to be a Communist today now means to live as a Communist' (Negri 1991: xvi).

The vision in *Empire* often looks like a recoding of Marx's *Capital* read a little superficially. Capitalism/empire is a product of class struggle and in turn creates the conditions via a global market, technological development and the construction of new subjectivities for its own destruction and the introduction of communist utopia. Sometimes *Empire* looks like a parody rather than a recoding, a giant joke from the post-modern Marxist anarchist intellectuals at the expense of the rest of us. For example, towards the end of *Empire*, having long rejected notions of liberal democracy such as universal rights, parliamentary representation and the mediation of political organisations, Hardt and Negri suddenly produce three political demands to petition from representative governments. The sudden insertion of reforms to be gained from the state or empire seems to cut across all the militancy and sophistication of their prose, suggesting that they don't take their profoundest ideas seriously and are merely testing us with contradiction to see if we can read a big book to the end.

Perhaps the joke is really upon the moderate defenders of capitalism, the likes of Soros and Stiglitz whom we met in Chapter 2. The three demands are: the right to universal migration, a basic income scheme, and the right to economic re-appropriation, control over and self-management of one's economic existence (Hardt and Negri 2001a: 396–407). Each demand is 'reasonable' and follows from the economic case made in *Empire*. How can capital, which demands the dismantling of borders for goods and finance, fix peoples in one place? The basic income scheme, long promoted by social creditors, Greens and other radicals, is almost mainstream. In a mild form, it was supported by Milton Friedman, and in the form of tax credits by British Labour governments from 1997 to 2010. Robert van der Veen and Philippe Van Parijs, in contrast, and like Hardt and Negri, have argued that basic income provides *A Capitalist Road to Communism* (1996). Given the nature of the social factory where society as a whole helps produce all goods and services, why should those outside the formal economy not be paid as they help sustain economic activity, particularly where they care for others such as elderly relatives and children? Finally, individuals should control the process by which they produce goods and services. Three very moderate demands that cannot reasonably be denied, but lead to a society where individuals are free to move where they like, where income is separated from work and work is controlled by the multitude.

Hardt and Negri seem to have produced a set of anti-capitalist demands that can be put to the mainstream. Autonomism has long advocated the virtues of refusal, seeing resistance as productive. Resistance rather than negotiating for rights is a feature of the more radical elements of the anti-capitalist movement. The astonishing growth of social media since *Empire* was published suggest that a central thesis of Hardt and Negri – that value is produced socially by affective labour – has strengthened their analysis. Perhaps another world is possible. Ryan, for example, has argued, 'Productive force, once liberated from the constraints of bourgeois productive relations, shows itself to be immediately constitutive, and it shows the possibility that the world can be transformed according to desire' (Ryan 1991: 219).

Critics have challenged *Empire* in a number of ways. First, Hardt and Negri have been seen as promoting the hyper-globalist thesis that is put most strongly by the fervent defenders of capitalism. Indeed, Ellen Meiksins Wood asks whether they have produced 'A Manifesto for Global Capitalism' (Wood 2003a). If markets are all-powerful, it is impossible to defend welfare states and workers' rights, or to prevent environmental standards from sliding. Hardt and Negri provide an exaggerated and pessimistic account borrowed from the political enemies of the left.

The strategic assumptions of autonomism can also be challenged. Negri, in particular from the 1970s to date, has overestimated the militancy of the working class. In an era where the traditional left has appeared to suffer defeat time after time, autonomism reminds us that capitalism is shaped by the resistance it faces. Is it not also a secular Marxist sin to reverse Gramsci's dictum that proclaims the need for 'optimism of the will, pessimism of the intellect'? Whatever happens, the working class is strong and the autonomists keep smiling as the police smash down their doors, burn their books, bulldoze their squats, kill their pets and imprison their children. Have Hardt and Negri re-imported the Hegelian grand narrative of capitalism as a process that creates its own collapse? Indeed, Sergio

Bologna, who coined the term 'tribe of moles', criticised Negri along these lines, noting:

> There have been many small (or big) battles, but in their course the political composition of the class has changed substantially in the factories, and certainly not in the direction indicated by Negri … In sum there has been a reassertion of reformist hegemony over the factories, one that is brutal and relentless in its efforts to dismember the class left and expel it from the factory. (quoted in Callinicos 2001: 44)

Empire finishes both beautifully and (for those with a distaste for theology) rather alarmingly, with a comparison between St Francis of Assisi and the communist militant:

> Consider his work. To denounce the poverty of the multitude he adopted that common condition and discovered there the ontological power of a new society. The communist militant does the same, identifying in the common condition of the multitude its enormous wealth. Francis in opposition to nascent capitalism refused every instrumental discipline, and in opposition to the mortification of the flesh (in poverty and in the constituted order) he posed a joyous life, including all of being and nature, the animals, sister moon, brother sun, the birds of the field, the poor and exploited humans, together against the will of power and corruption. Once again in postmodernity we find ourselves in St Francis's situation, posing against the misery of power the joy of being. This is a revolution that no power will control – because biopower and communism, cooperation and revolution remain together, in love, simplicity, and also innocence. This is the irrepressible lightness and joy of being communist. (Hardt and Negri 2001a: 413)

Despite its flaws, *Empire* and the broader autonomist tradition should be praised as intellectually productive and engaged. The autonomists are orientated to activism and will work to promote the analysis appropriate to accelerate change. In exploring autonomism, one is provoked to reflect deeply, which can be no bad thing.

Autonomism is hostile in one important sense to the very notion of economics. Economics, rather than being a neutral method of regulating activity to produce goods and services as efficiently as possible, is simply a method of control. The insight/suggestion is that economics is in fact always a form of politics, a way of constraining the power of the working class/multitude to allow capitalism to survive. Marx, while he bitterly fought with anarchists like Bakunin, argued that the state would wither away in a communist order. Despite the authoritarianism developed in his name by the likes of Stalin, Marx was, in the everyday sense, an anarchist. Hardt, Negri, Marx, Deleuze and the black bloc have their differences, but all agree that both the state and the market prevent the realisation of human potential.

Despite the inadequacies of *Empire* and autonomism, at least two other important insights are provided. First, capital rules, to the extent it rules at all, virtually through markets, and such a mechanism, while far from complete, increasingly dominates global politics and society. The US invades, global trading blocs clash as in the old imperialism, nation states have some power, but the market creates global sovereignty above and beyond such localisms. This is *potestas* or constituent power: if one likes, it can be described as force, oppression or 'power over'. Also the notion of *potentia*, creative power, 'power to', rings true to participants of the kinds of protest outlined at the start of this chapter. Unmediated by formal organisation, the revolution is made by loose but intelligent militant networks. *Potentia* fuels empire and can transform it. The market faces the multitude. Since publishing *Empire*, Hardt and Negri have produce a vast tribe of books, updating and deepening their ideas. These books, including *Commonwealth* (2009) deserve to be read too; their revisions, arguing that Latin American left countries have delivered some progress for anti-capitalism, their discussions of the Occupy movement and inspiration in the work of Spinoza, are all of great value to serious anti-capitalists. The financial journalist Paul Mason, surveying the Arab Spring protests, Occupy and student uprisings, noted that while many participants rejected any ideology, autonomist, anarchist and situationist ideas were, in his opinion, influential (Mason 2013).

8

ECOSOCIALIST ALTERNATIVES: MARX'S ECOLOGY

At first sight, environmentalists or conservationists are nice, slightly crazy guys whose main purpose in life is to prevent the disappearance of blue whales or pandas. The common people have more important things to think about, for instance how to get their daily bread ... However, there are in Peru a very large number of people who are environmentalists ... they might reply, 'ecologist your mother', or words to that effect ... Are not the town of Ilo and the surrounding villages which are being polluted by the Southern Peru Copper Corporation truly environmentalist? Is not the village of Tambo Grande in Pirura environmentalist when it rises like a closed fist and is ready to die in order to prevent strip-mining in its valley? Also, the people of the Mantaro Valley who saw their little sheep die, because of the smoke and waste from La Oroya smelter. (Hugo Blanco, quoted in Guha and Martinez-Alier 1997: 24)

Anti-capitalism has an ecosocialist shade. Some socialist anti-capitalists are also green and some green anti-capitalists are also red. There are strong socialist currents in most Green parties around the world and there are a number of red-green organisations such as the Initiative for Catalonia Greens (ICV). Ecosocialists combine aspects of green and socialist thought to argue that capitalism is the cause of ecological crisis. Ecosocialists believe that the green approach has not gone deep enough, while they criticise many on the left for failing to take environmental destruction seriously. Nonetheless, there is a distinct, albeit a minority, ecosocialist tradition that can be traced back through history. The road to a society that is green and red will be a long and hard one, with no short cuts based on nationalising the banks or electing a few more green or socialist politicians to office.

The journal *Capitalism Nature Socialism* is one source of such an approach. Its founding editor, James O'Connor, has developed the concept of the second contradiction of capitalism, showing how environmental degradation caused by capitalism feeds back into economic crisis for the system (O'Connor 1991). Joel Kovel's book *The Enemy of Nature* provides a detailed ecosocialist account of globalisation (2002). Kovel, who stood unsuccessfully for the US Green Party presidential nomination in 2000 against Ralph Nader, argues that globalisation is fuelled by capitalism and gives rise to accelerated economic growth that is wrecking the planet. Such growth is not a by-product of corporations or the money powers but is built into the very DNA of our economic system. He argues that the basic contradiction between use values and exchange values identified by Marx is at the core of the crisis. John Bellamy Foster (2000, 2002) and Paul Burkett (1999) have suggested that Marx's ideas, especially his theme of a 'metabolism' or interaction between humanity and the rest of nature, is a rich source of ecological ideas.

Ecosocialism has deep roots. William Morris, the poet, designer and novelist, shaped a distinctly English school of ecosocialism in the 1880s and 1890s. Aran Gare has chronicled in some detail the activities of a generation of green scientists and thinkers, who tried to shape the Russian Revolution in a more ecologically sensitive direction before being purged (Gare 1996). During the early 1970s, Professor Barry Commoner developed a leftist response to the limits to growth thesis, suggesting that capitalist technologies rather than overpopulation threatened global ecosystems (1972). Rudolf Bahro, an East Germany intellectual, fused red and green in books such as *The Alternative in Eastern Europe* (1978) and *Socialism and Survival* (1982). In Australia, the Marxist theorist and activist Alan Roberts showed how unfulfilled human needs fuelled rampant consumerism (Roberts 1979). Another Australian, Ted Trainer in *Abandon Affluence!* (1985), has argued that socialists must embrace a society based on meeting need rather than the wants created by capitalism. Much theoretical work has been done by writers such as Ariel Salleh (1997) and Mary Mellor (1992) to develop a feminist-socialist approach to ecological concern. In many countries in the global South, activists have developed an environmentalism of the poor, which links ecosocialist sentiments to day-to-day struggles against globalisation (Guha and Martinez-Alier 1997).

This chapter provides a survey of the ecosocialist tradition and the environmentalism of the poor, moves onto the red-green approach to globalisation and makes a nod towards the ecological Marx, before evaluating ecosocialist alternatives.

The Anti-Capitalism of the Poor

Ecosocialists argue that the ecological crisis is already with us, particularly in the global South where the capitalist production of basic commodities is degrading the environment. Such degradation inevitably leads to poverty for much of the world's population. Crops produced for exports take water from subsistence agriculturalists, thereby increasing the incidence of hunger. Forests are enclosed, felled and replaced with fast-growing cash-crop species, such as eucalyptus. Such development, as we have seen in previous chapters, makes the poor poorer by separating them from their local means of production.

The enclosure of the commons, identified by both Marx and subsistence ecofeminists, is an extremely important theme for ecosocialists. They argue that economic growth and the expansion of capitalism, far from being necessary to remove poverty, leads to poverty. For ecosocialists, it is utterly inappropriate to think of a contradiction between zero growth as a means of reducing environmental damage and the need for increased production to remove the problems of the poorest. The 'poor' have access to the means of production they need to survive and even prosper, but such non-monetised communal means of production are unmeasured by GNP figures. Neo-liberal globalisation is part of the long struggle of the state and commercial interests to steal from those who subsist, it is destructive of the environment and as such removes access to the resources that sustain ordinary people across the globe.

Authors such as Ramachandra Guha and Juan Martinez-Alier argue in their 'varieties of environmentalism' thesis that there are two environmentalisms: the supposed environmentalism of the wealthy post-materialist North, and the environmentalism of the poor of the South. The 'environmentalism' of the North is partly a construct of academics and the media. It is based on the assumption that environmentalism is a non-essential and aesthetic demand of the relatively prosperous. As individuals become wealthier, they have the choice of being concerned with non-material issues. In the South, the environment is a source of communal wealth. Peasants and gatherers defend it because they know that if their environment is enclosed or destroyed they will find it difficult to survive. Globalisation stops people from producing for themselves, accelerates the creation of waste and then pushes the toxic waste onto the very poorest.

The End of the World?

Ecosocialists draw strongly upon the Marxist analysis identified in earlier chapters, yet while many Marxists celebrate economic growth as a means of raising the productive forces, ecosocialists are strongly critical of capitalist growth. James O'Connor argues that capitalist growth tends to degrade the environment it depends upon to sustain growth. Capitalism, by polluting drinking water, reducing soil fertility and breeding toxins, weakens the ability of both workers and nature to sustain growth. This second contradiction, like the primarily economic contradictions discussed by Marx, has a tendency to drive the system out of existence. O'Connor notes that to overcome environmental contradictions, capitalism introduces new technologies that solve old environmental problems at the expense of creating new ones; for example, nuclear power is posited as an alternative to greenhouse-gas-producing fossil fuels. O'Connor also quotes Gary Snyder's contention that capitalism 'spreads its economic support system out far enough that it can afford to wreck one eco-system, and keep moving on' (O'Connor 1998: 181).

Some ecosocialists fear that the globalised economy is running out of fresh ecosystems to kill. Kovel, echoing the criticism of economic growth by Greens noted in Chapter 4, observes:

> If the world were a living organism, then any sensible observer would conclude that this 'growth' is a cancer that, if not somehow treated, means the destruction of human society, and even raises the question of the extinction of our species. The details are important and interesting, but less so that the chief conclusion – that irresistible growth, and the evident fact that this growth destabilizes and breaks down the natural ground necessary for human existence, means, in the plainest terms, that we are doomed under the present social order, and that we had better change it as soon as possible. (Kovel 2002: 5)

While ecosocialists agree that capitalism is characterised in the third millennium by the activities of transnationals and finance capital, even without such forces the market would tend to be destructive.

Kovel argues that the distinction between exchange values and use values outlined by Marx in Chapter 1 of *Capital* is the essential insight for understanding both globalisation and the ecological and social ills that it unleashes. In an economy based upon the market, we do not directly produce goods because they are useful to us. We produce goods that we exchange for money that we can then use to exchange for other goods. This seems a sensible and convenient arrangement. However, we constantly have to sell if we are to buy. This means that we have to persuade others to buy our goods if we are to survive. A contradiction tends to develop between the usefulness of goods and their value from exchange. We thus have to sell goods that previously had no use to maintain our ability to buy goods and services. This process has a tendency to get out of hand.

In the third millennium, the contradiction between use and exchange values has accelerated to an astonishing gap. Abstract economic activity with no apparent use value commands billions, while concrete useful activity, particularly in the 'domestic' sphere of caring for children or relatives, and preparing basic foodstuffs (the subject of subsistence discussed in Chapter 4), is largely unrewarded. Producing for use is no priority at all. If goods were quite useless, one might be reluctant to exchange them and this would lead to economic problems; for the moment, however, society is focused on exchange. If you buy this book instead of borrowing it from the library, this increases exchange value, but it would be better ecologically and socially to provide books, children's toys, tools, and so on, via libraries because this would circulate use values more widely. Anything that increases exchange values is encouraged in our society because it allows the market economy to function; however, this means that use values are largely ignored or achieved through duplication and waste.

For ecosocialists, it is clearly not enough to reform the worst aspects of capitalism or to define capitalism in such a way that mild change is possible. Many of the anti-capitalists examined in these pages see capitalism as the poisoned out-growth of what is a basically sane system. The abolition of fractional reserve banking, localisation of economies, an element of state or community planning, for example, can be used to heal the system. Ecosocialists see the need for economic growth as built into the market. This takes us a long way from elite theories of capitalism. Such elite theories are political rather than economic. They suggest that a particular class or even group of conspirators get together to design a globalising system that brings them immense personal wealth and power at the expense of the poor and the planet. Ecosocialist approaches suggest that the reality is even more worrying. Rather than there being a particular group who could be replaced, the system tends to self-perpetuate and is driven by apparently extra-human forces.

Kovel illustrates this contention with a discussion of the 1984 Bhopal disaster in India, when a toxic gas leak at a Union Carbide plant led to the worst industrial accident of human history. This might be thought to be just another example of the many cases of transnationals wrecking people and planet for reasons of personal greed. Tens of thousands were killed and many more blinded, and over thirty years later the death toll is still mounting. Union Carbide blamed an unknown saboteur. Kovel has suggested that the reality is that a downturn in sales led to falling profits for the company. Like the virtual movements of power catalogued by Hardt and Negri, the malign magic of the stock market meant that falling profits were likely to translate into falling share values. Lower share values would encourage shareholders to sell, weakening the company. Therefore cuts were made in the operating costs of the Bhopal plant and, Kovel suggests, these cuts led to disaster: the abstract pressure of the market rather than the concrete activities of plotters led to this catastrophe. This is not to say that the catastrophe was inevitable, but it provides an example of how hunger for exchange values can lead to disaster (Kovel 2002: 28). John Bellamy Foster quotes Noam Chomsky to make this point:

> The chairman of the board will always tell you that he spends his every waking hour laboring so that people will get the best possible products at the cheapest possible price and work in the best possible conditions. But it is an institutional fact, independent of who the chairman of the board is, that

he'd better be trying to maximize profit and market share, and if he doesn't do that, he's not going to be chairman of the board any more. If he were ever to succumb to the delusions that he expresses, he'd be out. (Foster 2002: 48)

Kovel argues that capitalism is like a virus spreading through the world, that moves extensively through geographical space and intensively into our very souls. Globalisation is driven by the crises of capitalism. To maintain profit, firms must sell more and exploit labour with greater vigour. A falling profit rate can be overcome by a combination of exploiting labour more intensively (getting them to work harder) or extensively (getting them to worker for longer) and selling to new markets. To survive, capitalism therefore must grow forever. New economic niches must be exploited by constructing new needs. Capitalism, Luxemburg (1971) argued, needs an 'outside' to colonise. Nature must be commodified by enclosing and exploiting new habitats. People must constantly consume more and work harder. Capitalism has a psychological dimension. The system tends to select those who are most aggressive and inspired at increasing profit. Individuals in firms who decide that there is a kinder, gentler way of doing things, or who have priorities other than profit, for example, trying to produce what is most environmentally friendly or useful, either fail to rise to the top or are replaced:

People who are genuinely forthcoming and disinterestedly helpful do not become managers of large capitalist firms. The tender-hearted are pushed off far down the ladder on which one ascends to such positions of power. For capital shapes as well as selects the kinds of people who create these events. (Kovel 2002: 38)

Every member of a capitalist firm could be replaced by another and the system would still maintain its trajectory. Capitalism colonises us internally and makes us dream of shopping.

Capitalism is a system that has evolved out of human action but seems to have developed its own inhuman power. Capitalists recognising that the end of the world may ultimately be bad for business will try to find ways of creating sustainable growth. Companies will seek corporate solutions to the ecological crisis. However, as far as market players are concerned, declining profits are a threat today and pollution a threat tomorrow, so share values are likely to take precedence over indices of species destruction.

John Bellamy Foster summarises the ecosocialist account of capitalism by comparing it to a giant treadmill:

First, built into this global system, and constituting its central rationale, is the increasing accumulation of wealth by a relatively small section of the population at the top of the social pyramid. Second, there is a long-term movement of workers away from self-employment and into wage jobs that are contingent on the continual expansion of production. Third, the competitive struggle between businesses necessitates on pain of extinction of the allocation of accumulated wealth to new, revolutionary technologies that serve to expand production. Fourth, wants are manufactured in a manner that creates an insatiable hunger for more. Fifth, government becomes increasingly responsible for promoting national economic development, while ensuring some degree of 'social security' for a least a portion of its citizens. Sixth, the dominant means of communication and education are part of the treadmill, serving to reinforce its priorities and values.

... Everyone, or nearly everyone, is part of this treadmill and is unable or unwilling to get off. Investors and managers are driven by the need to accumulate wealth and to expand the scale of their operations in order to prosper within a globally competitive milieu. For the vast majority the commitment to the treadmill is more limited and indirect: they simply need to obtain jobs at liveable wages. But to retain those jobs and to maintain a given standard of living in these circumstances it is necessary, like the Red Queen in *Through the Looking Glass*, to run faster and faster in order to stay in the same place. (Foster 2002: 44–5)

The market keeps us marching to the clock, ecosocialists are at one with the autonomists and subsistence ecofeminists on this point. Boredom, the commute to work, Export Processing Zones and injury due to poor health and safety conditions are just some of the symptoms of a disease called 'paid employment'. The market must be broken not only because it kills the planet, but also because it kills those of us who work every day.

Socialism and Ecology

Simply moving to a planned socialist economy will not suffice for thinkers like Kovel and Bellamy Foster. Environmental concern seems to be on a tick list of modern socialist virtues, but rarely goes very deep. Kovel notes how David McNally in his book *Against the Market* (1993) argues that production should not be expanded without any thought of the subsequent environmental ill effects (Kovel 2002: 209). For example, the need for a car, let alone a four-wheel-drive, should be questioned given the ecological and social costs.

Ecosocialists are somewhat divided on the question of Marx's green credentials. He can be interpreted as a productivist concerned only with expanding the economy (see Chapter 6); indeed, Marx argued that capitalism created the expansion of the means of production necessary to create a surplus. Without surplus, communism would simply be the sharing of poverty. Capitalism creates poverty and need, subsuming the whole globe to the dictates of profit. Equally, it breaks up settled hierarchical communities, sweeps away petty tyrants, expands human need positively, removes superstitions, creates a communication system and finally puts together the multitude/working class who will introduce a new society. Perhaps communism is impossible without capitalism.

However, Marx noted, in Russia it might be possible for the peasant *mir*, a form of communal village, to provide the basis for communism without a previous capitalist mode of production (Desai 2004: 98). While this may have been a throwaway thought in a draft of a discarded letter, there is more solid evidence for a greener Marx. In one of his earliest essays he noted:

> The view of nature which has grown up under the regime of private property and of money is an actual contempt for and practical degradation of nature … In this sense Thomas Müntzer declares it intolerable that 'all creatures have been made into property, the fish in the water, the birds in the air, the plants on the earth – all living things must become free.' (Marx 1977: 239)

For Marx, capitalism and globalisation, produced from the expansion of the market, are both good and bad. The green Marx would only be a half-Marx, and so too the productivist Marx. Even if Marx was no Green, his analysis of how capitalism works, his philosophy based on subtle dialectics and his vision of a society no longer dominated by economics makes him indispensable to any form of green anti-capitalism. In contrast, John Bellamy Foster and Paul Burkett argue that Marx was an early Green. Foster notes:

> I discovered that Marx's systematic investigation into the work of the great German agricultural chemist Justus von Liebig, which grew out of his critique of Malthusianism, was what led him to his central concept of the 'metabolic rift' in the human relation to nature – his mature analysis of the alienation of nature. To understand this fully, however, it became necessary to reconstruct the historical debate over the degradation of the soil that had emerged in the mid-nineteenth century in the context of the 'second agricultural revolution,' and that extends down to our time. Herein lay Marx's most direct contribution to the ecological discussion. (Foster 2000: ix)

Ecosocialists argue that his notion of a metabolism between humanity and the rest of nature is vital to recreating a more ecologically conscious connection. Marx's materialism, based on sensuous interaction with the rest of nature, is vital to green awareness. Marx and Engels also made numerous statements on ecological issues; indeed, Engels was politicised partly as a result of concern over river pollution, while soil erosion and sewage were significant issues for both writers (Parsons 1977). Engels noted:

> Let us not, however, flatter ourselves overmuch on account of our human victories over nature. For each such victory nature takes its revenge on us. Each victory, it is true, in the first place brings about the results we expected, but in the second and third places it has quite different, unforeseen effects which only too often cancel the first. The people who, in Mesopotamia, Greece, Asia Minor and elsewhere, destroyed the forests to obtain cultivable land, never dreamed that by removing along with the forests the collecting centres and reservoirs of moisture they were laying the basis for the present forlorn state of those countries. When the Italians of the Alps used up the pine forests on the southern slopes, so carefully cherished on the northern slopes, they had no inkling that they were thereby depriving their mountain springs of water for the greater part of the year, and making possible for them to pour still more furious torrents on the plains during the rainy season ... Thus at every step we are reminded that we by no means rule over nature like a conqueror over a foreign people, like someone standing outside nature – but that we, with flesh, blood and brain, belong to nature, and exist in its midst, and that all our mastery of it consists in the fact that we have the advantage of all other creatures of being able to learn its laws and apply them correctly. (Quoted in Foster 2000: 235–6)

While there is a minority ecosocialist tradition and more recently mainstream Marxists from Castro onwards have been showing a green side, Kovel suggests that socialists need to catch up. He believes that socialism without ecological concern is no basis for a sane world, and that socialists need to take their founding concepts and apply them far more deeply.

Malthusianism as Murder

Ecosocialists certainly see a range of opinions with the green movement as regressive and damaging. As we have seen, green politics at its most radical can engage a very fundamental critique of economics. However, particularly as regards an ideology that is put into practice by politicians struggling to change the society we live in on a daily basis, according to ecosocialists other Greens step back or are even ignorant of their radicalism. Localism, support for small businesses and demands for a range of ecotaxes are the kind of policies that can be used to gather votes without alienating support. Demands for zero growth, opposition to the tyranny of the clock and fears that quantitative measurements are leading to an instrumental and arid way of living are not the stuff of local election leaflets. Equally green policies have often been subverted, for example, biofuels were a green idea that went wrong, leading to energy crops replacing food, inputs of polluting fertilizers and pesticides and land grabs by corporations. Climate change has been tackled by market-based instruments such as tradable quotas that, while green inspired, have enriched bankers but failed to halt emissions. Ecosocialists suggest that Greens need a harder edge, a strong awareness of the dangers of the market and the problems of cooption.

Environmental concerns with population growth inspired by the economics of Malthus are also strongly criticised by ecosocialists (Kovel 2002: 23; Foster 2002). Thomas Malthus, a nineteenth-century clergyman, argued that poverty could not be removed by social reform; the poor would always tend to use up their resources and remain in misery because of their fertility. Paradoxically, ecosocialists like many political Greens can be easily labelled as neo-Malthusian because they criticise growth. Malthus was stringently criticised by Marx for blaming poverty not on class injustice but upon the breeding habits of the poor. Neo-Malthusianism tends to suggest that natural resources are running out and ecosystems are being devastated because people (especially poor people) have too many babies. Human greed, rather than a system that nurtures over-consumption, is also blamed.

Ecosocialists point out that Malthus had nothing to say about ecology himself and that his ideas were used to force peasants from the land into workhouses. The notion of the tragedy of the commons, developed by Garrett Hardin, is a key neo-Malthusian notion used to justify enclosure. Hardin argued that overgrazing would occur if common land was not owned privately. Herders would graze as many animals as possible, even though they knew this would result in soil erosion and disaster, and a free-rider problem would prevent conservation. For example, if any one herder were to graze their cattle less, others would exploit their good will by putting more of their cattle on the common. The solution is to abolish all commons and turn them into private property, which will not be abused. Hardin's ecological solution is a clarion cry for the privatisation of the last bits of non-commodified land or heavy-handed state control.

Guha and Martinez-Alier, in arguing for the often mistakenly termed Malthusian demand to limit capitalist growth, believe that the commons rather than private property are likely to lead to conservation. This is because market-based decision makers tend to value short-term gain rather than thinking of longer-term needs. In reality, commons regimes have been managed locally by stints or systems of communally agreed use to prevent disaster. There are thousands of examples of well-maintained commons throughout history and around the world:

[In] Torbel in Switzerland, a village of some 600 people ... grazing lands, forests, 'waste' lands, irrigation systems and paths and roads connecting

privately and communally owned property are all managed as commons ...
Under a regulation which dates back to 1517, which applies to many other
Swiss mountain villages, no one can send more cows to the communal
grazing areas than they can feed during the winter, a rule that is still enforced
with a system of fines. (*Ecologist* 1992: 128)

The real tragedy of the commons has been the fact that communal resources have
been taken from local people to help create markets and accelerate neo-liberal
globalisation (Roberts 1979; *Ecologist* 1992). Elinor Ostrom, while not an
ecosocialist, won a Nobel Prize in economics for arguing that commoners could
find ways of protecting local commons and she was critical of Malthusian ideas
(Wall 2014). A review written with the late Walt Sheasby puts these struggles for
the commons in context:

Communes formed more or less briefly under the maverick Wyclifite John
Ball in Kent, England, in 1381–82; the Hussite Jan Zizka in Tabor, Bohemia,
in 1420–24; the Anabaptists Thomas Muenzer of Muelhausen, Thuringia,
in 1524–25, Jacob Hutter in Moravia in 1526–36, Bernard Rothmann in
Muenster in 1533–35; and the Quaker layman Gerard Winstanley of the
Diggers in Surrey, England, in 1649. A recurrent theme in various European
locales over hundreds of years was the attempt to reclaim the 'commons.'

The Taborite communism that sprang up briefly in Bohemia in the 1420s
proclaimed: 'As in the city of Tabor there is no "mine" and no "yours" but
all is in common, the like it shall be everywhere and nobody shall have a
special property, and those who have such property commits a mortal sin.'
The Hutterites likewise proclaimed, 'Private property is the enemy of love.'
John Ball supposedly preached that 'Things cannot go well in England, nor
ever will, until everything shall be in common.' (Sheasby and Wall 2002: 160)

Ecotopia

Kovel is fascinated by a variety of ecological ensembles. Each such ensemble
bring together human activities in interaction with the rest of nature. For Kovel,
these ensembles can be green or destructive, ranging from a community based
around nuclear power to permaculturalists. Ecology ensembles that create
environmental sustainability put use value before exchange value. As we have
noted, this is because exchange values demand continual economic growth,
which wrecks ecosystems. Ecosocialists argue that with 'usufruct', the principle
of using but not privately owning goods, we could all have access to far more
useful things without expanding production. To achieve ensembles that are

ecologically sustainable demands not only removing the market but engaging with psychological issues, as well as constructing new practices.

Kovel concludes that we need to create or re-create a sensual concern with our surroundings and our products. This radical materialism values what is physically present rather than viewing consumption, production and distribution as goals in themselves or ways of sublimating hidden or semi-hidden psychological needs. Kovel moves on to an implicit theological critique that argues that over centuries we have tended to ignore the real material world of living things.

Ecosocialism draws consciously or unconsciously upon Freud as well as Marx and the Greens. Norman O. Brown's book *Life Against Death* (1960) illustrates the theme that unconscious drives are sublimated into the desire for consumer items and economic power. Ecosocialists use Marx to show that capitalism, far from being rational and based on maximising human benefit, is a system of organised chaos. Kovel argues that the dynamics of a capitalist economy tend to encourage the growth of a specifically capitalist personality based on competitiveness, violence and greed:

> The domain of use-values will be the sight of contestation. To restore use-value means to take things concretely and sensuously, as befits an authentic relation of ownership – but by the same gesture, lightly, since things are enjoyed for themselves and not as buttresses for shaky egos. Under capital, as Marx famously saw, what is produced is fetishized by the shroud of exchange-value – made remote and magical. In the fetishized world, nothing is ever really owned, since everything can be exchanged, taken away and abstracted. This stimulates the thirst for possessions that rages under capitalist rule. The unappeasable craving for things – and money to get things – is the necessary underpinning of accumulation and the subjective dynamic of the ecological crisis. The circuits of capitalist society are defined by having – and excluding others from having – until we arrive at a society of gated communities inhabited by lonely egos, each split from all and the atomised selves split from nature. They can only be resolved in a society that permits this hunger to wither, and this requires the release of labour from the bondage imposed by exchange values. (Kovel 2002: 239–40)

Ecosocialism in the Twenty-first Century

Ecosocialist strategies are diverse. Guha and Martinez-Alier celebrate struggles to maintain and restore the commons, an approach largely shared with the subsistence ecofeminism of authors like Vandana Shiva, discussed in Chapter 9. Other ecosocialists have looked to the traditional working class. After all, toxic industrial processes most directly affect workers and there is a history of working-class resistance to ecologically destructive processes. Australian ecosocialists, for example, have been associated with the green ban movement, where workers in the construction industry refused to build projects that were environmentally damaging (Roberts 1979). Globalisation makes these struggles potentially more difficult, because firms can move to areas of the globe where resistance is weaker, playing communities off against one another. However, as the autonomists have noted, new technologies including social media have the potential to create powerful global solidarity.

Kovel argues for working-class action and the construction of ecosocialist parties, although in practice this mainly involves the difficult task of making Green parties greener. He suggests that prefigurative projects must also be constructed around forms of production based on use values to provide examples of a post-capitalist world. He cites Indymedia, the Internet-based alternative media network and other projects associated with anti-globalisation protest. Religious communities, such as the Hutterite Bruderhof who seem to exist outside of capitalist consciousness, also fascinate him.

Since the publication of Joel Kovel's *The Enemy of Nature* (2002) and Foster's *Marx's Ecology* (2000), there has been an explosion of ecosocialist activism, especially in Latin America among indigenous peoples and social movement. Perhaps the strongest and most militant ecosocialist political organisation is the Revolutionary Workers Party of Mindanao, former guerilla fighters who have established an ecosocialist economy and society on part of the island in the Philippines (Wall 2010). The Fourth International, headed by the economist Ernest Mandel until his death, has declared itself ecosocialist, rejecting economic growth and advocating workers' control for green production. Trade union campaigns such as the 'One Million Green Jobs' project in the UK have also been growing. And ecosocialists have gained influence in some Green Parties, particularly in the UK and the US.

Ecosocialism provides a critique of what is wrong with contemporary globalisation by bringing together both red and green insights. Kovel and other ecosocialists take from the most radical elements of both to show that not only is neo-liberal globalisation profoundly destructive, but that a deep critique of economics is needed if we are to heal the world. Nonetheless, while ecosocialism is necessary, it is not sufficient; to transcend capitalist globalisation, it is crucial to go further still. Another necessary element is the feminist challenge to capitalism, which is discussed in the next chapter.

9

WOMEN OF THE WORLD UNITE: FEMINIST ECONOMICS

Feminism does indeed have something to say about the objectivity of economics.
By adopting a cultural value system that puts undue emphasis on masculine-associated traits and experiences, a concern for objectivity has been allowed to degenerate into a rigid objectivism, and a concern for reliable explanation of human behaviour has been allowed to collapse into a dogmatic focus on constrained maximization. (Nelson 1996: 150, original emphasis)

Feminist economists have challenged the discipline of economics as sexist, while ecofeminists, Marxist feminists and other revolutionary or radical feminists have attacked capitalism as oppressive to women. However, there are a number of contradictions and problems in describing an anti-capitalist feminism. Like green politics or socialism, with which some feminisms overlap, feminism is a complex discourse. For example, many feminist economists broadly support a capitalist or market-based economy; nor does feminism neatly intersect with gender. One of the most important feminist economists is a man (Amartya Sen), while another is a transgender woman who was identified as male at birth (Deirdre McCloskey). Feminist thought is increasingly intersectional, rejecting one-dimensional approaches and demanding that trans inclusion, sexuality, class, ethnicity and ability/impairment are addressed. However, all feminist economists agree that while economics claims to be objective, it is not; that while it claims to be gender neutral, it has a male bias, and that economic systems, both market-based and non-market, tend to exploit women. Feminist economists are variously pro-capitalist, anti-capitalist and reformist. There is also the vexed dilemma of essentialism. Gender is not the same as sex, and confusing gender with a fixed identity risks re-importing sexism into feminist analysis. This chapter introduces feminisms, outlines Amartya Sen's important but reformist approach, examines the feminist critique of economics and explores the varied contributions of ecofeminists, Marxist feminists, autonomists and others. The contribution of Elinor Ostrom, in 2009 the first woman to win the Nobel Prize in economics, summarises some key elements of a feminist economics.

Feminist Revolutions

The feminist economist Deirdre McCloskey observed, 'Feminism,' says the bumper sticker on my old Buick, 'is the radical notion that women are people' (2000: 363). Feminisms are, however, varied. Literary theorists have identified distinct French, Anglo-American and English feminisms. Radical, liberal and revolutionary feminisms have been distinguished. Historical analysis has given us first, second and third wave feminisms. Anti-feminism has been seen as resting on advances made by feminists, P.J. Goodman writing in *Pirate Jenny* magazine observed:

> Let me have a moment here with those of you who have no idea the price your First and Second Wave Sisters paid so you could enjoy the benefits of saying you are not a feminist. Need I remind you that LESS THAN 40 years ago a women could not get a credit card unless her husband cosigned for it. It has been LESS THAN 30 years since women have been admitted to graduate programs ... sister, someone cleared that path for you and paid dearly for it ... Do the right thing at your next gig, your next gallery show, your next art house screening, your next rock opera premier, the birth of your baby, or at the b'ris of your son and raise your fist, your glass, or your voice to the women who cut a swathe through this jungle for us so we could saunter along in their clear path and dare to say we aren't feminists. (Quoted in Redfern and Aune 2013: xi)

Feminist economists are also very varied in their assumptions. Typically, Amartya Sen, a colleague of Elinor Ostrom, mixes a radical commitment to opposing inequality including gender inequality, environmental destruction and exclusion, with a basic belief in the market. A combination of market economics and feminist commitment has also been proposed by Deirdre McCloskey, who combines it with a fundamental critique of the methodology of economics (McCloskey 1998). Both market-based and anti-capitalist feminists share a scepticism of mainstream economic methodology.

Deirdre McCloskey and the Methodological Challenge to Economics

Feminist economists are united in challenging the basic assumptions and methods of economics. Marilyn Waring, a former New Zealand Nationalist MP, noted that domestic labour, such as housekeeping and caring for children and the sick and elderly, and traditionally carried out mainly by women, was not valued by economists. Economics does not value economic activity, however vital, that is not exchanged for money. Waring suggested that GDP and similar methods of measuring economic growth needed to be replaced with indicators that included domestic labour (1989). The academic journal *Feminist Economics* and various professional groups of feminist economists have noted that the assumptions made by economists about the nature of 'rational economic man [*sic*]' are sexist and unrealistic. Katrine Marçal (2015) noted that while the grandfather of economics Adam Smith argued that the butcher and baker were motivated by money, Adam lived with his mother in Edinburgh, who served him dinner every evening for love rather than cash gain. Julie Nelson, a professor of economics from California, has shown that economics is far less 'objective' than it purports to be:

> The feminist interpretation advanced in this book does not depend on a world view that sees current economic practitioners as individually malicious, or sees formalism as a source of pure evil. It does not argue for a feminine economics, or for a new economics to be practiced only by females. What it argues for is a change in the value system of economics, so that economics can become flexible, as well as hard, contextual as well as logical, human as well as scientific, and rich as well as precise. Such an economics would be more adequate for analysis of the economic behaviour of both women and men, and by both male and female practitioners. (Nelson 1996: 150)

Deirdre McCloskey is a leading exponent of such a methodological challenge. She argues that economists ignore social distinctions between different groups in society, and are too dependent on formal mathematical models. She also believes that gender influences economic decision making. A post-modern economist, she defines post-modernism as both anti-essentialist and interpretative. She does not believe that it is useful to apply one underlying, fixed definition to feminism, or to anything else that we seek to understand:

> People are always getting into quarrels about the Essential Meaning of X. Never mind that if 20th-century philosophy has taught us anything (there is some debate among critics of 20th-century philosophy) it is that meanings do not lie around like pebbles to be picked up but are social agreements, like definitions of the word 'hominid' or 'income'. Yet it is still the case that one of the most effective rhetorical devices is to define away your opponent with an Essential Meaning. You know the device. If someone defines what you do as 'not [Essentially] economics' then she doesn't have to listen to you. Or answer your objections. (McCloskey 2000: 363).

For McCloskey, meaning is relational and based on family resemblances. She notes that economists claim to be 'scientific', but in reality, science is less easily separated from literary approaches than is often understood. Metaphors abound, for example, physicists use metaphor, and indeed the concept of the atom is a metaphor. Economists use metaphors; for example, she notes, no one has seen a demand curve. The literary quality of intellectual activities does not indicate 'anything goes' relativism for McCloskey, but nor does she feel that they can be ignored. She believes that economists need to be sensitive when it comes to the words they use, and more self-aware about the limits of their understanding transmitted as it is in words whose meaning can be resistant to theory and transparency.

McCloskey might be seen at first sight as an economic radical, and in many ways she is. Her thoughtful work on the commons contrasts with that of many economists who reject the concept of common property as inevitably flawed (McCloskey 1991). She is a strong defender of radical figures such as US Army intelligence analyst and whistleblower Chelsea Manning, imprisoned for 35 years for releasing thousands of classified documents; however, she combines methodological boldness with support for market economics. She is a strong advocate of many features of mainstream economics, believes in the efficiency of markets, and defends capitalism as advancing the position of women. She draws upon Adam Smith, noting that he believed in both market mechanisms and moral sentiment, thus having room for both self-interest and love of others. Indeed, academic feminist economists are often strong advocates of the market; however, some feminists have combined revolutionary aspiration with their critique of economics.

Amartya Sen's Reformist Feminism

Born in India, Amartya Sen won the 1998 Nobel Prize in economics for challenging Kenneth Arrow's impossibility theorem. Arrow argued that any form of democracy was undemocratic in some sense; however the rules of a system were constructed, some individuals would inevitably be excluded. His abstract approach was used to justify a rejection of government action to deal with social welfare, because it was impossible to decide between different groups. Sen showed that while formally correct, the impossibility theorem did not remove the need for governments to tackle poverty.

Sen's work is sophisticated and varied – it would be difficult to summarize it even in a whole book, let alone a few paragraphs; his approach to gender, though, is clear. A reformist liberal, he argues that the market is economically vital, suggesting that opposition to market exchange is as realistic as opposition to conversation. Like Adam Smith, he believes that exchange is an essential characteristic of human beings. Sen's perhaps best-known book, *Development as Freedom*, argues that development is only possible if freedom grows (Sen 1999). He rejects the narrow pursuit of GDP economic growth, arguing that prosperity must involve all-round human flourishing. Drawing upon Aristotle, he argues that we must grow not only in the quantity of goods and services, but in our capabilities as individuals. He argues that, for markets to work, we must have access to them, thus land redistribution, good education and healthcare and effective, inclusive social policies are necessary. Uniquely, he champions market mechanisms, but notes that markets only work well in societies where all have access to the market. He is a strong advocate of environmental policies and redistribution. While far from being a critic of capitalism, he has argued that rapid economic growth, if it degrades the environment and increases inequality, is damaging.

Like other feminist economists, Sen argues that mainstream economics ignores gender, and argues for inclusive social policies so that women can gain autonomy. He suggests that both sexist cultural traditions and the specific traditional role of women in family units, where domestic labour has been undervalued, have led to immense suffering among women. Most shockingly, through infanticide and gender-selective abortion, there has been a war against the female sex. In his essay '100 Million Women are Missing', he argued that women were not only being excluded from social institutions and economic equality, but were being excluded from existence.

The Unhappy Marriage of Frederich Engels and Revolutionary Feminism

Marxist and socialist feminists might agree with the methodological critiques of thinkers like Nelson and McCloskey, however they also argue that capitalism oppresses women. Marxist feminism emanates from Frederich Engels's *The Origin of the Family, Private Property, and the State* written in 1884 (Engels 2010). Marx and Engels became increasingly interested in anthropology and were inspired by Lewis Morgan's book *Ancient Society*, first published in 1877. Morgan studied the Iroquois Confederacy, a group of six indigenous nations who lived in what in Morgan's time was northern and western New York State, and part of Quebec. The Iroquois were a communal, self-governing democracy, where women enjoyed much great power and status than was found amongst Europeans at that time. Engels believed that, in prehistory, matriarchal societies were universal, with women enjoying equal status with men and being politically powerful. Such societies rejected the nuclear family and private property. What Engels classed as a world historic defeat for womenkind involved the emergence of private property, monogamous relationships, the nuclear family and the oppression of women. In prehistoric communist societies, women were free. According to Engels, the oppression of women was necessary for private-property ownership, with male heirs inheriting property and accumulation occurring. In a future communist society, women would once again be free.

Engels and succeeding Marxists argued that property rights were at the heart of women's oppression, and that women's liberation required a revolution to create communism. Engels was sincerely concerned with feminist goals, but he and other Marxists have been seen as oversimplifying the oppression of women. Marxist feminists such as Selma James, who in her book *Marx and Feminism* (1980) advocates wages for housework, have stressed that capitalist production requires the reproduction of workers, hence domestic labour undertaken by women is functional to capitalism. Other feminists have argued variously that capitalism has increasingly integrated women into paid employment, freeing them from patriarchy and unpaid labour, at least partially. Liberal feminists argue that better pay and conditions for women workers, rather than revolution, is the path to liberation. Marxist approaches may ignore the independently gendered role of oppression by centring on class struggle, the abolition of private property and the creation of communism (Sargent 1986). Ecofeminists have argued that both patriarchy and capitalism must be challenged if women are to be liberated, arguing that, even if capitalism was abolished, men might continue to benefit from the oppression of women.

Ecofeminism

Ecosocialist feminists argue that the material circumstances of women's existence from giving birth to largely sustaining economic activity via care and subsistence activities mean that women carry the burden of ecological crisis and enclosure (Mellor 1992, 1997).

Ecofeminists have developed a fundamental critique of economics in general, and globalisation in particular. Vandana Shiva, the Indian physicist, is very much at the forefront of the anti-globalisation movement. Her subsistence perspective turns economic wisdom on its head, not merely criticising economic growth, but arguing that growth fuels poverty. Where Soros, Stiglitz and the NGOs call for reform to achieve speedier development, she and her colleagues see the development process as one of enclosure. Economic 'development' occurs when ordinary people are forced from the land and made to take part in market economic activity. They lose their freedom and health, and their standard of living falls as they are denied access to economic resources, such as common land used for grazing animals. Forests that produce fuel, food and medicine are enclosed, literally and legally. As private property, they can be used to grow crops for export; which can be measured in monetary terms and lead to economic growth, despite rising real poverty (Shiva 2000).

Gross national product fails to measure what is economically important. From the subsistence perspective, what matters is the domestic work of women, which, like the backs of elephants in certain cosmologies, support the weight of the universe. The bulk of important work, such as gathering firewood, growing crops, herding animals, cooking meals, repairing and caring, has been completed in most societies in most parts of the world for most of human history by women. The male, who makes politics, drinks and gambles, has long been redundant in the world of subsistence.

Shiva criticises the predominantly male economic community for having no insight into real economic activity. She sees globalisation as a means of waging war on the poor by driving peasants from the land. The political economy espoused by Shiva echoes the complaints of the Zapatistas who, as we noted in Chapter 1, launched a revolution because they feared the effects of the North America Free Trade Agreement. Peasant opposition to globalisation is both more radical and more conservative than other strains of anti-capitalism. These are people who quite like mobile phones and the Internet but are very keen to be left alone to live in an informal village economy. They believe in a revolution that rejects almost all aspects of economics, practical and conceptual, so they can live in conditions that are often seen as 'primitive'.

GM crops and other high-tech solutions to the problem of hunger are a particular source of anger to peasant farmers. Numerous studies have suggested not that there is an absolute shortage of food in the world but that distribution is a problem. Free trade is one means of making life difficult for peasant farmers, because their crops may be more expensive than the products of large-scale agribusiness. They cannot sell their surpluses and find it more difficult to maintain independence. Agribusiness and big landowners gain most from new technologies and can out-compete peasant farmers. Modern agriculture demands neat rows of single crops for the export-led growth advocated by globalists. But monoculture farming is more vulnerable to pests and diseases, thus requiring ever increasing use of pesticides. Monoculture also results in declining soil fertility, so the need for more fertilizers. It prevents the growth of local crops for local use. The alternative to this type of farming is multicropping, that is, garden-style diversity producing the foods, medicines, building materials, fuel and many other 'products' needed by ordinary people. Shiva observed during her 2000 BBC Reith lecture on globalisation:

> Research done by FAO has shown that small biodiverse farms can produce thousands of times more food than large, industrial monocultures. And diversity in addition to giving more food is the best strategy for preventing drought and desertification.
>
> What the world needs to feed a growing population sustainably is biodiversity intensification, not the chemical intensification or the intensification of genetic engineering. While women and small peasants feed the world through biodiversity we are repeatedly told that without genetic engineering and globalization of agriculture the world will starve. In spite of all empirical evidence showing that genetic engineering does not produce

more food and in fact often leads to a yield decline, it is constantly promoted as the only alternative available for feeding the hungry.

(news.bbc.co.uk/hi/english/static/events/reith_2000/lecture5)

The examples Shiva gives can be multiplied. For example, Bettina Maag illustrates how the Tamang of Central Nepal have a tree-based commons economy:

> A Tamang, when asked about the use of the forest, will immediately answer 'the forest gives us timber, fuel wood and fodder.' Indeed, a wide spectrum of tree species found in the Tamang region is used to satisfy various local needs. Almost every species is in some way incorporated in the farming system. (Maag 1997: 114)

Subsistence ecofeminists can give an almost infinite number of examples of networks of women peasant producers actively resisting the march of modern economics. In Germany, they point to self-help socialist cooperatives that grow food. In Japan, there are the Yabo farmers, who live in cities and often work in high-tech sectors like IT, and many of whom are single parents. The Yabo farmers compost kitchen waste, cooperate to grow food in urban areas such as Tokyo, and share their crops. They grow up to 100 per cent of the vegetables and 70 per cent of the rice they need (Bennholdt-Thomsen and Mies 1999: 137). Shiva claims that:

> Indian women have been in the forefront of ecological struggles to conserve forest, land and water. They have challenged the western concept of nature as an object of exploitation and have protected her as Prakriti, the living force that supports life. They have challenged the western concept of economics. (Quoted in Dobson 1991: 50)

Subsistence ecofeminists argue that neo-liberal globalisation leads to poverty, trade leads to reduced choice and growth results in eco-catastrophe. Shiva notes:

> So no matter where you look, the World Bank is basically taking away the resources of the people, putting it in the hands of global capital, destroying the livelihoods of people in the name of efficiency and forcing destitution on millions and billions of people. Its policies are nothing short of genocide.
>
> Of course the World Bank and the IMF officials visit the Third World, but they do not know the realities because all they look at is the returns on investment calculations that they have already made in Washington before they made their trips.
>
> (Interview in Indymedia, archives.lists.indymedia.org/imc-houston/2001-January/000353)

Many feminist ecosocialists are wary of the essentialist claims of subsistence ecofeminists, suspicious of statements that women are essentially greener than men and critical of the peasant path to utopia. However, neither differences over the epistemological status of gender nor geographical separation should prevent global ecofeminists' solidarity and ecosocialist networks from actively resisting neo-liberalism. Calling for a revolutionary ecology movement, Carolyn Merchant notes:

> A socialist ecofeminists movement in the developed world can work in solidarity with women's movements to save the environment ... It can support scientifically-based ecological actions that also promote social justice. Like cultural ecofeminism, socialist ecofeminism protests chemical assaults on women's reproductive health, puts them in the border context of the relations between reproduction and production. It can thus support point of production actions such as the Chipko and Greenbelt movements in the Third World, protests by Native American women over cancer-causing radioactive uranium mining on reservations, and protest by working class women over toxic dumps in urban neighbourhoods. (Merchant 1992: 200)

The Indian novelist Arundhati Roy has shown how the construction of huge dams like that in Narmada displace millions of people from villages which are subsequently flooded. The dams also prevent fertile mud from being deposited on riverbanks which have been farmed for thousands of years, causing further displacement, further poverty and major environmental problems (Roy 1999, 2002). The lowest-caste dalits suffer while the huge energy corporations profit (Roy 2001). Roy's book *Capitalism: A Ghost Story* suggests that while GNP in India has increased, this has led to worse suffering for indigenous and lower-caste Indians (Roy 2014).

Autonomist Feminism and Zerowork

Much discussion from feminist economists has focused on the role of work and in particular domestic labour. Marxist feminists have noted that women's often unpaid labour is necessary for social reproduction, and while not measured in the production process, is essential to it. Thus, as we noted, the Wages for Housework campaign was created, so as to reward women for their labour. Other feminists, from Marxists to market-based, have seen formal paid employment as a path to liberation. Indeed, with globalisation, more and more women are working in paid employment; however, women are still paid less on average for the same work, recession has impacted more heavily on women, and women often work in the formal sector and then return home to complete their domestic labours.

Kathi Weeks has argued that traditional Marxists, and even many feminists, wrongly value work. She argues that work is far from necessary. Work is valued morally and absence of work is seen as damaging. She notes that, in fact, capitalists value work, but that we should not. Rather than being paid for domestic labour, we should reject work altogether. Work cannot be abolished, but it should not be seen as a social goal: technological advance allows us to reduce the work we do. She hints that Marx's son-in-law Paul Lafargue was a better communist than Karl because he wrote *The Right to be Lazy* (Lafargue 2011).

The painter Sunny Taylor argues that disability occurs not because of impairment, but because of social opposition to those who do not 'work'. Powerfully supporting such zero-work feminism, she adds another dimension to intersectionality:

> I have a confession to make: I do not work ... I am a drain on our country's welfare system. I have another confession to make: I do not think this is wrong, and to be honest, I am very happy not working. Instead I spend the majority of my time doing the activity I find the most rewarding and valuable, painting ... [what] people ask me when I say I am a painter is 'Do you sell your work?' ... I hate this question and I feel ashamed no matter how I answer it. This is because I always feel like this question is a test; a test to see whether my lifestyle and hobby are legitimate; and money is the gauge of this legitimacy. Is money really where all value lies? Are my art and my lifestyle really less meaningful because I do not support myself financially?
>
> Due to my disability (arthrogryposis multiplex congenita), I paint holding the paintbrush in my mouth instead of my hands; I use an electric wheelchair for mobility. When I first realized that due to my impairment I might be unable to work in a traditional job, I was worried about my financial future, but it never occurred to me to worry about my life's value as a 'nonproductive' citizen. However, I think that I am unusually fortunate to have been raised with a belief in my own inherent value, because many disabled people seem to carry a deep 'non-working guilt,' even if they are successful in other areas.
>
> (http://monthlyreview.org/2004/03/01/the-right-not-to-work-power-and-disability/)

Autonomist Marxists argue that work is like imprisonment, that the factory is a prison, and increasing value is produced, as we noted in the work of Negri and Hardt, in a social factory. With the arrival of the World Wide Web and three-dimensional printers, Weeks (2011) argues that work can be reduced and gender-specific roles can be largely removed. Rather than a wage for housework, she argues for a basic income to be paid to all, freeing us all to choose how we work and reward us for socially produced use value in society. Weeks defines capitalism by the existence of work, others argue that if property is owned communally, a post-capitalist society can be achieved. Perhaps the most important theorist of common pool property is Elinor Ostrom, whose insights may contribute to a feminist economics.

The Ostrom Alternative

Elinor Ostrom, who worked closely with her partner, the political scientist Vincent Ostrom, brings much to the debate about an anti-capitalist and feminist economic alternatives. She was very much a champion for what we might now call 'intersectionality'. She did not seek to explain inequality in terms of one dimension, but worked practically for women, minorities and others excluded from participation.

Ostrom faced prejudice in her early years. Her mother was Protestant, her father Jewish. She was brought up as a Protestant, yet she remembers children shouting 'Jew' at her in the Sunday school playground:

'I got circled in the schoolroom, out on the playground.'
"'You Jew! You Jew!'" she recalled, her voice rising, imitating the taunts. 'Having that experience as a kid and being a woman, and having that challenge as it has been at different times to be a woman, I've got pretty good sympathy for people who are not necessarily at the center of civic appreciation.' (Leonard 2009)

Interviewed shortly before her untimely death in 2012 by *Feminist Economics*, she noted the challenges she and other women faced in trying to build academic careers:

I do know a bit about the career of one other woman graduate student who was in my entry class. She did become so depressed over academic problems that she took a draft of her dissertation and burned it and moved out of academia entirely. (May and Summerfield 2012: 28)

She and Vincent stressed that economics moved beyond the market and the state. Her detailed work on the management of common pool resources such as fisheries and forests won her a Nobel Prize in economics. She argued that there were no panaceas, rejecting the idea that commons always worked and that non-state/non-market alternatives were always best. She was also methodologically sophisticated: echoing the critique that mainstream economics is crude, she worked hard to create more inclusive and rigorous research methods to discover how economic systems worked in reality as well as in theory. She and Vincent saw economics as about 'provisioning' or 'sustaining'. While neither of them were anti-capitalists and in many respects were critical of the left, especially of a left that trusts the state, alternatives to both market and state were a living practical reality for the Ostroms. In the concluding chapter I will examine how we can promote alternatives to capitalism that are democratic, just, efficient, work practically to produce and distribute goods and services, and are above all, ecologically sustainable. Elinor's work is a good starting point for doing so.

10

LIFE AFTER CAPITALISM: ALTERNATIVES, STRUCTURES, STRATEGIES

BLOOM: I stand for the reform of municipal morals and the plain ten commandments. New worlds for old. Union of all, jew, moslem and gentile. Three acres and a cow for all children of nature. Saloon motor hearses. Compulsory manual labour for all. All parks open to the public day and night. Electric dishscrubbers. Tuberculosis, lunacy, war and mendicancy must now cease. General amnesty, weekly carnival with masked licence, bonuses for all, esperanto the universal language with universal brotherhood. No more patriotism of barspongers and dropsical impostors. Free money, free rent, free love and a free lay church in a free lay state. (Joyce 2000: 610)

Would you like some comforting lies? I could tell you that capitalism has made nearly all of us richer, can solve environmental problems and overcome financial crisis. Or I could suggest that better government regulation would make markets work efficiently. I might indicate that promoting local currencies or introducing taxes on land, as Henry George suggested, would be sufficient to solve our problems. I am not going to express any of these thoughts. Capitalism has promoted economic expansion, but it is an ecologically unsustainable system. We cannot consume, produce and throw away at ever faster rates without catastrophe. Capitalism, as even its strongest supporters admit when pressed, promotes inequality and is fundamentally unstable. Rather mild reformists like Keynes and his followers, including Stiglitz and Soros, show that by promoting speculation, the spread of market forces promotes volatility. Defenders of the market who call for a smaller state to make the market pure, can make some interesting points. State power often promotes monopoly, concentrates wealth and power, drives war and, via protection for banks which are 'too big to fail', fuels financial catastrophe. Moral hazard is product of state action. The market versus state opposition is a false one. Violence from the state, as Marx noted, is needed to promote the primitive accumulation necessary for the market. Markets rely on property rights, which in turn, along with other institutions, are created by the state. Nation states and markets work together. It is thus wrong to say that when markets fail we should call in the state – often the state makes things worse. Nation states are not a magic solution. Like markets, they tend to work for the rich and the powerful, despite being wrapped in an ideology of good intentions.

Capitalism is cancerous, and there are fundamental reasons why we must oppose it. Human life should not be about promoting some kind of extra-human process. Economics should be a means, not an end. In capitalism, everything revolves around accumulating more and more cash. Music, football, cooking, wedding ceremonies – all become about the accumulation of cash in the market. All intrinsic and diverse human desires are simplified into collecting more exchange value. Marx studied capitalism in such obsessive detail because he felt that, fundamentally, it put a blind process in charge and made actual humans, even the rich and especially capitalists, into capitalism's tools. Likewise, if we construct a state and tell it to take charge, we remain like infants, controlled by abstract parents who care little for our needs. Institutions like the National Health Service have provided good, state-constructed, alternatives, but these need more room for popular involvement. Likewise attempts to reduce the welfare state via austerity have nothing to do with community provision; they have been introduced instead to provide tax cuts for an elite. Nonetheless, less capitalism does not simply mean more state!

To prosper, we need diverse ecologically sustainable systems, but capitalism in its drive for profit simplifies while it commodifies. The advance of capitalism is the destruction of diversity and threatens our basic life support systems on this planet. The need to make short-term profit is the entire goal of a system that has grown out of human action to dominate life on earth.

Providing alternatives to capitalism, especially if we reject technofixes and are sceptical of markets and states in general, is hard. However, it is necessary. Capitalism is not money in your bank account, but instead a gun held to your head – so this chapter is about disarmament. What are the alternatives and what are the strategies? How do we build and change, not just by slogans or outrage, but via practical political work, to construct an economy that does not threaten life, and does not put human desires second to a system of accumulation. Unsurprisingly, I am going to be name-checking Elinor Ostrom and Karl Marx rather a lot in this concluding chapter.

Marx, Ostrom and the Commons

Marx was a fiery revolutionary, buried in his books, who studied capitalism and advocated communism. Elinor Ostrom was, in contrast, a mild-mannered, grandmotherly woman, who came from a liberal tradition based on thinkers such as de Tocqueville and James Buchanan. She believed in a mixed economy and was sceptical of the state. I suspect there are very few people who study both Ostrom and Marx. In many ways they seem divergent thinkers; however, their ideas are often similar. They both believed in promoting self-governing societies, in which people make the rules and power is democratically shared. They were also passionately concerned about ecology. Marx was not a statist, despite this being a value often associated with socialism and communism. Ostrom and Marx believed not only that economic activity extended beyond states and markets, but also studied this in some detail. There are ways of embedding markets to make them more democratic and ecological. States can also be made more democratic. From farmers' markets, to trade unions to participatory budgets and fair trade, there are ways of making markets and states work less badly. Yet while it is impossible to wave a magic wand and abolish states and markets, there are alternatives that go beyond them. Marx wished to see a 'free association of labour', where people cooperate to produce what they want. Ostrom and her husband, and their network of associates, promoted self-government and democratic ownership. Ostrom was not fundamentally against either the state or the market but she was aware of alternatives. Economics to her was never about commodities alone, that is, goods and services produced to be exchanged, but was instead about sustaining or provisioning. This is a useful perspective. We need money to buy goods and services, and we need goods and services to sustain us. Economics should be about sustaining, meeting diverse human needs and wants, but in the twenty-first century it is no longer even about the goods and services that sustain us, it is about abstracts such as GNP and the accumulation of money.

Both Marx and Ostrom thought beyond the commodity. This is rare, even on the left, and very important. Ecosocialists like Kovel argue, as I have noted, that we can focus on use rather than exchange. This bridges the gap between unsustainable growth and ecological catastrophe. Once we reject accumulation as the goal of society, we can make goods to last longer, make them easier to repair, and build a social, sharing economy, where we can have more access to what we need with less resource use. If the convincing and sophisticated advocates of capitalism like Deirdre McCloskey think an economy based on rent can provide an alternative, their case would be worth hearing! An ecological economy is about promoting common property, so that we share our way to sustainability. This does not mean the disappearance of personal property, but it does mean sharing more, to sustain us with less effort, alienation and ecological damage.

Both Marx and Ostrom were hostile to utopias and panaceas. Marx lost patience with the socialist tailor Wilhelm Weitling, when Wilhelm and his comrades started discussing what kind of cutlery would exist in a communist society (Wheen 2000: 100). The idea that we can, or should, come up with a plan for everything, or a general blueprint for society, struck both Ostrom and Marx as ridiculous. Ostrom felt that distant planners would always make mistakes. Both thinkers believed that it is for people to democratically debate what they want, rather than for experts or prophets to construct a future for others. Likewise economic/social systems don't evolve according to a set plan; no one designed feudalism, for example.

However, the notion of commons was important to Marx and Ostrom. The nuances of Ostrom's approach – she focused, for example, on common pool resources rather than common pool property – are discussed, at length, in another of my books (Wall 2014). A good starting point for a practical anti-capitalism is to promote the commons.

Ostrom was interested in practical change rather than broad slogans, and tried to understand how people made things work. She studied hundreds of actual commons to find out why some were successful and why others failed; as a result, she came up with some design rules, although she stressed that these were general guidelines and subject to change (Ostrom 1991). Marx was greatly inspired by the Paris Commune and seemed to believe that communism was literally the commons. He and Engels noted that in the past, and amongst indigenous people, commons worked well. In the future, the communist commons would allow large-scale human cooperation and international economic activity to be used for the common good. This is, of course, extremely challenging, and generally Marxist-inspired social transformation has instead reproduced the state rather than commons.

Ostrom believed in a diverse economy. Both ecological and social/economic diversity were important to her. She believed in experimentation, pluralism and social learning. She felt that monocultures are dangerous and her favourite anti-slogan was 'No panaceas!' So for her, a mixture of common property, state intervention and markets provided the potential for greater diversity, democracy and ecological sustainability. The problem with this is that markets may evolve into monocultures and money tends to drive out non-commodified activity.

Though obviously my survey is very simplified, I think that both Marx and Ostrom grappled with the problems of human freedom, collectivism vs individualism, ecological sustainability and economic systems that work. They did so, despite their many differences, in a rather more sophisticated way than many other thinkers. To repeat, both were relaxed about the existence of non-market, non-state economic activity, and this is pretty radical. Most thinkers argue that if we brought in a technofix or a small reform, basically the system would work, with a combination of market and state, rather than including non-market and non-state institutions. However, both Marx's broad approach (commons at a macro level) and Ostrom's approach of a mixed economy of commons, market and state, can be challenged. I do think that trying to deepen our understanding of their work, and taking both Marx's and

Ostrom's work seriously, is productive for thinking about a post-capitalist world. The concept of the commons should be explored in detail by all who advocate an alternative to capitalism.

Defend, Extend and Deepen the Commons

While state provision can be humanised and markets tamed by the social, the more fundamental task requires that both the state and the market are rolled back. The commons provides an important alternative to both. The anti-capitalist slogan above all others should be 'Defend, extend, and deepen the commons.'

Throughout history, the commons has been the dominant form of regulation, providing an alternative almost universally ignored by economists, who are reluctant to admit that substitutes to the market and the state even exist. Within the commons, scarcity, if it exists, is usually managed and resources conserved through allocation systems arranged by users.

The commons works best by consensus and, unlike capitalism, does not depend upon constant growth. It provides shared access to important resources so that human needs can be met with potential equity. Anti-capitalist globalisation could be labelled positively as the movement for the commons. Where anti-capitalists lose, the neo-liberals will constantly advance. Their demands are unlimited because capitalism, to survive, needs constant commodification. Capitalism seeks to extend commodification; the anti-capitalist movement resists by conserving the commons. For example, in South America and South Africa, grass-roots protest seeks to prevent water being privatised. In cyberspace, downloaders, hackers and open source designers seek to maintain free access. Greens and subsistence ecofeminists preserve communal land from private corporations.

Some commons demand little or no regulation, merely preservation from such corporate assaults. However, there are numerous well-documented accounts of commons regimes where regulation occurs through local bargaining and shared use. In Canada, the Ojibway Nation of Ontario still harvests wild rice from Wabigoon Lake using commons principles (*Ecologist* 1992: 127).

Commons are surprisingly common, around 90 per cent of inshore fisheries are regulated by commons. Depletion is a product of high-tech hoovering by unregulated Japanese and European fleets keen to increase profit, rather than of more local abuse (*Ecologist* 1992: 127). In Maine, lobster fisheries have long been preserved by the commons; in Finland, many forests are communally regulated, and in Switzerland, grazing is often controlled by commoners to prevent 'tragedy' through overexploitation:

The importance of the commons is noted, as we have seen, by Greens, autonomists, anarchists and many Marxists from Marx onwards, and Elinor

Ostrom. There is no space here to examine the encyclopaedic variety and success of commons regimes, but work by scholars such as Ostrom (1991) can provide the basis for deepening the commons. The best anarchist experiments, from the Spanish Civil War to contemporary squatting, are based on the re-invention of the commons. However, there has been a long war against the commons. The earliest poems depicting Robin Hood (long before the inclusion of Maid Marion and Friar Tuck), are about a yeoman resisting enclosure. Where I live in the Windsor Forest, the royal family privatised the land for hunting. E.P. Thompson in *Whigs and Hunters* recorded how 'the blacks' who darkened their faces before 'poaching' game and resisting the royals fought gun battles in Winkfield and Wokingham parishes (Thompson 1977). A few miles away at St George's Hill, the Diggers briefly established a communal farm in 1649 (Brockway 1980). Wherever you live, there will, if you dig deep enough, have been a struggle between commoners and the monopolising state or market for control. New commons regimes are created with technological and social change. The Internet has heralded the arrival of open source, a new form of commons regime in cyberspace. Software is designed and put on the web free of charge (Moody 2001: 3). The open source movement produces programmes, recipes, designs and other forms of information which are developed, passed around, adapted and used freely. There is no lone genius creating in isolation, huge projects can be undertaken and flexibility is key – Wikipedia is a great example.

Open source is an excellent example of how something that does not directly increase GNP can fuel real prosperity: for example, it provides citizens and governments in developing countries with free access to vital computer software. Open source is, of course, contested; it is part of a wider struggle between corporations and the rest of us for power over the Internet, as some wish to institutionalise and commercialise it. From music companies who prosecute free file users to hackers who assault Microsoft, cyberspace provides one front in an open, global struggle, one in which almost all of us can participate. Instruments such as copy left and 'creative commons' allow individuals to copy software, recipes, articles and much else for free, thus being released from the prison of individual ownership. Open source encourages users to add their own touches, focusing attention on the quality of the product. It is a stunning example of how both the market and the state can be bypassed by cooperative creativity. The barrier between user and provider is eroded; a direct agreement between society members is maintained.

Marx links the open source principle to socialism and use: we should take what we want, but nurture what we use for the benefit of the next generation:

From the standpoint of a higher economic form of society, private ownership of the globe by single individuals will appear quite absurd as private ownership of one man by another. Even a whole society, a nation, or even all simultaneously existing societies taken together, are not the owners of the globe. They are only its possessors, its usufructuries, and like *boni patres familias*, they must hand it down to succeeding generations in an improved condition. (Marx, quoted in Kovel 2002: 238)

In similar fashion, Ostrom advocated a 'seven-generation' rule, noting that all policies should be considered as to how they would affect people and the environment seven generations into the future (Wall 2014).

Alternatives

There have been a number of attempts to build anti-capitalist alternatives. These are flawed, but while remaining critical, we have to respect them for trying. Fierce criticism is often used, not to create better alternatives, but as a way of destroying any who dare to resist. Yet, of course, the lessons of the Soviet experience are sadly largely negative, decent housing and healthcare was combined with poor planning, political tyranny and the destruction of the environment, from nuclear disasters to the draining of the Aral Sea to grow cotton. Starting in Venezuela, the Latin American left have taken state power in a number of countries and renewed socialist hopes. Wounded by both a Stalinist model and a vicious US blockade, which only in 2015 looks likely to be lifted, Cuba has, despite its flaws, also contributed to a new anti-capitalist model. Cuba, Venezuela, Bolivia, Ecuador and other allied countries have pushed all of Latin America a little to the left, creating some interesting economic alternatives and promoting a model of anti-capitalism that reflects many of the essential priorities. We can't just wait for the whole world to become anti-capitalist, so it is important to defend those who try, even if it is close to impossible to build alternatives.

Attempts to build alternatives are encouraging, yet in a capitalist system they tend to get drawn into the system and destroyed. In a market economy, there is pressure to work harder and lower standards. Even without the pressures of the market, communal alternatives would be likely to fail. The question of social cooperation is important and again this is a good point at which to return to the work of Elinor Ostrom, who dealt primarily with the micro and the local, whereas Marx addressed the macro of whole systems. When we explore real alternatives to capitalism, we should keep Ostrom's and Marx's approaches in creative tension. Thus institutions in, say, Venezuela still exist in a larger capitalist reality, which distorts them – this is a basic insight we can derive from Marx's analysis. Ostrom suggests that at a micro level, whatever the wider system, things can go wrong and human cooperation often fails. When she looked at the commons, she did not embrace broad solutions or statements, but examined various case studies in great detail. She studied commons that had been maintained for, in some cases, over a thousand years. This longevity was itself an impressive achievement, because mainstream economics suggests that commons always tend to collapse. Even more importantly, she looked at commons that failed. Backed up with a range of sophisticated techniques in social science, she developed some basic ideas, at a micro level, of what made commons work, why they failed and how human cooperation could be promoted. Whether examining the experience of the British National Health Service, cooperatives in Cuba, or German co-housing, Ostrom's broad approach, institutional analysis and development framework can be applied to communal institutions to seek how they might be made more resilient. Her methodology provides a pragmatic way of examining how democratic institutions and ownership might work.

Because I am sceptical that we can simply call in the state or revert to a central plan, practical policies beyond defending and extending the commons may seem distant. Without embracing utopianism, designing a blueprint, or rejecting the need for a different system, a number of additional practical examples of anti-capitalist economic instruments and proposals can be cited. From community-owned football teams to collective three-dimensional printing labs, common ownership can be extended. The right of workers to buy up the firms for which they work might be one line of change. Community renewable energy in Scotland is an example of ecological anti-capitalism in practice. The Swedish Meidner plan, where trade unionists and local communities were given shares in corporations, worked so well that when a right-wing party came to power in 1992, it was swiftly abolished:

> Rudolf Meidner's share levy, unlike so many modern taxes, was extraordinarily difficult to evade ... According to the original plan every company with more than fifty employees was obliged to issue new shares every year equivalent to 20 per cent of its profits. The newly issued shares – which could not be sold – were to be given to the network of 'wage earner funds', representing workplaces and local authorities. The latter would hold the shares, and reinvest the income they yielded from dividends, in order to finance future social expenditure. As the wage earner funds grew they would be able to play an increasing part in directing policy in the corporations which they owned.

(http://www.counterpunch.org/2005/12/22/a-visonary-pragmatist)

Green strikes and workers' plans to transform production in socially and ecologically useful directions deserve exploring too. From a basic income scheme to wealth taxes, a less corporate and unequal society can be built.

In 2014, the Green Party leader Natalie Bennett hit the headlines in the UK with her plans for a wealth tax to shift resources from the 0.1 per cent (www. theguardian.com/politics/2014/jul/24/green-party-calls-wealth-tax-assets-multimillionaires). A modest 2 per cent tax on the wealth of those with assets worth £3 million or more would, it has been claimed, raise £4 billion, which could be redistributed or invested in services. This is a starting point but no more; in a post-capitalist economy, there would be no millionaires. Equally, the market socialism based on such practical policies as described by David Schweickart in his book *After Capitalism* (2011), while often impressive, does not advocate a society which is commons-based and decommodified. Nonetheless, such measures can help by making space, inspiring imagination, and promoting a transition to a different kind of economy.

Positive state solutions, from health services to social housing and public transport, should be defended against the onslaught of the market the world over. Public services are the result of a long history of popular struggles and indicate a social recognition of the need to meet essential needs outside of the market, whether individuals can pay or not. However, the top-down nature of much state provision demands localisation and democratisation. Hilary Wainwright argues that innovative participatory mechanisms can be used to embed the state in society, reclaiming decision making for ordinary people. Strong extra-state institutions can also make successful state resistance to neo-liberalism easier. She cites the citizens' budgets introduced by the Brazilian Workers Party as one example of such a mechanism, noting 'participatory decision making has turned out to be a more socially efficient way of running things, delivering, by all accounts, a better city in which to live' (Wainwright 2003: 68).

Markets can be embedded in society. A strong example comes from Stan Thekaekara, who worked with Indian *adivasis*, 'first inhabitants', a marginalised group kicked off their land by higher caste groups. Once they had reclaimed their land, they grew tea and sold it directly to fair trade outlets in India and the UK. Face-to-face contact was made with working-class communities in Easterhouse, Glasgow who were sold ethical and cheap tea. Social preference rather than profit maximisation socialised economic activity (Thekaekara 2003: 9). Granted, we can't shop our way to utopia, and within capitalism, cooperation is so often distorted, but such projects have value in pointing us to a different world, a world that works for all, not just a minority.

The Mirror Stage

In a capitalist system, all alternatives tend to get corrupted, destroyed, or used to strengthen the system. Jodi Dean has written persuasively about how the extension of commons-based social media can be used to strengthen markets and hierarchy (Dean 2012). While Wikipedia has grown dramatically and continues to be free and open, in contrast, new social media platforms such as Google, Facebook and Twitter have become corporate instruments and have been used to spy on us, as whistleblower Edward Snowden revealed when in 2013 he released thousands of classified documents from the US National Security Agency (NSA). Cementing the worst of state and corporate control, commons too can be corrupted. Commons in history have also been associated with feudalism and supported elite users. Today, so-called 'platform capitalism' selectively frees and encloses: workers are deskilled and thrown out of work, as information technologies allow labour to be made voluntary, while licences for the technology apps to make this possible create new billionaires. Academics write journal articles without being paid (commons) and these articles are then placed behind pay walls (enclosure). Taxi drivers are driven out of work by the online Uber taxi-booking service, while Uber's CEO Travis Kalanick stood at 290 in Forbes's '400 Richest Americans' list, with an estimated fortune of $3 billion in 2014 (http://www.forbes.com/sites/forbespr/2014/09/29/forbes-announces-its-33rd-annual-forbes-400-ranking-of-the-richest-americans/). Given that even commons can be used to make many of us poorer and the 0.00001% obscenely rich, how do we advance? As noted earlier, nobody designed feudalism. Changes in institutions, and sets of rules, especially around property rights, can be understood as the DNA of social systems. The advocates of capitalism are flexible, they react to changing circumstances and keep revolutionizing what they do. The 2008–09 financial crisis can be seen as a failure of capitalism, inequality led to falling incomes for many, increasing credit allowed consumption to continue. This, combined with ever more complex financial instruments, led to disaster. It destroyed the intellectual credibility of neo-liberalism. The neo-liberals picked themselves up, dusted themselves down and used the resulting debt as a means of promoting even more privatisation, deregulation and capitalist expansion. They, of course, are tremendously well resourced. Economics preaches more growth, more profit, more commodities and more disaster. The mass media, funded by advertising, is pro-capital. Political parties are dominated by the right. Politicians who understand economics beyond the market and the state are rare, even on the far left.

The neo-liberals work to extend the rule of capital. For example, as I write, new trade and investment treaties, such as the Transatlantic Trade and Investment Partnership (TTIP) that allows corporations to sue states that damage their profits, are being rolled out across the globe. While our resources are fewer, we anti-capitalists have to keep working for new institutional rules that promote commons and democratic ownership of the means of production. We need to look constantly at how changing circumstances provide new opportunities. We must work tirelessly to protest and promote institutional alternatives. Opposition to corporate monopolies is popular, and increasing economic democracy is attractive. It is hard but we can work in practical ways for alternatives. Successful alternatives provide resources that can be used to promote further change.

We must have tenacity, flexibility, and persistently keep burrowing away. This is the mirror stage: the neo-liberals have these qualities and in this regard we need to reflect their behaviour. This precludes two failed alternative strategies. One is to say that we have a basically fair, but flawed system. With this sentiment, one regards corporations as an outrage to the competitive market and calls for reform. Or, as we have seen, perhaps the debt-based money system is the root of an evil and can be uprooted with community currencies. None of this works because we have a system, with a dynamic, that is a complex whole that needs replacing with something else. From exclusively private property to ideas of 'rational economic [sic] man', the system demands transforming.

The second failed alternative is to say no change is possible until everything changes. This is the ideology of the dogmatist, an imaginary solution to a real problem. Yes, all alternatives tend to be corrupted in the force field of capital, but if we don't start somewhere, we are unlikely to arrive in the different place we desire. We need to keep digging away, building and changing; revolution is necessary and by revolution I mean a basic and essential change in the structures of our society. However, revolution does not happen in one go – it is a process. One builds towards it, and if it contains an event, that event must be proceeded by continual transformation. It is not enough to say a discrete reform can cleanse a system that does not work, or to say 'let's do nothing until the glorious day.' We have to get to work now.

This highlights the significance of class, and other structural inequalities. Social classes are difficult to describe with precision, and social class does not capture all sources of injustice, power and potential for change at an aggregate level. An intersectional approach is needed. However, the rich and the powerful act together, on the whole, to preserve privilege. Anti-capitalism requires broad democratic ownership, capitalism concentrates ownership and therefore power in the hands of an ever smaller minority. The dominant class or classes wage class warfare against the rest of us. The recent lessons of austerity show this most clearly. This is not a book about class, but events do occur in a class context. The rich seek to preserve their gains and keep the rest of us distracted with bread and circuses to let them get on with it.

The political struggles to win power to create change and take on the powerful need to be discussed in detail. From class composition to political parties, there are many questions that need researching. The question of ideology, our imagined relationship to real world conditions, is also vitally important to discuss. There are many more books to write, but material political practice is of greater necessity. Let's continue the intellectual task of understanding capitalism and alternatives to capitalism in necessary detail. Let's challenge the 0.001%, who currently run the world, and let's grow a new system. The future of capitalism is inequality, instability, ecocide and, even where it seems to work, it's a system, invented by humans, that uses (and abuses) us as tools. We can do better. A democratic and ecologically sustainable future is necessary and possible, but we will have to fight for it. Let's build it now.

BIBLIOGRAPHY

ACME (1999) *Against Capital and the State*. Seattle: ACME Collective.

Albert, M. (2004) *Parecon. Life After Capitalism*. London: Verso.

Albritton, R. (1999) *Dialectics and Deconstruction in Political Economy*. London: Palgrave.

Anon. (1998) Behind the Balaclavas: Breaking Bread with the Zapatistas., *Do or Die!*, 5: 110–17.

—— (1999a) Friday June 18th 1999 Confronting Capital and Smashing the State, *Do or Die!*, 8: 1–12.

—— (1999b) Globalisation: Origins-History-Resistance, *Do or Die!*, 8: 35–55.

—— (2000) Resisting the WTO, *Do or Die!*, 7: 111–39.

—— (ed.) (2001a) *On Fire: The Battle of Genoa and the Anti-Capitalist Movement*. London: One-Off Press.

—— (2001b) Genoa: War Against Capitalism, *Fight Racism Fight Imperialism*, 162: 1–3.

—— (2001c) Vampires, *Do or Die!*, 9: 133–5.

—— (2003) Down with the Empire, Up with the Spring, *Do or Die!*, 10: 1–102.

Avineri, S. (1972) *Hegel's Theory of the Modern State*. Cambridge: Cambridge University Press.

Bahro, R. (1978) *The Alternative in Eastern Europe*. London: New Left Books.

—— (1982) *Socialism and Survival*. London: Heretic.

Balakrishan, G. (2003) *Debating Empire*. London: Verso.

Bell, E. (1993) *Social Classes and Social Credit in Alberta*. Montreal: McGill-Queens University Press.

Bennholdt-Thomsen, V. and Mies, M. (1999) *The Subsistence Perspective: Beyond the Globalised Economy*. London: Zed Press.

——, Faraclas, N. and von Werlhof, C. (2001) *There is an Alternative: Subsistence and Worldwide Resistance to Corporate Globalization*. London: Zed Press.

Benton, E. (ed.) (1996) *The Greening of Marxism*. London: Guilford Press.

Berlet, C. and Lyons, M. (2000) *Right-Wing Populism in America*. New York: Guilford Press.

Bhagwati, J. (2004) *In Defence of Globalization*. New York: Oxford University Press.

Bhaskar, R. (1989) *Reclaiming Reality*. London: Verso.

Birchall, J. (1997) *The International Co-operative Movement*. Manchester: Manchester University Press.

Black, E. (2001) *IBM and the Holocaust*. London: Little, Brown and Co.

Bookchin, M. (1974) *Post-Scarcity Anarchism*. London: Wildwood.

Boyle, D. (ed.) (2002) *The Money Changers: Currency Reform from Aristole to E-Cash*. London: Earthscan.

Braverman, H. (1974) *Labour and Monopoly Capitalism*. New York: Monthly Review Press.

Brewer, A. (1990) *Marxist Theories of Imperialism: A Critical Survey*. London: Routledge.

Brockway, F. (1980) *Britain's First Socialist: The Levellers, Agitators and Diggers of the English Revolution*. London: Quartet.

Bronner, S. (1987) *Rosa Luxemburg: Revolutionary For Our Times*. New York: Columbia University Press.

Brown, B. (1974) *Protest in Paris: Anatomy of a Revolt*. Morristown, NJ: General Learning Press.

Brown, N. (1960) *Life Against Death: The Psychoanalytical Meaning of History*. London: Routledge and Kegan Paul.

Bruce, I. (2008). *The Real Venezuela: Making Socialism in the 21st Century*. London: Pluto Press.

Buchan, J. (1997) *Frozen Desire: An Inquiry into the Meaning of Money*. London: Picador.

Bukharin, N. (1973) *Imperialism and the World Economy*. New York: Monthly Review Press.

Bull, M. (2003) You Can't Build a New Society With A Stanley Knife, in Balakrishnan, G. (ed.) *Debating Empire*. London: Verso.

Burgin, A. (2009). The Radical Conservatism of Frank H. Knight, *Modern Intellectual History*, 6: 513–38.

Burkett, P. (1999) *Marx and Nature: A Red and Green Perspective*. New York: St. Martin's Press.

Callinicos, A. (2001) Toni Negri in Perspective, *International Socialist*, 92: 33–67.

—— (2003) *An Anti-Capitalist Manifesto*. Cambridge: Polity Press.

Canovan, M. (1981) *Populism*. New York: Harcourt Brace Jovanovich.

Castro, F. (2003) *On Imperialist Globalization: Two Speeches*. London: Zed Press.

Caulfield, C. (1997) *Masters of Illusion: The World Bank and the Poverty of Nations*. New York: Henry Holt.

Chossudovsky, M. (1997) *The Globalisation of Poverty: Impacts of IMF and World Bank Reforms*. London: Zed Press.

Christian Aid (2000) *Mind the Gap: How Globalisation is Failing the World's Poor*. London: Christian Aid.

Chua, A. (2003) *World on Fire: How Exporting Free Market Democracy Breeds Ethnic Hatred and Global Instability*. New York: Doubleday.

Cleaver, H. (1981) Technology as Political Weaponry, in Anderson, R. (ed.) *Science, Politics and the Agricultural Revolution in Asia*. Boulder, CO: Westview Press.

—— (1991) Introduction to Negri, A., *Marx Beyond Marx: Lessons on the Grundrisse*. London: Pluto Press.

—— (2000) *Reading Capital Politically*. Leeds: Antithuses.

—— (2003) Marxian Categories, the Crisis of Capital, and the Constitution of Social Subjectivity Today, in Bonefeld, W. (ed.) *Revolutionary Writing*, New York: Autonomedia.

Commoner, B. (1972) *The Closing Circle*. New York: Alfred A. Knopf and Bantam.

Dale, G. (2010) *Karl Polanyi: The Limits of the Market*. Cambridge: Polity Press.

Dean, J. (2012) *The Communist Horizon*. London: Verso.

de Angelis, M. (2001) Marx and Primitive Accumulation: The Continuous Character of Capital's 'Enclosures', *The Commoner*, 2.

de Brie, C. (2000) Crime, the World's Biggest Free Enterprise, *Le Monde Diplomatique*, April.

Deleuze, G. and Guattari, F. (1988) *A Thousand Plateaus: Capitalism and Schizophrenia*. London: Athlone Press.

Desai, M. (2004) *Marx's Revenge: The Resurgence of Capitalism and the Death of State Socialism*. London: Verso.

Devine, P. (1988) *Democracy and Economic Planning*. Cambridge: Polity Press.

Dobson, A. (1991) *The Green Reader*. London: Andre Deutsch.

—— (2000) *Green Political Thought*. London: Routledge.

Doherty, B. (2007) *Radicals for Capitalism*. New York: Public Affairs.

Dolgoff, S. (ed.) (1990) *The Anarchist Collectives*. New York: Black Rose Books.

Dostoevsky, F. (1993) *Crime and Punishment*. London: Vintage.

Douglas, C. (1979) *The Monopoly of Credit*. Sudbury: Bloomfield Books.

Douthwaite, R. (1993) *The Growth Illusion*. Bideford: Green Books.

—— (2000) *The Ecology of Money*. Totnes: Green Books.

Drakeford, M. (1997) *Social Movements and Their Supporters: The Greenshirts in England*. Basingstoke: Macmillan.

Dyer-Witheford, N. (1999) *Cyber-Marx: Cycles and Circuits of Struggle in High-Technology Capitalism*. Urbana and Chicago: University of Illinois Press.

Ecologist (1992) Whose Common Future? *Ecologist*, 22, 4.

Elliot, D. (2003) *A Solar World: Climate Change and the Green Energy Revolution*. Totnes: Green Books.

Engels, F. (2010) *The Origin of the Family, Private Property, and the State*. London: Penguin.

Fast, H. (1970) *Spartacus*. London: Panther.

—— (1990) *Being Red*. Boston, MA: Houghton Mifflin.

Fine, B. and Saad-Filho, A. (2004) *Marx's Capital*. London: Pluto Press.

Firor, J. and Jacobsen, J. (2002) *The Crowded Greenhouse. Population, Climate Change, and Creating a Sustainable World*. New Haven, CT: Yale University Press.

Foster, J. (2000) *Marx's Ecology*. New York: Monthly Review Press.

—— (2002) *Ecology Against Capitalism*. New York: Monthly Review Press.

Foucault, M. (1979) *Discipline and Punish: The Birth of the Prison*. Harmondsworth: Penguin.

—— (1980) *Power/Knowledge: Selected Interviews and Other Writings*. New York: Pantheon.

—— (1991) Governmentality, in Burchell, G., Gordon, P. and Miller, P. (eds) *The Foucault Effect*. London: Harvester.

Friedman, T. (1999a) *The Lexus and the Olive Tree*. New York: Farrar, Strauss and Giroux.

—— (1999b) Manifesto for a Fast World, *New York Times*, 28 March.

Fromm, E. (1979) *To Have or To Be?* London: Abacus.

Fuller, J. (2001) The New Workerism: The Politics of the Italian Autonomists, *International Socialist*, 92: 63–76.

Galbraith, J. (1975) *Money: Whence it Came, Where it Went*. Harmondsworth: Penguin.

Gare, A. (1996) Soviet Environmentalism: The Path Not Taken, in Benton, E. (ed.) *The Greening of Marxism*. London: Guilford Press.

George, S. and Sabelli, F. (1994) *Faith and Credit: The World Bank's Secular Empire*. New York: Penguin.

German Green Party (1983) *The Programme of the German Green Party*. London: Heretic.

Goldman, E. (1906) Observations and Comments, *Mother Earth*, 1: 2.

Goldsmith, E. (ed.) (1972) *A Blueprint for Survival*. London: Tom Stacy.

—— (1988) *The Great U-Turn: De-Industrializing Society*. Bideford: Green Books.

Goldsmith, J. (1994) *The Trap*. London: Macmillan.

Gott, R. (2005). *Hugo Chávez and the Bolivarian Revolution in Venezuela*. London: Verso.

Gray, J. (2002) *False Dawn*. London: Granta.

Graeber, D. (2011) *Debt: The First 5,000 Years*. New York: Melville House.

Greco, T. (2001) *Money: Understanding and Creating Alternatives to Legal Tender*. New York: Chelsea Green Publishing.

Greenpeace (2001) *Getting to Zero Waste: A Citizens' Resource Recovery Strategy for Anyshire County Council*. London: Greenpeace.

Guérin, D. (1973) *Fascism and Big Business*. New York: Pathfinder Press.

Guha, R. and Martinez-Alier, J. (1997) *Varieties of Environmentalism: Essays North and South*. London: Earthscan.

Hardt, M. (2004) Intermezzo, in Passavant, P. and Dean, J. (eds) *Empire's New Clothes*. London: Routledge.

—— and Negri, A. (2001a) *Empire*. Cambridge, MA,: Harvard University Press.

—— (2001b) From Movement to Society, in Anon. (ed.) *On Fire: The Battle of Genoa and the Anti-Capitalist Movement*. London: One-Off Press.

Harman, C. (2000a) Globalisation: A Critique of a New Orthodoxy. *International Socialist*, 73.

—— (2000b) *The IMF, Globalisation and Resistance*. London: Socialist Worker.

Harvey, D. (1990) *The Condition of Postmodernity*. Oxford: Blackwell.

—— (1999) *The Limits to Capital*. London: Verso.

—— (2014) *Seventeen Contradictions and the End of Capitalism* London: Profile Books.

Hawken, P., Lovins, A.B. and Hunter Lovins, L. (1999) *Natural Capitalism – The Next Industrial Revolution*. London: Earthscan.

Hayek, F. (1976) *The Road to Serfdom*. London: Routledge and Kegan Paul.

Henwood, D. (1998) *Wall Street*. London: Verso.

Hertz, N. (2001) *The Silent Takeover*. London: Heinemann.

Hilferding, R. (1981) *Finance Capital: A Study in the Latest Phase of Capitalist Development*. London: Routledge.

Hines, C. (2000) *Localization: A Global Manifesto*. London: Earthscan.

Hirst, P. and Thompson, G. (1999) *Globalization in Question: The International Economy and the Possibilities of Governance*. Oxford: Polity Press.

Hiskett, W. and Franklin, J. (1939) *Searchlight on Social Credit*. London: P.S. King and Son Ltd.

Holloway, J. (2002) *Change the World: Without Taking Power*. London: Pluto Press.

—— and Pelaez, E. (eds) (1998) *Zapatista! Reinventing Revolution in Mexico*. London: Pluto Press.

Huber, J. and Robertson, J. (2000) *Creating New Money: A Monetary Reform for the Information Age*. London: New Economics Foundation.

Hulme, D. and Mosley, P. (1996) *Finance Against Poverty*. London: Routledge.

Hutchinson, F. and Burkitt, B. (1997) *The Political Economy of Social Credit and Guild Socialism*. London: Routledge.

——, Mellor, M. and Olsen, W. (2002) *The Politics of Money: Towards Sustainability and Economic Democracy*. London: Pluto Press.

James, S. (1980) *Marx and Feminism*. London: Crossroads.

Jay, M. (1973) *The Dialectical Imagination. A History of the Frankfurt School and the Institute of Social Research, 1923–1950*. London: Heinemann Educational Books.

Joyce, J. (2000) *Ulysses*. London: Penguin Modern Paperbacks.

Katsiaficas, G. (1997) *The Subversion of Politics: European Autonomous Movements and the Decolonization of Everyday Life*. Atlantic Highlands, NJ: Humanities Press.

Keynes, J. (1960) *The General Theory of Employment, Interest and Money*. London: Macmillan.

—— (1972) *Essays in Persuasion. Volume IX, The Collected Works of John Maynard Keynes*. Cambridge: Cambridge University Press.

King, J. (1988) *Economic Exiles*. London: Macmillan.

Klein, N. (2001a) *No Logo*. London: Flamingo.

—— (2001b) Reclaiming the Commons, *New Left Review*, 2, 9 (May–June): 86.

—— (2008) *The Shock Doctrine*. London: Penguin.

—— (2014) *This Changes Everything*. London: Allen Lane.

Kolakowski, L. (1988) *Main Currents of Marxism: The Founders*. Oxford: Oxford University Press.

Korten, D. (1998) *The Post-Corporate World – Life after Capitalism*. West Hartford, CT: Kumarian Press.

—— (2001) *When Corporations Rule the World*. San Francisco, CA: Kumarian Press.

Kovel, J. (2002) *The Enemy of Nature*. New York: Zed Press.

Kropotkin, P. (1972) *The Conquest of Bread*. New York: New York University Press.

Laclau, E. and Mouffe, C. (1985) *Hegemony and Socialist Strategy: Towards a Radical Democratic Politics*. London: Verso.

Lafargue, P. (2010) *The Right to Be Lazy*. Oakland, CA: AK Press.

Lang, T. and Hines, C. (1993) *The New Protectionism*. London: Earthscan.

Lebowitz, M. (2010) *The Socialist Alternative: Real Human Development*. New York: Monthly Review Press.

Lenin, V. (1982) *Imperialism: The Highest Stage of Capitalism*. Moscow: Progress.

Leonard, M. (2009) Nobel winner Elinor Ostrom is a gregarious teacher who loves to solve problems, Bloomington, IN: *Herald Times* online: http://www.heraldtimesonline.com/stories/2009/12/06/news.qp-7916285.sto.

Leval, G. (1990a) Collectivization in Magdalena de Pulpis, in Dolgoff, S. (ed.) *The Anarchist Collectives*. New York: Black Rose Books.

—— (1990b) Industrial Collectivization, in Alcoy, Dolgoff, S. (ed.) *The Anarchist Collectives*. New York: Black Rose Books.

—— (1990c) The Peasant Federation of Levant, in Dolgoff, S (ed.) *The Anarchist Collectives*. New York: Black Rose Books.

Lewis, M. (2010) *The Big Short*. New York: W.H. Norton and Co.

Lietaer, B. (2001) *The Future of Money: A New Way to Create Wealth, Work and a Wiser World*. London: Century.

Lomborg, B. (2001) *The Skeptical Environmentalist*. Cambridge: Cambridge University Press.

London Mayday Collective (2001) *Mayday Monopoly Game: Anti-Capitalist Actions Across London on Tuesday, 1 May 2001*. London BM Mayday.

Luxemburg, R. (1971) *The Accumulation of Capital*. London: Routledge.

Lyotard, J. (1984) *The Postmodern Condition*. Manchester: Manchester University Press.

Maag, B. (1997) Forests and Trees in the World of Two Tamang Villages in Central Nepal: Observations with Special Reference to the Role of Tamang Women in Forest Management, in Seeland, K. (ed.) *Nature is Culture: Indigenous Knowledge and Socio-cultural Aspects of Trees and Forests in Non-European Cultures*. London: Intermediate Technology Publications.

Macpherson, C. (1953) *Democracy in Alberta*. Toronto: Toronto University Press.

Mander, J. and Goldsmith, E. (eds) (1996) *The Case Against the Global Economy: And for a Turn Towards the Local*. San Francisco, CA: Sierra Club.

Marçal, K. (2015) *Who Cooked Adam Smith's Dinner?* London: Portobello Books

Marcuse, H. (1964) *One-Dimensional Man*. London: Routledge and Kegan Paul.

Marx, K. (1973) *Grundrisse*. Harmondsworth: Penguin.

—— (1977) *Early Writings*. Harmondsworth: Pelican.

—— (1979) *Capital*. Vol. 1. Harmondsworth: Penguin.

—— (1987) *Marx and Engels Collected Works*. Volume 42. New York: International Publishers.

—— and Engels, F. (1985) *The Communist Manifesto*. Harmondsworth: Penguin.

Mason, P. (2013) *Why It's Still Kicking Off Everywhere*. London: Verso.

May, A.M., and Summerfield, G. (2012) Creating a Space where Gender Matters: Elinor Ostrom (1933–2012) talks with Ann Mari May and Gale Summerfield, *Feminist Economics*, 18, 4: 25-37.

McCaughan, M. (2004) *The Battle for Venezuela*. London: Latin America Bureau.

McCloskey, D (1991) The Prudent Peasant: New Findings on Open Fields, *Journal of Economic History* 51 (2) June 1991: 343–55.

McCloskey, D.(1998) *The Rhetoric of Economics*. Madison: University of Wisconsin Press.

—— (2000) Others Things Equal: Free-market Feminism 101, *Eastern Economics Journal*, 26, 3: 363–5.

McLellan, D. (1980a) *Marx before Marxism*. London: PaperMac.

—— (1980b) *Marxism after Marx*. London: PaperMac.

McMurtry, J. (1999) *The Cancer Stage of Capitalism*. London: Pluto Press.

—— (2002) *Value Wars: The Global Market Versus the Life Economy*. London: Pluto Press.

McNally, D. (1993) *Against the Market: Political Economy, Market Socialism and the Marxist Critique*. London: Verso.

—— (2002) *Another World is Possible: Globalization and Anti-Capitalism*. Winnipeg: Arbeiter Ring Publishing.

Meadows, D. (1974) *Limits to Growth: A Report for the Club of Rome's Project on the Predicament of Mankind*. New York: Universe.

Mellor, M. (1992) *Breaking the Boundaries: Towards a Feminist, Green Socialism*. London: Virago.

—— (1997) *Feminism and Ecology*. Cambridge: Polity Press.

Melucci, A. (1989) *Nomads of the Present*. London: Radius.

—— (1996) *Challenging Codes*. Cambridge: Cambridge University Press.

Merchant, C. (1992) *Radical Ecology*. London: Routledge.

Mies, M. (1986) *Patriarchy and Accumulation on a World Scale*. London: Zed Press.

Moggridge, D. (1976) *Keynes*. London: Fontana.

Mol, A. and Spaarrgaren, G. (2000) Ecological Modernisation Theory in Debate: A Review, *Environmental Politics*, 9, 1: 17–49.

Monbiot, G. (2003a) *Captive State: The Corporate Takeover of Britain*. London: Macmillan.

—— (2003b) *The Age of Consent: A Manifesto for a New World Order*. London: Flamingo.

Moody, G. (2001) *Rebel Code: Linux and the Open Source Revolution*. London: Penguin.

Moody, K. (1997) *Workers in a Lean World*. London: Verso.

Moody, R. (1992) *The Gulliver File: Mines, People and Land*. London: Pluto Press.

Mooney, C. (2005) *The Republican War on Science*. New York: Basic Books.

Moore, M. (1996) *Downsize This! Random Threats from an Unarmed American*. New York: Crown Publishers.

Morris, D. (1996) Free Trade: The Great Destroyer, in Mander, J. and Goldsmith, E. (eds) *The Case Against the Global Economy: And for a Turn Towards the Local*. San Francisco, CA: Sierra Club.

Mosler, W. (2010) *The Seven Deadly Innocent Frauds of Economic Policy*. St Croix, US Virgin Islands: Valance Co.

Nader, R. (1965) *Unsafe at Any Speed: The Designed-in Dangers of the American Automobile*. New York: Grossman.

—— (2002) *Crashing the Party: Taking on the Corporate Government in an Age of Surrender*. New York: St. Martin's Griffin/Thomas Dunne.

Negri, A. (1991) *Marx Beyond Marx: Lessons on the Grundrisse*. London: Pluto Press.

—— (1989) *The Politics of Subversion*. Oxford: Polity Press.

Nelson, J. (1996) *Feminism, Objectivity and Economics*. London; Routledge.

Nelson, R. (2001) *Economics as Religion: From Samuelson to Chicago and Beyond*. University Park, PA: Penn State Press:

Notes from Nowhere (ed.) (2003) *We Are Everywhere*. London: Verso.

O'Connor, J. (1973) *The Fiscal Crisis of the State*. New York: St Martin's.

—— (1984) *Accumulation Crisis*. Oxford: Blackwell.

—— (1991) On the Two Contradictions of Capitalism, *Capitalism Nature Socialism*, 2, 3: 107–9.

—— (ed.) (1995) *Is Capitalism Sustainable? Political Economy and the Politics of Ecology*. New York: Guilford Press.

—— (1998) *Natural Causes: Essays in Ecological Marxism*. New York: Guilford Press.

Ostrom, E. (1991) *Governing the Commons: The Evolution of Institutions for Collective Action*. Cambridge: Cambridge University Press.

Palast, G. (2003) *The Best Democracy Money Can Buy*. London: Robinson.

Parsons, H. (ed.) (1977) *Marx and Engels on Ecology*. Westport, CT: Greenwood Press.

Passavant, P. and Dean, J. (2004) *Empire's New Clothes*. London: Routledge.

Patomaki, H. (2001) *Democratising Globalization: The Leverage of the Tobin Tax*. London: Zed Press.

Pearce, F. (1976) *Crimes of the Powerful. Marxism, Crime and Deviance*. London: Pluto Press.

Perirats, J. (1990) The Aragon Federation of Collectives: The Final Congress, in Dolgoff, S. (ed.) *The Anarchist Collectives*. New York: Black Rose Books.

Perlman, F. (1992) *Anything Can Happen*. London: Phoenix Press.

Petras, J. and Morley, M. (1975) *The United States and Chile: Imperialism and the Overthrow of the Allende Government*. New York: Monthly Review Press.

—— and Veltmeyer, H. (2001) *Globalisation Unmasked*. London: Zed Press.

—— (2003) *System in Crisis*. London: Zed Press.

Piketty, T. (2014) *Capital in the Twenty-First Century*. Cambridge, MA: Harvard University Press.

Plant, S. (1992) *The Most Radical Gesture*. London: Routledge.

Poguntke, T. (1993) *Alternative Politics: The German Green Party*. Edinburgh: Edinburgh University Press.

Polanyi, K. (1957) *The Great Transformation*. Boston, MA: Beacon Press.

Porritt, J. (1984) *Seeing Green: The Politics of Ecology Explained*. Oxford: Blackwell.

Price, W. (1981) *Social Credit and the Leisure State: Key to the Green Revolution*. Hebden Bridge: Social Credit Union.

Read, J. (2003) *The Micro-Politics of Capital*. Albany: State University of New York Press.

Redfern, C. and Aune, K. (2013) *Reclaiming the F word: Feminism Today*. London: Zed Books.

Rich, B. (1994) *Mortgaging the Earth*. London: Earthscan.

Ritter, G. (1997) *Goldbugs and Greenbacks: The Antimonopoly Tradition and the Politics of Finance in America*. Cambridge: Cambridge University Press.

Ritzer, G. (1995) *The McDonaldization of Society*. London: Pine Forge Press.

Roberts, A. (1979) *The Self-Managing Environment*. London: Allison and Busby.

Rosset, P. and Benjamin, M. (1994) *The Greening of the Revolution: Cuba's Experiment with Organic Farming*. Melbourne: Ocean.

Rowbotham, M. (1998) *The Grip of Death: A Study of Modern Money, Debt Slavery and Destructive Economics*. Charlbury: Jon Carpenter Books.

—— (2000) *Goodbye America: Globalisation, Debt and the Dollar Empire*. Charlbury: Jon Carpenter Books.

Rowe, J. (2002) The Majesty of the Commons: A Review of David Bollier's *Silent Theft*, *Washington Monthly* (April).

Roy, A. (1999) *The Cost of Living*. London: Flamingo.

—— (2001) *Power Politics*. Boston, MA: South End Press.

—— (2002) *The Algebra of Infinite Justice*. London: Flamingo.

—— (2014) *Capitalism: A Ghost Story*. Chicago, IL: Haymarket Books..

Rupert, M. (2000) *Ideologies of Globalization: Contending Visions of a New World Order*. London: Routledge.

Russell, P. (1995) *The Chiapas Rebellion*. Austin, TX: Mexico Resource Center.

Rustin, M. (2003) Empire: A Postmodern Theory of Revolution, in Balakrishnan, G. (ed.) *Debating Empire*. London: Verso.

Ryan, M. (1991) Afterword, in Negri, A. (1991) *Marx Beyond Marx: Lessons on the Grundrisse*. London: Pluto Press.

Sahlins, M. (1972) *The Original Affluent Society*. Chicago, IL: Aldine Atherton.

Salleh, A. (1997) *Ecofeminism as Politics: Nature, Marx and the Postmodern*. London: Zed Press.

Sargent, L. (ed.) (1986) *The Unhappy Marriage of Marxism and Feminism: A Debate on Class and Patriarchy*. London: Pluto Press.

Schlosberg, D. (1999) *Environmental Justice and the New Pluralism: The Challenge of Difference for Environmentalism*. New York: Oxford University Press.

Schumacher, E. (1978) *Small is Beautiful. A Study of Economics as if People Mattered*. London: Abacus.

Schweickart, D. (2011) *After Capitalism*. Lanham, MD: Rowman and Littlefield Publishers.

Search, R. (1977) *Lincoln Money Martyred!* Hawthorne, CA: Omni Publications.

Seeland, K. (ed.) (1997) *Nature is Culture: Indigenous Knowledge and Socio-cultural Aspects of Trees and Forests in Non-European Cultures*. London: Intermediate Technology Publications.

Sen, A. (1999) *Development as Freedom*. Oxford: Oxford University Press.

Seymour, R. (2014) *Against Austerity*. London: Pluto Press.

Sheasby, W. (2003) George Soros and the Rise of the Neocentrics, *Change Links* (December).

—— (2004) Karl Marx and the Victorians' Nature: The Evolution of a Deeper View: Part One: Oceanus, *Capitalism Nature Socialism*, 15, 2: 47–64.

—— and Wall, D. (2002) The Enemy of Nature and the Nature of the Enemy, *Capitalism Nature Socialism*, 11, 4: 155–66.

Shiva, V. (1988) *Staying Alive: Women, Ecology and Development*. London: Zed Press.

—— (2000) *Stolen Harvest: The Hijacking Of The Global Food Supply*. Cambridge, MA: South End Press.

Sklair, L. (2001) *The Transnational Capitalist Class*. Oxford: Blackwell.

Sklar, H. (1980) *Trilateralism*. Boston, MA: South End Press.

—— (1995) *Chaos or Community: Seeking Solutions, Not Scapegoats for Bad Economics*. Boston, MA: South End Press.

Smart, D. (1978) *Pannekoek and Gorter's Marxism*. London: Pluto Press.

Snyder, G. (1974) *Turtle Island*. New York: New Directions Books.

—— (1999) *The Gary Snyder Reader: Poetry, Prose, and Translations*. Washington, DC: Counterpoint.

Soros, G. (1998) *The Crisis of Global Capitalism*. London: Little, Brown and Co.

—— (2004) *The Bubble of American Supremacy*. London: Weidenfeld and Nicolson.

Souchy, A. (1990a) The Collectivization of the Metal and Munitions Industry, in Dolgoff, S. (ed.) *The Anarchist Collectives*. New York: Black Rose Books.

—— (1990b) Collectivization in Catalonia, Dolgoff, S. (ed.) *The Anarchist Collectives*. Black Rose Books: New York.

Stiglitz, J. (2001) Foreword to Polanyi, K., *The Great Transformation*. Boston, MA: Beacon Press.

—— (2002) *Globalization and its Discontents*. London: Allen Lane.

—— (2003) *The Roaring Nineties: Seeds of Destruction*. London: Allen Lane.

—— (2010) *Freefall*. New York: W.H. Norten and Co.

—— (2013) *The Price of Inequality*. London: Penguin.

Stingel, J. (2000) *Social Discredit: Anti-Semitism, Social Credit, and the Jewish Response*. Montreal: McGill-Queen's University Press.

Strayer, J. (1991) *The German Peasants' War and Anabaptist Community of Goods*. Montreal: McGill-Queen's University Press.

Taylor, K. (1982) *The Political Ideas of the Utopian Socialist*. London: Cass.

Thekaekara, S. (2003) *Beating the System: Local Solutions to the Globalisation Crisis*. London: New Economics Foundation.

Thompson, E. (1976) *William Morris: From Romantic to Revolutionary*. New York: Pantheon Books.

—— (1977) *Whigs and Hunters: The Origin of the Black Act*. Harmondsworth: Penguin.

Tilly, C. (1978) *From Mobilization to Revolution*. Englewood Cliffs, NJ: Prentice-Hall.

—— (2003) A Nebulous Empire, in Balakrishnan, G. (ed.) *Debating Empire*. London: Verso.

Tokar, B. (1992) *The Green Alternative*. San Pedro, CA: R. and E. Miles.

Toke, D. (2000) *Green Politics and Neoliberalism*. Basingstoke: Macmillan.

Trainer, E. (1985) *Abandon Affluence!* London: Zed Press.

—— (1989) *Developed To Death!* London: Green Print.

Tronti, M. (1976) Workers and Capital, in *The Labour Process and Class Strategies*. London: Conference of Socialist Economics.

UNCTAD (2002) *Are Transnationals Bigger than Countries?* (TAD/INF/PR/47). Geneva: UNCTAD.

van der Veen, R. and Van Parijs, P. (1986) A Capitalist Road to Communism, *Theory and Society* 15, 5: 635–55.

Veblen, T. (1994) *The Theory of the Leisured Class*. New York: Dover.

Vonnegut, K. (1971) *Cat's Cradle*. London: Penguin, 2000.

Wainwright, H. (2003) *Reclaim the State: Experiments in Popular Democracy*. London: Verso.

Walker, M. (1977) *The National Front*. London: Fontana.

Wall, D. (1990) *Getting There: Steps to a Green Society*. London: Greenprint.

—— (1993) *Green History*. London: Routledge.

—— (1994) *Weaving a Bower Against the Endless Night*. London: Green Party.

—— (1999) *Earth First! and the Anti-roads Movement*. London: Routledge.

—— (2003) The Ecosocialism of Fools, *Capitalism Nature Socialism*, 14, 2: 99–122.

—— (2004) Bakhtin and the Carnival Against Capitalism, in Carter, J. and Morland, D. (eds) *Anti-Capitalist Britain*. London: New Clarion Press.

—— (2010) *The Rise of the Green Left*. London: Pluto Press.

—— (2014) *The Sustainable Economics of Elinor Ostrom*. London: Routledge.

Waring, M. (1989) *If Women Counted: A New Feminist Economics*. London: Macmillan.

Warren, B. (1980) *Imperialism: Pioneer of Capitalism*. London: New Left Books.

Weeks, K. (2011) *The Problem with Work*. Durham, NC: Duke University Press.

Weizsacker, E., Lovins, A. and Lovis, H. (1997) *Factor Four: Doubling Wealth, Halving Resource Use*. London: Earthscan.

Went, R. (2000) *Globalization: Neo-liberal Challenge, Radical Responses*. London and Sterling, VA: Pluto Press.

Wheen, F. (2000) *Karl Marx*. London: Fourth Estate.

Wilkinson, R. and Pickett, K. (2010) *The Spirit Level*. London: Penguin.

Williams, R. (1982) *Socialism and Ecology*. London: Socialist Environmental and Resources Association.

Wilpert, G. (2007). *Changing Venezuela by Taking Power: The History and Policies of the Chávez Government*. London: Verso.

Wilson, E.O. (2002) The Bottleneck, *Scientific American* (February).

Wolf, M. (2004) *Why Globalization Works: The Case for a Global Market Economy*. New Haven, CT: Yale University Press.

Wolfe, T. (1988) *The Bonfire of the Vanities*. London: Pan.

Wood, E. (2003a) A Manifesto for Global Capitalism? in Balakrishnan, G. (ed.) *Debating Empire*. London: Verso.

—— (2003b) *Empire of Capital*. London: Verso.

Woodcock, G. (1963) *Anarchism. A History of Libertarian Ideas and Movements*. Harmondsworth: Penguin.

Woodin, M. and Lucas, C. (2004) *Green Alternatives to Globalisation: A Manifesto*. London: Pluto Press.

Wright, S. (2002) *Storming Heaven: Class Composition and Struggle in Italian Autonomist Marxism*. London: Pluto Press.

Zerzan, J. (1999) *Elements of Refusal*. Columbia, MO: Columbia Alternative.

INDEX